D0915495

Irish Literature, History, & Culture
Jonathan Allison, General Editor

Advisory Board
  George Bornstein, University of Michigan
  Elizabeth Butler Cullingford, University of Texas
  James S. Donnelly Jr., University of Wisconsin
  Marianne Elliott, University of Liverpool
  Roy Foster, Hertford College, Oxford
  David Lloyd, University of California, Berkeley
  Weldon Thornton, University of North Carolina

But the Irish Sea Betwixt Us

Ireland, Colonialism, and Renaissance Literature

Andrew Murphy

THE UNIVERSITY PRESS OF KENTUCKY

Publication of this volume was made possible in part
by a grant from the National Endowment for the Humanities

Editorial and Sales Offices: The University Press of Kentucky,
663 South Limestone Street, Lexington, Kentucky 40508-4008

03 02 01 00 99   5 4 3 2 1

Library of Congress Cataloging in Publication Data

Murphy, Andrew.
   But the Irish Sea betwixt us : Ireland, colonialism, and
renaissance literature / Andrew Murphy.
       p.   cm. — (Irish literature, history, and culture)
   Includes bibliographical references (p.   ) and index.
   ISBN 0-8131-2086-1 (cloth : alk. paper)
   1. English literature — Early modern, 1500-1700— History and
criticism.   2. English literature — Irish influences.
3. Shakespeare, William, 1564-1616 — Knowledge — Ireland.   4. Spenser,
Edmund, 1552?-1599— Knowledge — Ireland.   5. Jonson, Ben, 1573?-1637—
Knowledge — Ireland.   6. Ireland— Foreign public opinion, British.
7. Ireland — Historiography.   8. Colonies in literature.   9. Ireland—
In literature.   10. Renaissance — England.   I. Title.   II. Series.
PR129.I7M87   1999
820.9'32417'09031— dc21   98-41607

Designed & set in Adobe Garamond & Catull
by Books International, Inc.

For Charonne Ruth

Contents

But if that land be there (quoth he) as here,

And is theyr heaven likewise there all one?

And, if like heaven, be heavenly graces there,

Like as in this same world where do we wone?

— Edmund Spenser

Colin Clouts Come Home Againe

Acknowledgments

This book began life as an exercise in reinventing the wheel. As a first-year graduate student at Brandeis University in Boston, I discovered Edmund Spenser's *View of the Present State of Ireland* and promptly set about writing a long seminar paper on the inscription of colonialist discourse in *The Faerie Queene*. I am grateful to Billy Flesch for bearing with that paper's shortcomings and for gently prompting me to think through in more complex ways the issues I was beginning to explore. I am also grateful for guidance and encouragement given at this stage by Allen Grossman, Anne Janowitz, and Alan Levitan.

The Ph.D. thesis that eventually arose from the original seminar paper was jointly supervised by Gary Taylor and Mary Campbell, both of whom were exemplary mentors throughout the whole process. They were prompt and thorough in responding to my work and struck a perfect balance between criticism and encouragement.

Various people have read sections of the book and have helped to shape and focus it and, indeed, at times to save me from my own ignorance and folly. I would especially like to thank Eibhlín Evans, Alan Ford, Nicholas Grene, Tom Healy, Geraldine Higgins, Liz Hodgson, Margaret Rose Jaster, Arthur Kinney, Bernhard Klein, and Elizabeth Sagaser. I am also very grateful to the many people who provided me with copies of unpublished materials relevant to my topic — in particular, Alan Ford and Tom Healy (again) and also Dympna Callaghan, Chris Highley, and Willy Maley. Special thanks go to Andrew Hadfield, for sending me a set of proofs for his *Spenser's Irish Experience*.

I am especially grateful to Kentucky's series editor, Jonathan Allison, and to his anonymous referees for the encouragement and feedback that they provided and for the efficient manner in which the book was handled.

I also owe a great debt to the many non-Renaissance, or nonacademic friends whose support and encouragement sustained the project from its inception.

My particular thanks in this regard go to Bonnie Burns, Amy Curtis-Webber, Tina Kelleher, Eileen McKeith, Nancy Nies and Andrew Roberts.

Two people have done more to sustain both this book and myself than I can fully articulate here. One is Gerard Murphy, whose support has been a gift without measure. The other is the book's dedicatee, for whom this effort is a slender enough return for all that she has given.

University of St. Andrews

Introduction

In the Spenser chapter of his 1984 book, *Poetry and Politics in the English Renaissance,* David Norbrook is almost apologetic about his dedication to tracing the political and historical lineages of Spenser's poetic career, as he observes, "This book is not exclusively concerned with topical issues, and it has become unfashionable to pay close attention to Spenser's political allegory" (1984, 125). More than a decade later, this touch of reticence on Norbrook's part may feel rather surprising. In general terms, the 1980s witnessed the phenomenal rise of a revitalized historicist criticism on both sides of the Atlantic, with the ascendancy of New Historicism in North America and of Cultural Materialism in Britain.[1] Attention to Spenser's "political allegory" formed a significant part of this new critical program—as we can see, for instance, from the fact that one of the foundational texts of the New Historicism—Stephen Greenblatt's 1980 study *Renaissance Self-Fashioning*—takes up, among other issues, the politics of Spenser's *Faerie Queene.*

In their respective chapters on Spenser, both Greenblatt and Norbrook draw attention to the connections between the allegory of the *Faerie Queene* and a political tract that Spenser composed while he was working on the poem—his *View of the Present State of Ireland*. Their analyses of these texts signaled what would become a steady stream of engagements with Spenser's Irish context by literary critics over the course of the next decade,[2] including a collection of essays dedicated precisely to *Spenser and Ireland* (Coughlan, 1989) and a special issue of the *Irish University Review* (*IUR*) (Autumn/Winter 1996) dedicated to the related topic, "Spenser in Ireland."[3] Indeed, the extent of this outpouring of material on Spenser's Irish connections has been such as to prompt the editor of this latter collection (Anne Fogarty) to observe that "the current urge, inspired by the vogue for materialist and contextual readings prompted by new historicist criticism, to see Spenser solely in terms of his connection with Ireland has become so commonplace that it is in danger of blinding us to the complexity of history on the one hand and of *The Faerie Queene* on the other. The lapidary slogan, 'Spenser and Ireland,' brandished by so many recent investigations of the poet's work, runs the risk of ushering in a new critical orthodoxy which may turn out to be just as restrictive as the interpretative approaches which it is trying to replace" (204).

This great revival of literary critical interest in Spenser's Irish politics has run in parallel with a general resurgence of interest in early modern Ireland among historians. Looking back on two decades of Irish historical studies, Steven Ellis commented in 1990 that "the past twenty years have witnessed something of a renaissance in the history of Tudor Ireland" ("Economic," 239). Much of this renewal of historical interest has both intersected with and entered into dialogue with the work of literary scholars. Historian Nicholas Canny, for instance, contributed an article on Spenser to the *Yearbook of English Studies* in 1983 and also contributed an introduction to Coughlan's 1989 volume. Further articles on Spenser followed from historians such Ciarán Brady, Brendan Bradshaw, and Canny himself.

Whereas Spenser has held center stage throughout this period, the critical focus has also broadened to take in the Irish dimension of other Renaissance writers, with analyses of the Irish context of the work of Shakespeare, Johnson, Milton, and others also appearing in print. The broader issue of Ireland and the Renaissance has, like the issue of Spenser and Ireland, prompted an anthology of essays: Bradshaw, Hadfield and Maley's 1993 *Representing Ireland: Literature and the Origins of Conflict, 1534-1660*. A volume dedicated to Shakespeare's Irish connections (*Shakespeare and Ireland: History, Politics, Culture*) has also recently appeared.[4]

There has, then, clearly been no shortage of accounts of the intersections of English literature and Irish politics in the Renaissance period. So, why is this present book—yet another contribution to a debate that has been ongoing now for more than a decade—necessary? What does *But the Irish Sea betwixt Us* have to offer that has not already been said by other critics? The answer lies in the framework that has been brought into play in many of the analyses of Renaissance Ireland published to date. The earliest literary scholars to write on early modern Ireland tended to come to their subject from a broader interest in the field of Renaissance colonialism. Stephen Greenblatt is a good case in point. His earliest book was a study of courtier, adventurer, and New World explorer Walter Raleigh; his chapter on Spenser in *Renaissance Self-Fashioning* includes among its reference points the experiences of Columbus and Cortés in the New World; and his more recent books (notably *Learning to Curse* and *Marvelous Possessions*) have been very much concerned with issues of discovery and colonial power.[5] Thus, for Greenblatt as for many of his successors, an interest in Ireland in essence amounts to an interest in a particular local instance of a larger global issue: Renaissance colonialism. We can see this process of contextualizing Ireland within a greater colonial framework at play in an article such as Paul Brown's groundbreaking 1985 study, "'This Thing of Darkness I Acknowledge Mine': *The Tempest* and the Discourse of Colonialism." Brown opens his article by attending to "Shakespeare's patronal relations with prominent members of the Virginia Company" (48) before going on to discuss the significance of contemporary seventeenth-century conceptions of Pocahontas. Having thus established a New World colonialist frame for his article, Brown turns to analyzing how Ireland can be seen as a kind of "semiperipheral" colonial instance, noting "a general analogy . . . between Ireland and Prospero's island" (57).

The thrust of much subsequent criticism has been, we might say, to pursue the "general analogy" between Ireland and the New World that motivated the work of both Greenblatt and Brown and the other early scholars to write on Ireland and Renaissance literature. What has often been lost sight of, in the process, is the extent to which Renaissance Ireland *differs* from the New World. We can get a sense of this difference being simultaneously both registered and denied in a quotation such as the following, from Patricia Coughlan's own contribution to her *Spenser and Ireland* volume:

Spenser's images of the Irish were . . . most assuredly formed by his intellectual and emotional familiarity with the Renaissance Christian typology of the wildness outside civil society. This set of representations has been well described by Hayden White, and one may form an impression of its interweaving with and modification by actual colonial activities by bringing general theoretical discussions such as White's into relation with specific case-histories of the various colonial fields, such as D.B. Quinn's on the Irish, James Muldoon's on the North American Indians, Peter Hulme's on the Caribbean, and Anthony Pagden's analysis of Spanish interpretations of South American indigenes in the context of their rule over them. In spite of the major actual differences between these various places and people, their colonizing interpreters came to be equipped with more or less the same model of civility *versus* barbarity, formed in the tradition of European classical and Christian thought. (48-49)

Coughlan is clearly correct here in proposing a Christian-European model of a civility-barbarism dichotomy that has been deployed at a variety of different cultural and historical moments and locations. However, the particular occasions of such deployment differ significantly in different circumstances. Coughlan recognizes this fact when she acknowledges "the major actual differences between" the various peoples who have been subject to the force of this dichotomy. But these differences are recognized only to be immediately erased, as all of the various subjects of early modern colonialism are conflated into a single community of the colonized. A sense of difference is not sustained, nor is any acknowledgment made of the crucial distinction separating the Irish on the one hand from the North American Indians, Caribbeans, and South American indigenes on the other. Unlike these peoples, who were all *newly encountered communities* in the early modern period, the Irish had, in this period, a relationship with their English neighbors stretching back over several centuries, and they shared a certain ethnic and religious heritage with them.

The aim of this book is to hold open that sense of Irish difference and to explore the way in which, as a result of this deep history, colonialism in Ireland necessarily took a unique form, so that English writers faced a rather different task in encountering their neighboring Irish Others than they did in encountering wholly alien communities in the New World. Though a very great deal of valuable work on early modern Ireland has been done by scholars such Patricia Coughlan, such critics have not always recognized the important distinguishing particularities of the Irish colonial experience. For the most part, such critics have seen the English as encountering (or forging) a purely dichotomous Otherness in Ireland, in terms such as those Coughlan herself delineates, when she observes that "Ireland constitutes a radical alterity, a challenging otherness" ("Secret" 1979, 46), or in the manner set out by Ann Rosalind Jones and Peter Stallybrass, when they similarly observe that "the weight [of English writing on Ireland] went into establishing the absolute otherness of the Irish" (1992, 158).

In part, the strict binarism of these writers arises out of their heavy reliance on the work of a relatively narrow range of Irish historians. In particular, the earliest literary scholars who wrote about Ireland and Renaissance literature tended to depend for their historical contextualizing on the work of David Beers Quinn and Nicholas Canny—pioneering writers who placed a heavy emphasis both on the links between the English project in Ireland and in the New World and on the fundamentally colonialist thrust of English policy in Ireland from the middle decades of the sixteenth century onward. However, as Hiram Morgan has observed, while "enormous credit is due to the scholarship of Quinn and Canny for having developed such an innovative perspective," nevertheless, "their thesis has now gained such widespread acceptance that Early Modern Ireland has been dragged into mid-Atlantic, cut off from Europe and left an English stepping-stone to North America" ("Mid-Atlantic" 1991-92, 50). Steven Ellis has offered a similar critique of a form of historiography that he suggests has set Ireland "adrift somewhere in the north Atlantic" and has argued that it may finally be the *differences* between Ireland and the New World that hold more significance than the similarities and continuities proposed by Quinn and Canny:

Ireland was not an unknown island 3,000 miles out in the Atlantic, waiting to be discovered and colonised. It had been linked by the Irish Sea into the British political system for hundreds of years, with strong cultural ties across the North Channel linking Ulster and Gaelic Scotland, and stable political connections of a different kind binding English Ireland to England and Wales. What occurred between 1534 and 1603 was not the forging of new ties between Britain and Ireland where none had previously existed but a radical redefinition of traditional relationships between the two islands and between the different peoples in the archipelago. ("Writing Irish History" 1996, 13)[6]

Thus, in recent years, the analyses put forward by Quinn and Canny have come increasingly under scrutiny, and historians such as Morgan, Ellis, T.C.

Barnard, Brendan Bradshaw, Ciarán Brady, and Karl Bottigheimer have argued for a more complex model of Anglo-Irish relations in the sixteenth century. In the case of many literary critics, however, acknowledgment of these complexities is again admitted only to be immediately suppressed, as in the case of Anne Fogarty's observation, in her otherwise impressive analysis of Spenser's *View* and *Faerie Queene,* that, "while it is recognized that the term colonialism can merely serve as an approximate and unsatisfactory description of the complexities of English policy in sixteenth-century Ireland, it will nonetheless be argued that the images of Otherness at the core of each of these works . . . are indicative of the writer's attempt to formulate and construe a rhetoric of colonial power" (1989, 77). Some recent critics have indeed attempted to move beyond what Willy Maley has called "the stultifying dualism" (Review of Cairns and Richards 1989, 293) of certain forms of literary analysis—analysis that sees English writing on Ireland as operating only through a fixed and stable colonial binarism. Maley's own work—together with that of, for example, Andrew Hadfield, David Baker, Chris Highley, and Michael Neill—has provided a more rich and complex model for interpreting English texts about Ireland.[7] This study aims to complement and build on that work and also, I hope, to offer something new to the debate.

While acknowledging that Ireland's experience in the Renaissance period is always in some fundamental sense colonial, I aim in this book to delineate the *complexities* of Ireland's colonial positioning, particularly as it is shaped by the extended relation of "proximity" between the two islands of Britain and Ireland. I will define what I mean by "proximity" in greater detail in my first chapter, but here I would just note that the term is intended to indicate a certain set of multiple resonances. Ireland and Britain are "proximate" in the sense that they lie close to each other geographically, but that geographical proximity has lead to a complex relationship of closeness between the populations, so that, even by the sixteenth century, they had shared an extended political, ethnic, and religious heritage.[8] The primary contention of this book is that these relations of geographic and cultural proximity rendered the Irish, for the English, as "proximate" Others rather than what Ann Jones and Peter Stallybrass might call "absolute" Others. The value of the term "proximate" in this latter sense is that it indicates, as well as a relationship of closeness, a certain kind of "*ap*proximateness"—the Irish are, in some respects, very like the English, but they are also distinctly different from them—being possessed of their own culture, language, legal systems, and traditions. They are, in other words, imperfect aliens. Adapting from Homi Bhabha, we could say that they are, in a complex sense, "almost the same, but not quite."[9] The significance of these various relationships of proximity is, I will contend, that the colonialist framing of Ireland in English writing is always a process fraught with hazards. Ireland is always a problematic instance for the English writer, because the standard tropes of colonial stereotyping are always likely to unravel in the encounter with the imperfect Otherness of the Irish.[10]

The principal focus of the book is on the Renaissance period. As Richard Helgerson has made clear in *Forms of Nationhood*, this period is crucial to the founding of an English sense of national identity—a process that, as writers such as Andrew Hadfield, Willy Maley, and Michael Neill have established, both drew on and was severely disrupted by England's relationship with Ireland.[11] The Renaissance period is also important from an Irish perspective in that, in this era, the Nine Years' War (1594-1603) signaled the possibility of an *Irish* national identity, as it also raised the possibility that the island of Ireland might, for the first time ever, become a united entity and that, in the process, it might achieve complete independence from Britain.

The textual analyses offered by this study begin, however, not with the Renaissance, but with Gerald of Wales' twelfth-century books on Ireland, the *Expugnatio Hibernica* and the *Topographia Hibernica*. Gerald is a much neglected figure—at least by comparison with his sixteenth- and seventeenth-century successors.[12] His work is, however, of central importance to the whole question of English engagements with Ireland, since it is foundational for much of what follows. As Andrew Hadfield has observed, "as late as the sixteenth- and seventeenth-centuries Giraldus defined the tradition of English writing on Ireland, being the most widely read authority on Irish customs as well as on Irish history" ("Briton and Scythian" 1993, 393). It is from this perspective that I approach his Irish writings, as I attempt to trace within his work many of the paradigms and problematics that would resurface again and again in the tradition of representations of Ireland. In this sense, I view Gerald as, effectively, the initiator of a tradition, rather than as in some way standing in for the entire medieval corpus of writing about Ireland emanating from the island of Britain. Much more work needs to be done on medieval representations of Ireland and Elizabeth Rambo has made a start on this task with her *Colonial Writing in Medieval English Literature*, published in 1994.[13] Other writers must carry this process forward.

As I have already indicated, my own primary interest lies in the Renaissance. In selecting texts from this period for analysis I am, in a sense, traversing ground that has already been mapped out for me by others. As Michael Neill has noted, "the English enterprize in Ireland seems, at first sight anyway, to have had remarkably little impact on imaginative literature"—"[g]iven the amount of political, military, and intellectual energy it absorbed, and the moneys it consumed, Ireland can seem to constitute . . . one of the great and unexplained lacunae" in the literature of the period ("Broken English" 1994, 10, 11).[14] There are a relatively small number of texts by Renaissance writers who substantially engage with the issue of Ireland, and this corpus of materials has long been established: Spenser's *View* and *Faerie Queene* book 5 (extended into book 6 by perceptive critics such as Anne Fogarty and Andrew Hadfield); Shakespeare's *Henry V;* and Jonson's *Irish Masque at Court.* These texts stand out as significant attempts to come to terms with England's relationship with Ireland; they are often supplemented by other works by the same three authors (for example, Spenser's *Colin Clouts Come Home Againe;* Shakespeare's *Tempest;* some of Jonson's other masques or minor poems) and by lesser known works by writers such as Ford, Donne, and Milton. For the purpose of the present study, I have devoted a chapter each to Spenser, Shakespeare, and Jonson, endeavoring to place their Irish work within the framework of my conceptions of proximity. I have also, however, tried to take in a number of other, less frequently examined, texts along the way, such as Daniel's *Panegyrike Congratvlatorie,* Donne's "H.W. in Hiber. Belligeranti," and Ford's *Fames Memoriall.* Literary scholars writing on Renaissance Ireland have always, of course, understood the necessity of engaging with texts that are not purely "literary," and, in common with these scholars, I incorporate within this study a broad range of other materials from the Renaissance period, including various journals and accounts from the Nine Years' War, pamphlets relating to the union of James VI and I's kingdoms and to the outbreak of hostilities in Ireland in 1641, and "histories" of various kinds, by writers such as William Camden, Thomas Gainsford, and John Davies.[15] I also consider some materials derived from the state papers of the period. My hope is that by both focusing on standard, canonical texts, and by engaging with a range of other materials, I can evoke a rich model of how the issue of proximity plays itself out across the Renaissance.

These, then, are my objectives in this study: to offer a theoretical model of the Anglo-Irish encounter, predicated on the notion of multiple "proximities";

to apply this theoretical model to what we might see as the foundational documents of the tradition of British imaginings of Ireland—Gerald of Wales's *Topographica Hibernica* and *Expugnatio Hibernica;* then to trace, in greater detail, the manner in which the issue of proximity manifests itself in a broad range of texts drawn from the Renaissance era, with particular attention to the work of three major literary figures from the period. In my conclusion, I sketch out how the issue of proximity remained central in the early decades of the seventeenth century and make some general suggestions as to how the concept might be employed more generally in relation to the post-Renaissance period.

If I have had one ambition in writing this book, it has been to attempt to offer a more complex account of how English writers in the Renaissance perceived Ireland, challenging the view that presents the sixteenth-century Anglo-Irish relationship in strictly binary colonialist terms. It goes without saying, of course, that this is only part of the story. Just as the English constructed images of the Irish in this period, so too did the Irish construct their own images of their neighbors in the island of Britain as they also constructed images of themselves. As I have already noted, the Nine Years' War raised the possibility of an Ireland that might well have been united and might have become independent of England. These events would appear to have given rise to the first attempts to construct a broadly based native sense of unitary Irish identity and a kind of native Irish discourse of nationalism. There is a great deal of work still to be done in this area. What we might characterize as a "subaltern history" of the period has yet to be written, delineating the native Irish response to the English project.[16] A study of native Irish historiography also needs to be written, as does a history of the responses of Irish elites to the Nine Years' War—a history that would engage with the work of seventeenth-century Irish writers such as Peter Lombard, Geoffrey Keating, Philip O'Sullivan Beare, and David Rothe.[17] Conrad Russell's assertion that the native Irish "are by far the most inaccessible to historians" ("British Background" 1988, 168) notwithstanding, an abundance of material is certainly available for anyone interested in undertaking such a study—Michelle O Riordan and Marc Caball (among others) have already taken the first steps in charting this territory.[18] Such work is of vital importance, but it lies outside the scope of the present study. It also lies outside the competence of this author, requiring, as it does, for an adequate engagement with the topic, a good knowledge of sixteenth- and seventeenth-century Irish. I do, however, hope that other, properly equipped, scholars will take up the challenge posed by these materials—perhaps, indeed, under the auspices of the current series—and that they might, in the process, find something of use to them in my present efforts.

One further reservation, or caveat, must be entered here. My desire to loosen traditional binaries notwithstanding, it will be noticed that the book itself—like this introduction—organizes itself very largely around the central divisions between England and Ireland, English and Irish. However, the frequency with which overlong footnotes throughout the text struggle to offer some accommodation to relations between England and Ireland (and the Anglo-Irish relationship) on the one hand and between Scotland, Wales and England (and Anglo-Scottish and Anglo-Welsh relations) on the other indicates a distinct shortcoming of my study: its failure adequately to engage with the greater *British* (in the broadest sense) dimension of the issues under discussion.[19] Willy Maley has observed, with characteristic wit, that "posting something through that letterbox between 'Anglo' and 'Irish' is not easy" ("Spenser and Scotland" 1996, 3), and, doubtless, I have contributed here to the occlusion of Scotland (and indeed of Wales) in discussions of the early modern Anglo-Irish relationship that Maley anatomizes in much of his work. A great deal of historical work on the "British" dimension of Irish, English, Scottish, and Welsh history has begun to appear in recent years.[20] It is to be hoped that the work of Maley and others will serve to extend the valuable insights offered by this work into the realm of literary studies.

Finally, I should say that, although this book in many ways sets itself in opposition to much of the work that has been done by my predecessors, I am perfectly well aware that anything I have to say that is of value has been made possible by the efforts of those writers in whose footsteps I am following. The frequency with which the work of a great many of these historians and critics is cited and invoked here should, in itself, make clear the extent of my indebtedness to them. In a very real sense, these scholars have served to map and define the territory in which this present study operates. If they find this book even in a small measure as useful as I have found their pioneering studies, I will consider my efforts to have been worthwhile.

1

"White Chimpanzees"
Encountering Ireland

She had an idea that he would have to be a foreigner: not an
Englishman, still less an Irishman. A real foreigner.
D.H. Lawrence, *Lady Chatterley's Lover*

I.

We begin with twentieth-century Dublin and a moment of cultural epiphany. In Roddy Doyle's novel, *The Commitments,* Jimmy Rabbitte astonishes his friends Derek Scully and Outspan Foster by declaring that "the Irish are the niggers of Europe, lads." This information comes as a revelation to Derek and Outspan: "They nearly gasped: it was so true" (1989, 9). In the novel, Jimmy's observation is turned to comic effect, as, on the strength of his insight, he goes on to proclaim James Brown's slogan: "Say it loud, I'm black an' I'm proud"— a phrase humorously inapposite in the context of a racially homogenous working class Dublin. For all the scene's humor, however, the observation itself and the comic incongruity of the situation indicate a deeper resonance at work in the episode.

To hear some of the historical and cultural echoes at play here, we must go back to the mid-nineteenth century and to the English writer Charles Kingsley, who visited Ireland shortly after the famine and wrote back to his wife in

England: "I am daunted by the human chimpanzees I saw along that hundred miles of horrible country. I don't believe they are our fault. I believe that there are not only many more of them than of old, but that they are happier, better and more comfortably fed and lodged under our rule than they ever were. But to see white chimpanzees is dreadful: if they were black, one would not feel it so much, but their skins, except where tanned by exposure, are as white as ours" (Kearney 1985, 7).

For Doyle, the multiply resonant term "nigger" provides a series of meanings, some of which are applicable to the Irish, but others of which are not, and this disjunction serves finally as a source of comedy—the Irish may be "niggers" of a sort, but they are, for the most part at least, not black.[1] For Kingsley, the disjunction serves rather as a source of profound anxiety. A certain kind of racial identity can be imposed on the Irish, but, disturbingly, they fail adequately to equate to the stereotype—"chimpanzees" they may well be but, "except where tanned by exposure," their skins are as white as the white skins of the English.

Turning back from Kingsley to *The Commitments* once more, we notice an odd doubleness in Doyle's phrase: "The Irish are the niggers *of* Europe." We might ask ourselves what force the word "of" has in this phrase. The answer, I would argue, is twofold. In the first instance, insofar as the phrase "nigger" can be appropriated as a generic term to describe any group that has been subject to colonial oppression and displacement, then the Irish are "Europe's niggers"—subjects of the English colonial enterprise. But, in addition to being "Europe's niggers," they are also "niggers" *of Europe,* which is to say, they are "niggers" who happen to be European, who belong to a greater social and cultural world that encompasses both England and Ireland.[2] This, of course, is precisely the source of Kingsley's great anxiety: the Irish can be classed as alien, but not wholly so. The term "nigger" is at one and the same time entirely apposite and altogether inapplicable when characterizing the Irish.

It is to this area of doubleness that my study is addressed—to the gap, we might say, that opens up between the apposite and the inapplicable or, more accurately, to the inhering of the inapplicable within the apposite. The territory I wish to explore is precisely that indicated by Kingsley when he registers his own anxiety concerning the failure of the Irish adequately to comply with the cultural and racial stereotype within which he would confine them. What I will wish to argue throughout is that this anxiety is not just an isolated experience of self-doubt encountered on a trip along a particular "hundred miles of horrible" Irish countryside; not just what Alan Sinfield would call a "fault-line" serving to expose a contradiction between the overlapping codes of imperial discourse.[3] Rather, I take Kingsley's letter as being indicative of a defining feature of English colonialist writing on Ireland generally: its encountering of sameness at the heart of presumed difference. Thus, where Michel de Certeau observes in *Heterologies* that "what is near masks a foreignness" (1986, 67), the thrust of my work here is to suggest that, in an Anglo-Irish context, what is foreign masks (or rather, more often, fails to mask) a nearness.

This aspect of English writing on Ireland has gone largely unattended. For the most part, literary critics analyzing such texts have tended to see them in terms of a clean and stable binary opposition between the colonizer and the colonized. Thus, for example, David Cairns and Shaun Richards open their seminal study, *Writing Ireland: Colonialism, Nationalism and Culture,* by asserting that "our beginning lies with the reality of the historic relationship of Ireland with England; a relationship of the colonized and the colonizer" (1988, 1).[4] In a similar vein, Richard Kearney, in commenting on the very passage from Kingsley quoted above, characterizes it as an example of "the colonial calibanisation of the Irish" (7). In saying this, Kearney misses the profound anxiety and ambiguity of the text; he sees it as a moment of coherent and unidirectional colonial definition—calibanization—whereas, in fact, as I have suggested, it actually indicates an instance of the *failure* of colonial definition to sustain itself.

Kearney's desire, of course—as his deployment of the term "calibanization" indicates—is to assimilate Ireland's colonial experience to that of other colonized territories elsewhere.[5] A similar desire can be seen at play in Terry Eagleton's contribution to the Field Day volume *Nationalism, Colonialism, and Literature,* in which he writes that "it was never of much interest to British imperialism whether the Irish were Irish or Eskimo, white or black, whether they worshiped tree gods or the Trinity. It is not their ethnic peculiarity but their territory and labor power that have entranced the British" (1990, 29). For Eagleton, Ireland's colonial experience is all of a piece with that of other territories that have been subjected to British imperialism. In this view, Ireland and the Irish are just so much grist to the imperial mill. Ireland might just as well be India or Africa for all that the agents of British imperialism care. But, again, this view of the Irish situation ignores—indeed, allows of no possibility of—the peculiar anxiety that Kingsley registers. Contrary to Eagleton's claim that "it was never of much interest to British imperialism whether the Irish were . . . white or black," Kingsley, as we have seen, exhibits a profound awareness of the fact precisely that the Irish are *not* black, and he finds this deeply troubling.[6]

Eagleton's determined stance here is characteristic of the general tone of the collection in which his piece appears. *Nationalism, Colonialism, and Literature* is uncompromising in its view of the Irish situation as wholly intelligible within a global colonialist frame. In part, the participants in the volume are driven to this stance by their understandable desire to resist what they perceive as a recent trend within Irish historiography that seeks to qualify radically the notion of colonialism.[7] As Seamus Deane ironically observes in his introduction to the volume, "ultimately, there may have been no such thing as colonialism. It is, according to many historians, one of the phantoms created by nationalism, which is itself phantasmal enough" (1990, 7). In Deane's view, the ultimate effect of this revisionism has been to "locali[ze] interpretation, confining it within groups, interests, classes, and periods" (6). In the face of this erosion, Deane feels compelled to state on behalf of Field Day that their analysis of the Irish political situation "derives from the conviction that it is, above all, a colonial crisis" (6).

The work of Field Day and others in insisting on the colonialist nature of the Anglo-Irish relationship and in the forging of links between Ireland's experience and that of other colonial territories has been necessary, important, and fruitful. But the danger of viewing Anglo-Irish history exclusively within a global colonialist frame is that it may lead to the loss of any adequate sense of the historical particularities of the Irish situation—rather as if the stand against the localized interpretation of some revisionists has prompted the jettisoning of that most famous maxim of one of the very contributors to *Nationalism, Colonialism, and Literature* (Frederic Jameson): "Always historicize."

We can see this clearly in the case of Eagleton's piece cited above, where Ireland becomes just another instance of a monolithic British imperialism in action—an instance no different from all of the others throughout the globe. We find a similar mindset at play in Edward Said's contribution to the same Field Day volume, when Said writes that "it is true that the connections are closer between England and Ireland, than between England and India, or France and Senegal. *But the imperial relationship is there in all cases*" (1990, 81 [emphasis added]). In the latter half of this quotation, Said, like Eagleton, unambiguously asserts the global imperial dimension of the Irish situation. But his linking of Ireland here to a greater general realm of imperialism is at the expense of the important insight of his initial assertion, in which he recognizes that, because of the closeness of the connections between Britain and Ireland, the colonial relationship between the two neighboring islands must needs be in some way different from other relationships of a colonial kind. Like Eagleton and Kearney, then, Said fails finally to engage with the *particularity* of the Irish situation—"the closeness of connections" that persists within the Anglo-Irish colonial relationship; the sameness that Kingsley troublingly discovers at the heart of Anglo-Irish colonial difference.[8]

Kingsley is greatly disturbed, as we have seen, by the fact that the Irish do not fully conform to his anticipated image of colonial difference. On his journey through Ireland, he comes to the shocking realization that Irish Otherness is at best partial. The Irish are curiously hybrid, approximating both to the colonial stereotype and, simultaneously, to the English themselves: "their skins . . . are as white as ours."[9] In one sense, Kingsley's realization is a rather simple one: the Irish are white, not black. But, of course, the strength of Kingsley's reaction indicates a set of deeper issues at play here. The white skin of the Irish signifies a certain connection of racial kinship between the colonizer and the colonized. We have already noted in relation to the Roddy Doyle phrase one dimension of this relation of kinship, in that the Irish can be seen as being both "Europe's niggers" and "niggers *of Europe,*" which is to say that even as they are the subjects of colonial oppression, they are still connected to a common European social and cultural realm, a realm to which England and Ireland jointly belong.

Said similarly notes such a relationship of commonality in registering the fact that "the connections are closer between England and Ireland, than between England and India, or France and Senegal." Although Said himself does not pursue this insight, preferring instead to assimilate Ireland's colonial experience to a greater global imperial paradigm, it is, nevertheless, worth asking what exactly might be meant by the closeness of connections that Said recognizes as existing between England and Ireland, and what the implications of that closeness and those connections might be.

England and Ireland are close to each other in a number of different ways and one purpose of this chapter is to provide an account of the constituent elements of this relationship of propinquity. I propose to reformulate Said's closeness, designating it as the category of "proximity." I choose this term for its multiple resonances, because it serves both to indicate that which is close — "proximate"—while at the same time retaining a sense of that which is "ap-proximate"—a relationship simultaneously of similarity and of difference.[10] We have already seen the effects of the emergence of a sense of proximity at play in Kingsley's text on Ireland. The category of proximity is central to virtually all English writing on Ireland, as it returns again and again in such discourse, taking different forms over time as the historical circumstances of the Anglo-Irish relationship change, but always serving to disrupt such discourse, in the way that Kingsley finds his text disrupted by his recognition of the implications of the white skins of the Irish.

My task here and throughout this book is, thus, not to deny the assertion of previous scholars that the colonial paradigm has dominated Anglo-Irish rela-tions and English writing about Ireland. The reality of dispossession and dis-placement certainly speaks against any such view.[11] For this reason, I regard Field Day's reassertion of the colonialist interpretation of Irish history as being both valid and necessary. However, it is also necessary to move beyond viewing this relationship in strictly binary terms and within a framework that assimi-lates Ireland's colonial experience to a general global imperialist experience. To do so is to overlook those aspects of the colonial situation that are unique to the Irish arena, in which English writers find themselves confronted by an Other who is neither fully alien nor yet wholly identical with the self. To do so is also, of course, to conflate the experiences of different peoples in a way that, while useful in producing a working model of imperialist ideology and prac-tice, nevertheless also serves to mask the real differences of individual ethnic histories and experiences. Because, finally, of course, Doyle's Jimmy Rabbitte is wrong: the Irish are *not* "niggers," and it is a disservice to black history and to black suffering to appropriate the term "nigger" as a description of the Irish, however much Ireland may have undergone a similar history of suffering and oppression over the course of its colonial experience.[12] Noting the extension of the colonial model to a variety of different scenes of oppression, Henry Louis Gates has been prompted to ask whether "we still need global, imperial the-ory—in this case, a grand unified theory of oppression" (1991, 470). The an-swer, I feel, is yes, in some sense, we do. But any such theory needs to be finely callibrated and must be as alert to difference as it is to commonality. It needs, in other words, to avoid what David Lloyd has noted as the risks of "discover-ing identity at the expense of significant difference" (1993, 9).[13]

II.

We began with the twentieth century and then stepped back to the nineteenth century. The body of this text will, as I have already noted in my introduction, take us back further still, first to the twelfth century and then on to the period that will be our main focus, the closing decades of the sixteenth century and the opening decades of the seventeenth — the period of the English Renaissance. In the late twelfth century, we find the first major texts written about Ireland by a native of the island of Britain — Gerald of Wales's *Topographia Hibernica* (*c.* 1187) and *Expugnatio Hibernica* (*c.* 1189). Gerald was related to many of the participants in the Norman-English invasion of Ireland in the twelfth century and in his texts we encounter the foundational documents of the tradition of British writing on Ireland.[14] Moving on to the sixteenth century, it is in the Renaissance period that we find the first great blossoming of texts about Ireland produced by writers from Britain. These texts are spread across a wide variety of types and genres, from official and quasi-official tracts and proposals, to memoirs and journals, to poems and dramatic works. Many English writers of the period spent time in Ireland in one capacity or another and the subject of Ireland seems in some measure to have occupied the minds of just about every early modern literary figure.[15]

The likely reason for the burgeoning British interest in Ireland in the Renaissance period lies in the fact that, just as this was a period of enormous change in Britain itself, so too was it an era of evolution and transformation within Anglo-Irish relations. In the century from 1541 to 1641 Ireland witnessed an unprecedented array of English initiatives aimed at consolidating and/or expanding crown control of the island.[16] This included, in the early decades of the seventeenth century, the plantation of the onetime Irish stronghold of Ulster. It is in the plantation of this territory and the consequent Catholic uprising in 1641 that the roots of the current crisis in Northern Ireland are to be found, lending the early modern period a special significance in the general history of Ireland.

The history of early modern Ireland has been the subject of considerable debate in recent years. Indeed, in 1990, T.C. Barnard was moved to observe that "in the last twenty years our knowledge, although not always our understanding, of sixteenth- and seventeenth-century Irish history has immeasurably increased" (1990, 39). It is to this historiographical debate that I will now turn. Having looked at the way in which literary scholars have viewed the colonial situation generally, I will now examine the historians' view of colonialism within the period that is the primary focus of this study.

One of the great pioneers among Irish early modern historians has been David Beers Quinn, whose academic publishing career has spanned some five decades.[17] During the course of his career as a historian, Quinn's primary interests lay jointly in sixteenth-century Ireland and in England's involvement in the New World, and he noted that, in many instances, much the same cast of characters was involved in colonial ventures in both places. In 1966, in response to a Folger Library commission, Quinn published his influential *The Elizabethans and the Irish,* which includes a chapter entitled "Ireland and America Intertwined." In this chapter Quinn argues persuasively for seeing a similarity in method and attitude among those involved in colonizing enterprizes on both sides of the Atlantic. The thrust of Quinn's work has thus been not just to affirm the predominance of the colonial paradigm within the early modern Anglo-Irish relationship but also to place Ireland's early modern colonial experience within a greater global context. In this his work has much in common with the more recent aims of the Field Day enterprise.

In the past two decades, Nicholas Canny has succeeded D.B. Quinn as the prime exponent of the colonialist reading of early modern Anglo-Irish relations. Like Quinn, he has been at pains to stress the need to see Ireland's colonial experience in the period within a greater global frame. In one of his earliest published articles—"The Ideology of English Colonization: From Ireland to America"—Canny has stated that "attempts to reassert English authority over Ireland produced under Elizabeth I a pattern of conquest, bolstered by attempts at colonization, which was contemporaneous with and parallel to the first effective contacts of Englishmen with North America, to plans for conquest and settlement there, and to the earliest encounters with its Indian inhabitants. The Elizabethan conquest of Ireland should therefore be viewed in the wider context of European expansion" (1973, 575). Furthermore, Canny has sought to carve out for Ireland a place of special significance in the history of British colonialism. Thus, in his groundbreaking study of late sixteenth-century Ireland, *The Elizabethan Conquest of Ireland,* he has written that "events in Ireland, 1565-1576, have a significance in the general history of colonization that transcends English and Irish history. The involvement of men in Irish colonization who afterwards ventured to the New World suggests that their years in Ireland [were] years of apprenticeship" (1976, 159).

Canny's enduring commitment to the view that Ireland's early modern colonial experience was all of a piece with a greater European colonial thrust in the period can be seen in, for instance, his participation as coeditor (with Anthony Pagden) of the 1987 collection of essays entitled *Colonial Identity in the Atlantic World, 1500 to 1800*. The "innovative feature of this book," according to J.H. Elliott in his Introduction to the volume, "is its attempt to portray the Atlantic colonial world from Ireland to Brazil as a relatively homogenous unit, moving in common response to common requirements and pressures" (1987, 4).

The Quinn-Canny view of Anglo-Irish history has not gone unchallenged among historians of early modern Ireland. None of the historians disputing their model has sought to deny that Ireland's situation in this period was indeed in some fundamental sense colonial; to do so, as T.C. Barnard rightly observes, "would be perverse" (1990, 42).[18] But such historians *have* challenged the assumptions of Quinn and Canny that Ireland can so readily be assimilated to a greater colonial "Atlantic World"—that "English expansion within and without the British Isles" can be viewed "as a single phenomenon" (Bottigheimer, "Kingdom" 1978, 45)—and that Irish history in this period is comprehensible exclusively within the terms of the colonial framework. In challenging the Quinn-Canny model, these historians have sought to bring to light some of the complexities of the Anglo-Irish relationship within the early modern period, noting ways in which Ireland's colonial experience differed from that of other territories colonized from western Europe during the course of the sixteenth and early seventeenth centuries.

One simple, but crucial, difference between Ireland and the New World has been noted by T.C. Barnard. We cannot, he writes, "entirely overlook geography while we wrangle over constitutions and political and economic systems. Propinquity if nothing else related Ireland and England" (43). As neighboring islands, Britain and Ireland are physically close to each other.[19] They are separated by the Irish Sea, which, at its widest point, is no more than about a hundred and thirty miles across. A typical crossing from Britain to Ireland would likely have involved a sea voyage of less than a hundred miles. As Barnard observes, "Travel between the two islands was quick, cheap and regular. The sea journey, although it could be frustrating and hazardous, did not excite the terrors, create the bonds or require the planning that the passage to North America necessitated; it did not in prospect lead to the making of wills or thalassophobia"[20] (43). Jane Dawson has likewise noted that an even clearer set of links existed between Ulster and western Scotland: "Geography, culture and strategy all helped to bind the Scottish and the Irish kingdoms together. The most obvious link was the simple geographical proximity of Ulster to Kintyre and Galloway. In the early modern centuries, the sea united rather than divided communities. Travel by water between the northern Irish coast and the Western Scottish Islands and mainland was much easier than the journey by land between different areas within Ireland or Scotland" (1987, 113-14). As such closely neighboring islands, Britain and Ireland thus inevitably shared an extended common history stretching back over several centuries. By the mid-Tudor period, Ireland, for four of those centuries, had been incorporated in one measure or another into a greater British realm. Thus, whereas the Americas constituted, in so many senses, a distant "virgin territory" for the English, Ireland was in no way a "New World."

One might note here, for example, the virtually ineffable strangeness that Europeans encountered in the New World during the early period of the colonization of the Americas—what Anthony Pagden calls "the very newness of the New World" (Introduction to Las Casas *Short Account* 1992, xxxiv). Pagden quotes Pedro di Quiroga, writing in 1551, "have no dealings with the things of this land until you understand them, because they are strange affairs and a strange language that only experience will reveal to you" (xxxiv). Likewise, Hernán Cortés, in his second letter from Mexico, writes, "I cannot describe one hundreth part of all the things which could be mentioned, but, as best I can, I will describe some of those I have seen which, although badly described, will, I well know, be so remarkable as not to be believed, for we who saw them with our own eyes could not grasp them with our understanding" (101-102).[21] Despite obvious linguistic and cultural differences from England, the familiar neighboring territory of Ireland could never be said to be so exotic—a point registered, in fact, by Francis Bacon, in his "Certain Considerations Touching the Plantation in Ireland":[22] "For *Pleasure,* in this *Region* or *Tract of Soyl,* there is no *Warm Winters,* nor *Orenge Trees,* nor strange *Beasts,* or *Birds,* or other Points of *Curiosity,* or *Pleasure,* as there are in the *Indies,* and the like; So as, there can be found, no Foundation, made upon Matter of *Pleasure,* otherwise, then that the very *Desire* of *Novelty,* and *Experiment,* in some *stirring Natures,* may work somewhat" (1657, 259-60). Likewise, the struggle that can often be discerned in the work of the early explorers of the New

World to rehearse the alien in terms of the familiar seems hardly so urgent or necessary in an Anglo-Irish context.[23]

Ciarán Brady has, in any case, challenged Canny's proposal of a clear English linking of Ireland with the New World and of a definite continuity of rhetoric between both colonial instances. As he observes, "overt comparisons with the new world experience were, as one of their most careful analysts [Nicholas Canny] has conceded, scattered, and lacking in coherent argument. In view of the obvious ideological advantages attached to such identifications, their relative scarcity is odd; and yet there were a number of important factors inhibiting the development of this line of argument" ("Road" 1989, 35). Among the "important factors" that Brady notes as serving to inhibit the establishment of a strong conceptual link between Ireland and the New World was the fact that "the English and the Irish did not meet across a frontier but mingled closely together in a manner that overcame or diluted such cultural differences as existed between them" (35)—again, as I have been suggesting, though Ireland certainly offered a markedly different culture, it was by no means as wholly alien a territory as the Americas.

Brady is also, however, one of a number of writers to have drawn attention to another feature of the sixteenth-century Irish scene that served to distinguish it clearly from the New World. Brendan Bradshaw, for instance, has argued that, in the middle decades of the sixteenth century, Anglo-Irish relations underwent a "constitutional revolution," promoted by a group of "commonwealth liberals" in Dublin and London. The aim of this "revolution" was to incorporate the Irish within the English polity. As part of this process, Henry VIII's title was amended, by the Irish parliament, from "Lord" of Ireland to "King" of Ireland. The intention of this move was, as Bradshaw has made clear, that, "by making explicit the sovereign status of the English crown in Ireland, [the reformers] repudiated the divided structure of the medieval Lordship and replaced it with a constitution that envisaged the island as a political unity, its inhabitants a single community of subjects, governed by the unilateral jurisdiction of the crown. By making the sovereignty explicit also they increased the crown's commitment to giving it reality" (*Constitutional Revolution* 1979, 238).

Elsewhere, Bradshaw has observed that "in taking the title of King, Henry had contracted an obligation to the whole of Ireland as his kingdom, and to all its inhabitants as his subjects. He was pledged, in effect, to the political unification of Ireland under the jurisdiction of the Crown" ("Beginnings" 1973, 76). Michael Neill has rightly pointed out that "it is difficult to overestimate the significance of this statute for the subsequent direction of Irish affairs, for it marks the point at which wholesale incorporation of the native Irish into the body politic defined by English settlement became, for the first time, legally enunciated policy" ("Broken English" 1994, 5). Steven Ellis makes clear the contrast that this offers with the English New World:

> In the case of north America, it was never seriously intended by the crown, as it was in Ireland, to incorporate the territory as a core region in the English state, and to turn the natives there into civil Englishmen . . . to be governed by the normal structures of English administration and law. . . . The depiction of Ireland as an Atlantic colony obscures [a] central feature of English rule there: it reduces English law and administration to an arbitrary external force, shaped simply by the need to control the natives, even though crown and community alike accepted that English administrative structures were supposed to operate in the same way in both England and Ireland. ("Writing Irish History" 1996, 14)

In constitutional terms, the effect of the 1541 legislation was to confirm Ireland's status as a kingdom, with all of the island's inhabitants being seen as the English king's subjects. Of course, this reconceptualization was never wholly conciliatory in its tone or thrust—as Brady has noted, the writings of those who supported the change "were rarely unalloyed and frequently they conceded the necessity of force and dispossession in some areas, and its desirability in others" ("Road" 1989, 26).[24] Likewise, Nicholas Canny is certainly correct in arguing that this policy of incorporation gradually gave way, as the century progressed, to a more clearly colonialist model. Nevertheless, as Karl Bottigheimer has argued in "Kingdom and Colony: Ireland in the Westward Enterprise, 1536-1660," a residual sense of Ireland's status as kingdom persisted throughout the period, serving always to complicate the way in which the island was perceived.[25] Thus, Bottigheimer observes that Ireland "could never escape its legacy as a kingdom of the realm, or its long history of prior connections with England (and Scotland) and the English monarchy" ("Kingdom" 1978, 55). There is, for Bottigheimer, always a certain fundamental English ambivalence in the period under discussion concerning the exact status of Ireland, an ambivalence that centers on the disjunction between English perceptions of the island simultaneously as kingdom and as colony.

In Raymond Gillespie and Ciarán Brady's coauthored introduction to *Natives and Newcomers*, Brady has picked up on Bottigheimer's distinction and suggested that the conceptions of Ireland as kingdom and as colony were not only copresent throughout the period but, indeed, that they were in some sense interpenetrative:

> From the beginning there was an element of colonial exploitation in the attempt to constitute Ireland as a kingdom, and even in periods of intense colonial activity Ireland's sovereign status never disappeared from the minds of either the monarchs or their various subjects in the land. . . . the relative strength of these images of Ireland as kingdom and colony varied among the different power groupings in the island, and over time. Neither ever held sway to the exclusion of the other, each rather coexisted in a delicate balance in the minds of political actors. The effect of each was at all times influenced by the presence of its rival. The course of Irish history between 1534 and 1641 was the result of the continuing interaction between the two, and it was this interaction that made Irish society so distinctive. (17)[26]

In Brady and Gillespie's view Ireland was "a constitutional anomaly, neither the 'kingdom' of England nor a 'colony' in north America" (17).[27]

T.C. Barnard, as we have seen, has joined with Brady and Gillespie and others in stressing the importance of the greater extended British context of Ireland's colonial experience in the sixteenth and seventeenth centuries. He has also drawn attention to another important factor at play in the Anglo-Irish relationship generally. "We should not be distracted," he cautions "from Ireland's place in the European world to which it belonged by tradition, history, culture, religion and trade" (1990, 44). Although Britain and Ireland were closely bound together as neighboring islands, both were also part of a greater European sphere—something that we have noted in our opening engagement with Roddy Doyle's novel. In this sense, too, Ireland must be distinguished from the New World. Ireland, like Britain, had its place in a greater Europe and, thereby, the English and the Irish shared a certain heritage, unlike European colonists in the New World, who found themselves confronted by alien civilizations in an alien land.[28]

Quite apart from any other connections with Europe, we should bear in mind that Ireland had long been involved in European trade of various kinds. To take just one example of such commercial connections, we might note

Hiram Morgan's observation of Hugh Roe O'Donnell's stronghold in Tirconnell, that its Atlantic coastline "made possible strong trading links with Britain and the Continent" and that "in 1560 O'Donnell was described as 'the best lord of fish in Ireland, and he exchangeth fish always with foreign merchants for wine by which [he] is called in other countries the king of fish'" (*Tyrone's Rebellion* 1993, 113).[29] Longstanding traditions of equitable trading such as this formed no part of Europe's relationship with the New World.

The significance of the European connection can also be seen in the area of religion. Britain and Ireland shared a common European Christian heritage extending back at least a thousand years from the Renaissance era.[30] Indeed, missionaries from the islands of Britain and Ireland had jointly played a large part in forging a European Christian community in the middle ages. As W.R. Jones has observed, "the success of Irish and Anglo-Saxon missionary efforts and of Carolingian imperialism broadened the extent of the Christian community and endowed it with a unified territorial existence. The idea of a more or less spiritually homongeneous Christendom, sharpened by attacks on its periphery by Avars, Slavs, Vikings, Magyars, and, occasionally, Arabs, evolved as a fact, if not as a name, during the eight, ninth, and tenth centuries" (1971, 390).

In the sixteenth century, of course, such religious commonality was sundered by the divisive issue of the Reformation.[31] The Reformation failed in Ireland (among both the Gaelic Irish and, for the most part, among the descendants of the original colonists also) and the religious rupture to which the Reformation gave rise was, in a certain measure, convenient for the English, because it provided them with a serviceable means for effecting a distinction between themselves and their fellow Christian neighbors.[32] Having said this, however, we should also note that the religious divisions of the sixteenth century should not be seen in the stark terms suggested by the unremittingly polar Catholic-Protestant divide of the Ireland of our own century. As many recent commentators have observed, the question of "why the Reformation failed in Ireland" is enormously vexed.[33] Indeed, Nicholas Canny has argued that the very framing of the question itself tends to posit an implacable opposition between a securely entrenched Catholicism and an alien, innovative Protestantism, denying any possibility that the Reformation might ever have succeeded. As Canny observes, at least as far as anglicized Ireland was concerned, "the failure of the state religion to win popular support . . . was by no means a foregone conclusion by the 1570s, most especially when we allow for the English experience where individuals and communities whose attachment was to pre-Reformation Christian practice, but who occasionally conformed to the state religion, were as liable to be fully absorbed into the Established Church as to be lost forever to the Counter-Reformation" ("Reformation" 1979, 434).[34] It may also be worth noting here that the issue of religion did not immediately serve as a clear and inevitable marker of difference in Ireland in this period. Ciarán Brady notes, for instance, that "the fact that, as late as 1569, Edmund Campion, a dangerous intellectual dissident, could be lodged consecutively in the houses of the speaker and the leader of the opposition of the Irish commons under the protective eye of the viceroy, is a curious indication of the lack of urgency with which the reformation was pursued by the government. Even after Elizabeth's excommunication in 1570 the level of tension remained low. Known recusants continued to occupy high places within the administration or to enjoy the patronage of government officials" (*Chief Governors* 1994, 211).

We should also note that, in this context, the Reformed community itself was by no means a monolithic entity, set in discrete opposition to its Catholic counterpart. Recent work by Thomas Healy is enormously instructive in this regard. Healy offers as an alternative to Benedict Anderson's (1979) conception of the nation as an "imagined community," the notion of a national identity predicated on the "sectarian community," suggesting that "what predominantly fashions the imagined organisations of integrated self or state in early modern England is a sectarian identity founded on religious difference."[35] But, as Healy makes clear, this "sectarian identity," even as it defines itself against its alien others, experiences difficulty both in isolating itself from its alien counterpart and in accommodating difference within its own boundaries:

The rhetoric of inclusion, the pursuit of wholeness in either self-definition or national identification, is matched by an uncertainty about communion. In part this disparity occurs because the rhetorical borders erected by sectarian positions to separate their identities from the alien were in actuality far more permeable than sectarian rhetoric can admit. The more claims to wholeness are made in the language of self-definition, the more forces are recognized, within and without the imagined national community, which disrupt a sectarian language's claims to accurate, hegemonic, self-representation.

As Healy indicates, the coherence of a centralized Protestant identity is challenged both by its encounter with alien others who cannot be fully excluded and by those communities within (for example, English recusants) that cannot be fully included within its terms. The Irish, in a sense, lie at the intersection of these two issues: like their Catholic counterparts in England itself, they are not assimilable to the community that defines itself on sectarian lines, but, at the same time, they cannot be securely excluded from that community either.

If we turn back to looking at the issue of religion in a broader European context, we might note that the persistence of Catholicism in Ireland tended to reaffirm the European lineage of the Irish, so that, in their conflicts with the English, they tended to look to the continent, seeking aid from and alliance with the European Catholic powers. We can see this connection most clearly when, during the course of the Nine Years' War against the English at the close of the sixteenth century, a group of Irish leaders elected to solicit military support from Catholic Europe in the name of the Counter-Reformation. In this sense, we might say that religion served as a marker of civil connectedness for the Irish within the greater European sphere as they forged alliances with their continental correligionists.[36] Once again, Ireland's position can be distinguished from that of the New World, where no such historical or religious links or alliances with the European powers could be claimed by the natives.

One of the Irish leaders who sponsored the approach to Christian Europe was Hugh O'Donnell. Morgan informs us that O'Donnell wrote to King Philip of Spain and "offered himself as facilitator . . . . He asserted that it was a propitious time for Philip to invade Ireland because it could be conquered at little cost and be used to divert the English from interfering in the affairs of France and Flanders" (*Tyrone's Rebellion* 1993, 141). The terms in which O'Donnell's approach are couched serve to highlight the manner in which the conflict in Ireland was seen as taking its place within a greater European political and military framework.[37] The war in Ireland is presented as being intimately connected with other struggles taking place elsewhere, and Ireland is aligned with the interests of a greater Catholic Europe.

The larger European framework is also highlighted by the case of O'Donnell's northern ally, Hugh O'Neill, who served as leader of the Irish forces in the Nine Years' War. Hans Pawlisch notes that O'Neill "maintained two agents, Peter Lombard of Waterford and Edmund MacDonnell, Dean of Armagh, at the courts of Rome and Spain" (1985, 64), and R.F. Foster has observed of O'Neill that he "was spoken of in Europe, and treated with as 'Prince of Ireland'" (1989, 5). The Spanish court made repeated efforts to supply O'Neill and O'Donnell with soldiers and munitions throughout the last decade of the sixteenth century, eventually succeeding in landing a substantial force of men at Kinsale in 1601. When he had finally been defeated and out-manuvered by the English, O'Neill went into exile on the continent and lived out the remainder of his life in Rome, the recipient of a papal pension.[38]

We have begun, thus, to map out some of the ways in which the particularities of Ireland's situation and history render deeply questionable any easy assimilation of Ireland's colonial experience to a greater global colonialism embracing the New World. The next task is to draw on this historiographical record in order to evoke a more formalized conception of the category of proximity.

III.

If we return for a moment to Edward Said, we will recall his noting that "it is true that the connections are closer between England and Ireland" than within other colonial relationships. We are now in a better position to provide an account of the particular ways in which England and Ireland are close and to suggest what the significance of that closeness is.

At the most basic level, T.C. Barnard reminds us that "propinquity if nothing else related Ireland and England." Unlike Europe and its transatlantic territories, the islands of Britain and Ireland lie in close physical proximity to each other. This physical proximity has resulted in an extended history of contact between the two islands, stretching over many centuries. From the late-twelfth century onward, Ireland was in one measure or another incorporated into a greater British realm. The nature of this "incorporation" certainly changed over the years, but it had the general effect throughout the centuries of formalizing a certain close relationship among the populations of the two islands.

But, as Barnard and others also remind us, Ireland and Britain are both part of a greater Europe—a world to which they belong "by tradition, history, culture, religion, and trade." Thus, whereas the Irish and the British share a certain history as peoples from the same island group, they also both participate in a greater "continental" identity and share an ethnic, cultural, and religious heritage. And though the religious issue served as a marker of division from the time of the Reformation forward, it also served to strengthen the links between the Catholic Irish and their European correligionists, thus highlighting Ireland's place within a greater European Catholic sphere.

The Irish and the British are thus bound together in a complex relationship of proximity: as European Christians living in neighboring islands with a long history of contact formalized into a series of arrangements aimed at absorbing one island into the dominion of the other. This, then, is the nature of Anglo-Irish proximity. But what are its implications? To recur to Barnard once again, we note that he has asserted that "it would be perverse to deny that in some ways Ireland was treated and behaved like a colony" (42). The nature of English intervention in the affairs of Ireland *is* always in some ways colonial. The English always behave in some ways like colonialists, and the Irish are always in some ways perceived as the colonized. But in other ways, the exact nature of the English initiative in Ireland is altogether more ambiguous. And, in some ways, though the English would construct the Irish as colonial Other, as we have already seen, the Irish — precisely because of their longstanding proximate relationship with the British — fail so easily to answer the English as one half of the colonial dyad. It is this failure that, as in the case of Kingsley, serves to disrupt the thrust of English colonial discourse on Ireland.

In his 1946 study, *Anti-Semite and Jew,* Jean-Paul Sartre characterized anti-Semitism as "at bottom a form of Manichaeism," observing that "it explains the course of the world by the struggle of the principle of Good with the principle of Evil. Between these two principles no reconciliation is conceivable; one of them must triumph and the other be annihilated" (1976, 40-41). Influenced by Sartre, Frantz Fanon adapted this same notion in *Black Skin, White Masks* (1986) and in *The Wretched of the Earth,* where he describes the colonial space as "a world cut in two" (1968, 38). "The colonial world," Fanon writes, "is a Manichean world. It is not enough for the settler to delimit physically, that is to say with the help of the army and the police force, the place of the native. As if to show the totalitarian character of colonial exploitation the settler paints the native as a sort of quintessence of evil" (41). Abdul JanMohamed has picked up on Fanon's analysis of colonial Manichaeism and has evolved from it a theory of "colonialist literary representation" arguing that "the dominant model of power- and interest-relations in all colonial societies is the manichean opposition between the putative superiority of the European and the supposed inferiority of the native. This axis in turn provides the central feature of the colonialist cognitive framework and colonialist literary representation: the manichean allegory—a field of diverse yet interchangeable oppositions between white and black, good and evil, superiority and inferiority, civilization and savagery, intelligence and emotion, rationality and sensuality, self and Other, subject and object" ("Economy" 1986, 82).[39]

Jan Mohamed's theory of colonialist literary representation is in many ways as applicable to Anglo-Irish colonialist writing (literary or otherwise) as it is to the colonial novels to which he applies it in his *Manichean Aesthetics.* There tends to be a recrudesence of English writing on Ireland in times of Anglo-Irish crisis, and such writing is often motivated by a desire to justify or advocate harsh measures against the population of the island. The grounds for this justification or advocacy are often derived from just such a Manichean formulation as Fanon and JanMohamed describe.[40]

However, even though it may well indeed be possible to trace a profound *desire* for Manichean order within Anglo-Irish colonialist writing generally, the attempted deployment of what JanMohamed isolates as the typical bipolar oppositions that have served historically as the basis of colonialist analysis ("white and black, good and evil, superiority and inferiority, civilization and savagery," and so on) invariably tends, in an Irish context, to be disrupted by the colonial text's inevitable encountering of the issue of Irish proximity. Many of the oppositional binaries that JanMahomed isolates here are either—as Kingsley discovers—not wholly applicable to the Irish situation or else can only be adapted to that situation by placing the terms of the dichotomy under considerable strain.

It should also be noted, in any case, that in recent years poststructuralist writers on colonialism have begun to challenge the notion of a relatively coherent set of binary oppositions that a strictly Manichean theory of colonialist discourse implies. Robert Young, for instance, has contrasted Edward Said's classic formulation of a totalized binary colonial system with "the Derridean account that draws attention to the ways in which totalizations never succeed in producing a perfect structure of inclusions and exclusions, with the result that the unassimilable elements determine (and disallow) any totality which seeks to constitute itself as a totality by excluding them" (1990, 137). Homi Bhabha has been in the vanguard of such critics, as he has attempted to provide a more complex model of colonial stereotyping, emphasizing the psychoanalytic component of Fanon's theorizing and taking account of poststructuralist theories of discourse.[41]

Bhabha clearly recognizes the *force* of colonialist discourse, observing that "the objective" of such discourse "is to construe the colonized as a population of degenerate types on the basis of racial origins, in order to justify conquest and to establish systems of administration and instruction" (*Location* 1994, 70). At the same time, however, he cautions against an overly simplified or schematic view of the mechanism of colonial stereotyping, arguing that "stereotyping is not the setting up of a false image which becomes the scapegoat of discriminatory practices. It is a much more ambivalent text of projection and introjection, metaphoric and metonymic strategies, displacement, over-determination, guilt, aggressivity; the masking and splitting of 'official' and phantasmatic knowledges to construct the positionalities and oppositionalities of racist discourse" (81-82). There is, for Bhabha, a certain profound "ambivalence" at the core of all colonialist construction. "The [colonial] stereotype," he argues, "is a complex, ambivalent, contradictory mode of representation, as anxious as it is assertive" (70).

To this extent, then, the fissures and instabilities of Anglo-Irish discourse — its inability to mobilize and sustain the kinds of clear dichotomies that Jan-Mohamed delineates — may be symptomatic of the kinds of splitting and ambivalences that Bhabha sees as fundamental to the ways in which *all* colonialist discourse inevitably and necessarily functions.[42] But in the Anglo-Irish instance, this process becomes, as it were, "redoubled," as the effort to evoke and sustain difference is further undermined by the ambiguous status of the Irish. Thus, if all binaries are constitutively unstable, we might say that, in an Irish context, the instabilities of the colonial binary are peculiarly hard to elude or elide, as the odd simultaneity of the likeness and otherness of the Irish (what I am calling "proximity") always serves to disrupt the desired exclusivist polarity of the colonialist paradigm. The colonialist writer on Ireland is thus, again and again — and in an especially forceful manner — brought up against the failure of discursive binaries to sustain themselves, as the proximate status of the Irish serves to undermine their intended colonial positioning.

Here we might usefully refer to Jonathan Dollimore's deployment of the concept of proximity in a different context — his analysis of constructions of homo/sexuality in *Sexual Dissidence*.[43] Dollimore notes that "within metaphysical constructions of the Other what is typically occluded is the significance of the *proximate*" (1991, 33). It seems entirely fitting that Dollimore should first introduce this notion into his analysis in a chapter on Oscar Wilde.[44] "For Wilde," Dollimore writes, "transgressive desire is both rooted in culture and the impetus for affirming different/alternative kinds of culture . . . [It] is because of and not in spite of this shared cultural dimension that Wilde can enact one of the most disturbing of all forms of transgression, namely that whereby the outlaw turns up as inlaw, and *the other as proximate proves more disturbing than the other as absolute difference*" (15 [emphasis added]). For Dollimore, then, Wilde is a kind of liminal figure who enacts transgression at the point of intersection of different cultural, sexual, and, we might add, *national* orders. He is the outlaw who turns up as inlaw, eliciting (and soliciting), in the process, profound anxiety and disruption.[45]

For Dollimore, the Wildean moment provides an instance of what he terms *transgressive reinscription*— "a *turning back* upon something and a perverting of it typically if not exclusively through inversion and displacement" (323). In English texts about Ireland, what we often find is a similar "turning back," but by the text itself, on the essayed system of difference. Thus, to recur to Kingsley again, the shock of the Irish encounter is that the Irish "except where tanned by exposure" turn out to be as white as the English, so that, in this instance, the expected outlaws turn out in fact to be inlaws of a kind. It is indeed true for Kingsley that "the other as proximate proves more disturbing than the other as absolute difference"; as Kingsley himself puts it, "If they were black one would not feel it so much." We might well ask, then, on behalf of Kingsley and his fellow English writers, the question posed by Dollimore elsewhere in *Sexual Dissidence:* "Finally, is it possible that we fear sameness as much as we fear difference?" (63).

IV.

In the introduction to their seminal essay collection, *Representing Ireland,* Andrew Hadfield and Willy Maley observe that, in the early modern period, "Ireland was both a mirror and a hammer—reflecting and fragmenting images of England" (1993, 15). The phrase is an evocative one, and the authors intend it as a comment on the way in which, during this period, English identity became oddly contingent on the process of representing Ireland. As Hadfield and Maley note, "One of the most important ways in which Ireland was read in this period was as a series of negative images of Englishness. Ireland, in this respect, as well as being a text, is a negative of a photograph of English identity which never comes into view; we have only the negative, not the original print" (7). Hadfield and Maley's real focus here is the process whereby "the development of 'Englishness' depended on the negation of 'Irishness'" (7), but their chosen metaphors have still deeper resonances. A photograph and its negative are different entities and carry different images. But those images are, of course, not entirely divorced from each other, and the negative image is always recognizable as a version of its "positive" counterpart. The territory of this study, in contrast (or, rather, I would say, in complement) to the work of scholars such as Hadfield and Maley, is precisely the space in which this recognition is encountered and engaged with—the moment in which it is realized, as it were, that the positive inheres in the negative. In this process, Ireland is indeed "a mirror and a hammer." In encountering Ireland, the English writer expects to find a sharply defined Otherness but instead finds, adumbrated within the outline of the Other, a certain image of the Self. That encounter, far from facilitating a kind of enabling "misrecognition," in fact serves to interrogate the desired misreading of colonial stereotyping. In this sense, Ireland is also, as Hadfield and Maley suggest, "a hammer . . . fragmenting images of England." But this "of" has the same double force as Doyle's "niggers *of* Europe," in that the images fragmented are at one and the same time images of the Other invoked by the English and images of the Self evoked by Irish proximity. It is that process of fragmentation that English writing on Ireland seeks—and finally fails—to contain.

2

"Ad Remotissimas Occidentis Insulas"
Gerald and the Irish

I.

In a much quoted remark in the essay "Anglo-Irish Attitudes," Declan Kiberd has observed that "the English did not invade Ireland—rather, they seized a neighboring island and invented the idea of Ireland" (1986, 83).[1] Insofar as there is an "originary" moment in that process of invention, it can be traced to the closing decades of the twelfth century and the arrival of the Norman-English in Ireland.[2] It is in this period that the cleric Gerald de Barri, or "Giraldus Cambrensis," became, as F.X. Martin has noted, "the first foreigner to write a book about Ireland" (1969, 279).[3] Gerald was a member of the extended Cambro-Norman family grouping (the Geraldines) who made up a large portion of the contingent of adventurers who initially came to Ireland from Britain in 1167 in support of the deposed Irish king of Leinster, Diarmait MacMurchada. This group eventually remained and settled in the country, to pursue their own territorial ambitions.[4]

Gerald actually wrote two books about Ireland: the *Topographia Hibernica* (*c.* 1187) and the *Expugnatio Hibernica* (*c.* 1189). The former is a general account of the island and its people, whereas the latter consists largely of a celebration of the history of Gerald's own family's intervention in Ireland. Taken together, these texts serve as the foundational documents of an extended tradition of writing on Ireland, providing succeeding generations of writers from Britain with sources of information about the land and its people. In addition, Gerald's texts represent a first attempt not just to write at extended length about the island of Ireland but also to meditate on Irish culture and heritage as well as the relationship of the Irish to the inhabitants of neighboring Britain.

A number of writers have noted that the Norman-English project in Ireland occurred against a background of significant colonialist expansion within Europe generally. Michael Richter, for instance, has suggested that the "invasion of Ireland may be profitably studied in a wider context . . . as an aspect of a more widely noticeable European phenomenon in a period of economic and demographic growth" (1985, 292). Anngret Simms, likewise, sees Ireland's experience as being all of a piece with a general process of expansion taking place within Europe, arguing that "medieval colonisation in Ireland was part of the wider process of people, settlement and agricultural and military innovations spreading from the European core areas to the more peripheral regions" (1988, 37). On this basis, Simms has noted certain key similarities in the situations and attitudes of Gerald and of other commentators of the period, such as Adam of Bremen, who wrote an account of the Scandinavians in the 1070s, and Helmold of Bosau, whose *Chronicle of the Slavs* was written in the 1170s.

There are, however, certain key distinctions that must be made between the Norman-English expansion westward and other contemporary expansionist projects. In the first instance, we might note that some historians have recently argued against seeing the advent of the Norman-English to Ireland unambiguously in terms of "invasion" or "conquest" and have stressed the prior history of contact between the Irish and their neighbors in Britain. In the volume on the medieval period of the 1987 Oxford *New History of Ireland*, for instance, F.X. Martin has written of Diarmait MacMurchada's soliciting of aid from Britain that it was "no mere leap into the unknown": "He was no barbaric native chieftain, crazed by defeat and blindly seeking a patron abroad among the superpowers. Two decades before he set out from Ireland he had already been associated with Henry II, to whom he had supplied ships for campaigns in Wales" (48).[5]

But just as the Irish and the Norman-English were in some degree united by a history of prior contact and alliance, so too were they related by their common participation in a greater European realm. This connection is particularly clear in the case of religion. At the time of the advent of the Norman-English to Ireland, Irish monks and missionaries had been playing an active and well-recognized role within the European Christian world for several centuries. Indeed, Irish clergy played a crucial part in helping to establish a greater Christian realm within Europe. As W.R. Jones has observed, "the success of Irish and Anglo-Saxon missionary efforts and of Carolingian imperialism broadened the extent of the Christian community and endowed it with a unified territorial existence" (1971, 390). Denis Bethell has also noted the strong tradition of Irish pilgrimage abroad and the establishment of communities of Irish monks in continental Europe, "The tenth and eleventh centuries saw . . . the foundation of wholly new communities on the continent, at Waulsort in the Ardennes by St Cadroe of Armagh in 946, which was followed by his making an Irish foundation at Metz in the 970s. At the same period we have a description of a crowd of Irish priests who were kept by St. Gerard of Toul, who died in 994. Gero, archbishop of Cologne, brought Irish monks to St Pataleon's 'Cologne' a little later" (1971, 113). With regard to Irish religious contacts with Britain, Bethell notes that "up to 1066 we can still say that English and Irish monks shared a common cultural world in which the Irish could still be teachers" (125) and, although the reputation of the Irish as teachers had declined by the twelfth century they nevertheless remained "important purveyors of romance and hagiography" (122).[6]

The significance of Ireland's strong Christian connection in the present context is that it served to distinguish Ireland's situation from that of other areas that experienced the press of expansion in the period. As Robert Bartlett has argued (writing of the Celtic territories generally), a distinction must be drawn "between the situation in the Celtic west, which was Christian, and in Eastern and Baltic Europe, where large numbers of pagans survived throughout the period. The Slav tribes between the Elbe and Poland, Baltic peoples such as the Prussians and Lithuanians, and a considerable proportion of the Scandinavians were pagan in the twelfth-century" (1982, 167-68). The importance of this distinction emerges precisely at the time of Gerald's writing of his Irish books, because in this period the preparations for the Third Crusade served to foreground a stark division between the Christian West and the "heathen" East. The effect of the fall of Jerusalem to Saladin in 1187 (very likely the year in which Gerald completed the first of his Irish books) can be seen in the writing of William of Newburgh, in which the Christian West becomes a single realm united in sorrow at the news from the Holy Land: "The sad rumour of these unfortunate events in the East spread quickly throughout the world and brought shock and horror to the hearts of all Christians" (quoted in Bartlett 78-79). In this context, we find that the foregrounding of the conflict between the West and the alien East serves to drive European Christians together as a single community, a community to which, of course, Ireland belonged.[7]

We might say, then, that even at the very moment of Gerald's inception of an British tradition of textualizing Ireland, the island and its people presented an anomalous case within the context of other, contemporary colonial endeavors. The Irish had a certain common history with their invading neighbors, as they also had a common religious affiliation with them and participated jointly in a greater religious and cultural world. This situation was further intensified by the fact that the Irish colonial venture was undertaken against the background of a greater split between East and West so that Ireland's alignment with a positive realm contradistinguished from the negatively valenced East becomes all the more apparent.

Thus, in writing about the Irish in this period, Gerald had not only to strive to evoke a sense of Irish Otherness, but also needed to engage with and account for the fact that, within that Otherness, there resided a certain profound and enduring element of proximite alignment. We can trace in Gerald's work the strategies he employs both for engaging with and disengaging an Irish sense of proximity, and also the residual inscription of that proximity within his narratives.

II.

Gerald's first Irish book is divided into three parts. Part 1 is largely traditional in its ambition and scope. Thus, for instance, where Bede opens his *History* by noting that "Britain, formerly known as Albion, is an island in the ocean, lying towards the north west at a considerable distance from the coasts of Germany, Gaul, and Spain, which together form the greater part of Europe" (1990, 44),[8] Gerald begins the *Topographia* by telling his readers that "Ireland, the largest island beyond Britain, is situated in the western ocean about one short day's sailing from Wales . . . This farthest island of the west has

Spain parallel to it on the south . . . Greater Britain on the east . . . and only the ocean on the west" (1982, 33).[9]

The initial purpose of the first part of Gerald's text is to provide an account of the geographic location and primary physical features of the island (for instance, *"The nine principal rivers and many others that have recently emerged"* [36])[10] and to log its various flora and fauna, checking them against the plant and animal stock of the British and greater western regions, and noting Irish novelties, absences, and similarities (*"Fish that are new and not found elsewhere"* [38]; *"Birds and those that are missing"* [38]; "Ireland has almost all the kinds of wild animals that are found in the western regions" [47]).

As a conclusion to his catalog of anomalies among the Irish fauna, Gerald notices the absence in Ireland of "all poisonous reptiles" (50). This too, in a sense, is traditional, and Gerald again follows Bede in further informing his readers that "if poison be brought in [to Ireland], no matter what it be, from elsewhere, immediately it loses all the force of its evil" (51) and in suggesting that certain items of Irish origin provide an antidote against poison (*"The dust of this land which kills poisonous reptiles"* [51]; *"The boot-thongs of this country used as antidotes against poison"* [51]). Gerald rejects the traditional explanation that poisonous reptiles are absent from Ireland because they were banished from the island by St. Patrick, and, again like Bede, instead suggests that their absence stems from the natural benignity of the territory and its climate: "Some indulge in the pleasant conjecture that Saint Patrick and other saints of the land purged the island of all harmful animals. But it is more probable that from the earliest times, and long before the laying of the foundations of the Faith, the island was naturally without these as well as other things" (50).[11]

The effect of Gerald's adoption of this particular explanation for the absence of reptiles in Ireland is to disjoin the island's benignity from the realm of Christian innovation and to assign it instead to a natural condition of the land itself. In this sense it may appear as if Gerald in some measure is seeking to de-emphasize the transformative effects of Ireland's Christian tradition — a tradition that it shares with the rest of the western European world.

However, at the very end of this first part of the *Topographia,* it is precisely a figuration of an Ireland incorporated into a positive West that emerges in the text. This vision of a positive western arena is achieved by the unexpected irruption into the text of a negatively charged East from which the West is contradistinguished. In the twenty-sixth chapter of the opening part, Gerald summarizes *"the many good points of the island and the natural qualities of the country"* (53). This chapter is then followed by a direct comparison of West with East:

> What riches has the East then to offer in comparison with these? It has, of course, many-coloured silken cloth produced by the silk-worm; it has precious metals of certain types, sparkling gems and aromatic spices. But what are these in comparison with the loss of life and health? They are obtained only by enduring constantly the enmity of an enemy that one cannot get away from — the air that is within, and that surrounds one. (54)

As Gerald continues, he elaborates further his sense of the strong dichotomy that separates East from West. It becomes clear that it is not merely a pestilential climate that threatens one in the East:

> The poisoned hand is to be feared there too: that of his step-mother by the step-son, of the enraged wife by her husband, and that of his wicked cook by the master. And not only food and drink, but also clothes, chairs and seats of all kinds. Poisons attack you from all sides, as also do poisonous animals. But the most harmful of all harmful things attacks you — man himself. Among so many dangers of death, what feeling can there be of security of life? Or rather, among so many deaths, what life can there be? (55)

Gerald next turns from his evocation of a ubiquitously toxic East to contemplate, in two chapters, the benefits of the West. In the first of these chapters, he writes of *"the incomparable mildness of our climate,"* noting that "We can safely take our rest in the open air, or upon bare marble. We have no fear of any breeze, piercing in its coldness, fever-laden with its heat, or pestilential in what it brings. The air, that by breathing in we encompass and which continually encompasses us, is guaranteed to us to be kindly and health-giving" (55). In the second chapter, he writes of *"certain deficiencies here that are in fact praiseworthy"* (55). The net effect of these two chapters — with, in the first instance, the insistent repetition of the first person plural and, in the second, of the repeatedly emphasized "here" distinguished from the implied "there" of the East — is to incorporate Ireland into a greater positive Western realm distinguished from a pernicious East.[12] So, we might say, Gerald begins the *Topographia* by actually acknowledging a relationship of proximity between

Ireland and the West, acknowledging an Irish "sameness" counterposed against an Eastern "difference."

In the closing chapter of part 1, Ireland is brought into a direct contrast with the East, as Gerald posits a general theory of the relationship between toxicity and geography: "The well of poisons brims over in the East. The farther therefore from the East it operates, the less does it exercise the force of its natural efficacy. And by the time it reaches these farthest parts, after having traversed such long distances, losing its force gradually, it is entirely exhausted—just as the sun, the farther from the zodiac it sends its rays, the less does it exercise the force of its heat; and so some of the farthest parts of the arctic regions are completely without the benefit of its warmth" (56). Here Ireland becomes, as it were, the absolute point of the positive West, since, as the farthest territory from the East, it provides a zone in which Eastern poison is so weakened as to be entirely ineffectual. In this sense, Ireland is more completely distinguished from the East than is any other part of the West and is thus set against the East in a relationship of direct opposition.

At the end of part 1 of the *Topographia,* then, Gerald acknowledges Ireland's relationship of proximity to the Western realm. Indeed, Ireland seems the very apotheosis of that Western positivity that is contradistinguished from the negative East. We notice, however, that, in thus positioning Ireland as the absolute zero point of a graduated scale that runs from East to West, Gerald, in a sense, also *disjoins* Ireland from a continuous East-West realm, since the island is presented as standing alone as that unique place where no poison prevails. Thus, though it would appear in one way to epitomize the positive West, Ireland can also be seen as being anomalous and discontinuous from the West.

It is this sense of Ireland's anomalous relationship to the rest of the world that Gerald picks up on as he begins to shift his focus at the opening of the second part of the *Topographia.* Where at the close of part 1 he unites Ireland with the West *against* the East, Gerald now, continuing to invoke the East-West dichotomy, turns to *aligning* Ireland *with* the East by presenting *both* realms as anomalous territories lying outside the central Western domain.

In this maneuver, Gerald embraces a longstanding tradition that associated those territories peripheral to the West (broadly defined—implying over time Greece, Rome, Christian Europe) with the anomalous and the marvelous. Herodotus, for instance, writing in the fifth-century B.C., observed that "the most distant parts of the world, as they enclose and wholly surround all other lands, should have those things which we deem best and rarest" (quoted in Hodgen 1964, 27).

Within the genre of European marvels literature, the traditional site of the marvelous had tended to be located in the East. As Mary Campbell notes in *The Witness and the Other World*, "The Greek authors who first promulgated the marvels material in Europe tended to concentrate on the Eastern 'Elsewhere' for historical reasons: they saw more of Asia than of other distant areas and came into political conflict with it. Their medieval inheritors and plagiarists continued what had become a traditional identification of monsters with the East—partly, at least at first, out of habit" (1988, 48).[13] In his opening address to Henry II at the very beginning of the *Topographia*, Gerald unites the marvelous East with an Ireland that is figured as something akin to the Far West: "Just as the countries of the East are remarkable and distinguished for certain prodigies peculiar and native to themselves, so the boundaries of the West also are made remarkable by their own wonders of nature. For sometimes tired, as it were, of the true and the serious, she draws aside and goes away, and in these remote parts indulges herself in these secret and distant freaks" (31).

In recurring to this notion at the opening of part 2 of the *Topographia*, Gerald points out that, in presenting his account of "things which, appearing to be contrary to nature's course, are worthy of wonder," he is actually embarking on a new departure within the marvels tradition: "For just as the marvels of the East have through the work of certain authors come to the light of public notice, so the marvels of the West *which, so far, have remained hidden away and almost unknown,* may eventually find in me one to make them known even in these later days" (57; my emphasis). In this sense, Gerald sees his gesture of uniting Ireland with the East as something novel. The effect of this gesture is in part to signal a shift in Gerald's conception of the East-West dichotomy so that Ireland now becomes realigned with an anomalous non-Western realm against which Western "orthodoxy" is defined. Over the course of the second part of the *Topographia*, Gerald deploys this realignment as a strategy for seeking to negate the relationship of proximity between Ireland and the positive West, which he initially acknowledged at the end of part 1.

III.

Although Gerald aligns Ireland with the East in the opening of part 2 of the *Topographia,* his account of Irish anomalies differs from the Eastern marvels tradition in one respect, in that his text actually consists of an intertwining of two separate strands of writing. In the first chapter of this part, Gerald proposes to provide an account, not only of "such things as are marvellous in themselves" but also to treat "of those exceedingly wonderful and miraculous deeds done through the merits of the saints" (57). In the *Topographia,* Gerald thus combines a version of the Eastern marvels tradition with a Christian tradition of miracle stories taken from the lives of the saints.

In one sense, the effect of this combination may be to undermine Ireland's Christian heritage by associating the works of the island's saints with the anomalous wonders characteristic of the heathen East. But Gerald's undertaking in part 2 of the *Topographia* is, in fact, more complex than this. The text does not provide simply a process of inversion whereby Ireland, having once been acknowledged as a proximate territory, is simply restored to the desired negative position through being brought finally into coherent alignment with the East from which it had initially been positively distinguished. In fact, what emerges over the course of part 2 of the book is that the strategic thrust of the text is, first, to evoke precisely Ireland's dual status of simultaneous alignment with East and West and, then, to follow this evocation of Ireland's double positioning with a meditation on the *implications* of such liminal status.

In effect, what we are presented with in part 2 of Gerald's book is a critique of the very position that Ireland occupies astride the East-West divide, conforming fully to neither Sameness nor Otherness but rather approximating simultaneously to each. Gerald provides this critique by evoking within his narratives of Ireland's miracles and marvels a set of strict dichotomies and by relating what happens when such dichotomies are transgressed—when definite boundaries are not sustained. The final effect of the cumulative set of anecdotes and stories presented in part 2 is to deny that any kind of mediate position is sustainable—indeed to suggest that the breaching of boundaries separating dichotomous realms is morally repugnant and is therefore subject to divine retribution. In the context of Ireland, it is as if Gerald, having presented the island as a territory that straddles two antithetical realms, now recruits the island's joint wonders tradition to the task of emphasizing the importance of maintaining strict distinctions, stressing that no mediate position is either feasible or morally allowable.

We can see Gerald's invocation of an essentially Manichean dichotomy most clearly in his tale of "a lake in Ulster which contains an island divided into two parts":

One part contains a very beautiful church with a great reputation for holiness, and is well worth seeing. It is distinguished above all other churches by the visitation of angels and the visible and frequent presence of local saints.

But the other part of the island is stony and ugly and is abandoned to the use of evil spirits only. It is nearly always the scene of gatherings and processions of evil spirits, plain to be seen by all. (61)

In a similar vein, he presents us with another island that "no woman or animal of the female sex could ever enter . . . without dying immediately." He goes on to tell us that "this has been proved many times by instances of dogs and cats and other animals of the female sex. When brought there often to make a trial, they immediately died" (60).

In these stories, Gerald provides us with a set of starkly dichotomous realms, and, in the case of the gender restrictive isle, he notes the fatal consequences that attend on any attempt to breach the boundaries of those dichotomies. Those belonging to one category simply cannot survive in its opposing realm. Such insistence on the consequence of transgression is characteristic of many of the other anecdotes that appear in part 2 of the *Topographia*. For instance, in *"A big lake that had a marvellous origin"* (64), Gerald rehearses the traditional story of the origins of Lough Neagh: how a young woman, drawing water from a well, is distracted by her crying child and, running to attend to the boy, she neglects the longstanding injunction that the well be kept covered at all times when not in use. As she is about to return to the well, she meets "such an overflow from that well that both herself and her boy were swept off immediately" and "the whole area was covered with a sea of water which remained there and made a permanent lake" (65).

Though the story itself is traditional, John O'Meara notes in the Introduction to his translation of the *Topographia* (132) that Gerald makes one significant new contribution to the narrative: he attributes the catastrophic effluxion of the well to the fact that the people of the region were "very much given to vice, and particularly addicted, above any other people in Ireland, to bestiality" (64). The inundation of the land thus becomes a punishment from God for "such filthy crimes against nature" (65).

What we can see in this anecdote is, once more, the consequences of transgressing a sharply demarcated boundary—this time the boundary between the human and other species. The marvels section of the *Topographia* contains quite a number of such stories concerning bestiality. In some cases, the bestial union produces offspring. These are monstrous progeny, neither one thing nor another, as in the case of the creature who "had all the parts of the human body except the extremities which were those of an ox" (73). Again, any positioning that attempts to bridge discrete, separated realms is either untenable or repugnant. The liminal fruits of such positioning are monstrous and repellant.

The anecdotes that Gerald produces from the lives of the Irish saints have a similar cast to them. Saints Nannan and Yvor are associated with tales of irrevocable banishment and the establishment of strict zones of exclusion. We learn of a certain village in Connacht where "there was such a multitude of fleas" that "the place was almost abandoned because of the pestilence, and was left without inhabitants, until, through the intercession of Saint Nannan, the fleas were brought to a certain neighboring meadow. The divine intervention because of the merits of the saint so cleansed the place that not a single flea could ever afterwards be found here. But the number of them in the meadow is so great that it ever remains inaccessible not only to men but also to beasts" (80-81). Likewise, in Ferneginan in Leinster, "the larger mice that are commonly called rats were entirely expelled by the curse of the bishop, Saint Yvor, whose books they had happened to eat. They cannot be bred nor can they live there, if brought in" (81).

In a series of stories concerning Saint Brigid, the consequences of transgressing stringent boundaries are once again stressed. In the area of County Kildare associated with Brigid, there is a fire *that never goes out and whose ashes do not increase*" (81). Gerald tells us that "this fire is surrounded by a hedge which is circular and made of withies, and which no male may cross" (82). The punishment for crossing (or even attempting to cross) this boundary is severe:

At Kildare an archer of the household of earl Richard crossed over the hedge and blew upon Brigid's fire. He jumped back immediately, and went mad. Whomever he met, he blew upon his face and said: "See! That is how I blew on Brigid's fire."

Eventually he . . . asked to be brought to the nearest water. As soon as he was brought there, his mouth was so parched that he drank so much that . . . he burst in the middle and died. (88)

And, again: "Another who, upon crossing over to the fire, had put one shin over the hedge, was hauled back and restrained by his companions. Nevertheless

"Ad Remotissimas Occidentis Insulas"   { 43 }

the foot that had crossed perished immediately with its shank. Ever afterwards, while he lived, he was lame and feeble as a consequence" (88).

Taking this set of narratives in the context of Gerald's exploration of the East-West divide, then, we can say that Gerald, at the end of part 1, presents us with an Ireland that is fully part of a postive Western realm; at the opening of part 2, by shifting his focus, he reorients his image of Ireland so that now, instead of being distinguished from the East, it is in fact aligned with it. In spanning these two positions, Ireland, we might say, becomes truly "proximate": neither completely identical with the Western realm nor yet wholly like its Other, the East. Thus, the project of much of part 2 of the *Topographia*—the thread running through its otherwise rather loose arrangement—becomes the reinvocation of strict dichotomies, so that the validity of the kind of mediate space occupied by a proximate Ireland is denied. The striking feature of this maneuver of Gerald's is that, in itself, it involves a welding together of two different traditions, which one might expect to be held in a dichotomous relationship to one another: the Eastern marvelous and the Western miraculous. It is also striking that, in deploying the stories of Ireland's miracles in this way, Gerald is effectively recruiting the *native* Christian tradition in order to denounce implicitly the island's own ambiguous position.

Perhaps it is all of a piece with this strategy that Gerald should part 2 of the *Topographia* with a criticism of the saints of Ireland: "This seems to me a thing to be noticed that just as the men of this country are during this mortal life more prone to anger and revenge than any other race, so in eternal death the saints of this land that have been elevated by their merits are more vindictive than the saints of any other region" (91). In a sense, Gerald's final gesture in second part is that, having once recruited Ireland's thaumaturgic Christian tradition to his own project, he ends by undermining that tradition in itself—by characterizing the Irish miracle workers as vindictive in their punishment of transgressors.

IV.

Gerald opens the third and final part of the *Topographia* by observing that, "For the rest, it now seems time to turn our pen to the description of the first inhabitants of this land, and take, one after the other, the arrivals of different peoples: how they came, and from where; how long they stayed in the island, and how they disappeared—we shall try to explain all this as briefly and as clearly as possible" (92). In this part of the *Topographia,* Gerald finally turns his attention to the general population of the island, providing an account of their history and an examination of their customs and culture. Having implied in part 2 that Ireland's mediate position relative to the West and the East is simply untenable, the thrust of Gerald's presentation and analysis in the part that follows is to discover, within Ireland's history, discontinuities that would serve to uncouple the island from the greater Western European Christian realm.

This process begins with the story that Gerald presents as the traditional founding moment of Irish history: "According to the most ancient histories of the Irish, Cesara, the grand-daughter of Noah, hearing that the Flood was about to take place, decided to flee in a boat with her companions to the farthest islands of the West, where no man had yet ever lived. She hoped that the vengeance of the Flood would not reach to a place where sin had never been committed" (92-93). Gerald notes that, "in spite of her cleverness," Cesara "did not succeed in putting off the general, not to say universal, disaster" (93). In this sense, he does not claim that the Irish are the direct descendants of Cesara, but he does, in presenting the Cesara story at the head of his Irish history, raise the specter of an Irish population radically uncoupled from the rest of the humankind—a disjunct branch of the family of Noah fled "to the farthest islands of the West" ("ad remotissimas occidentis insulas" [139]) to form their own independent community there.

In the chapters that follow, Gerald continues the narrative of Irish history through successive waves of settlers (Bartholanus "with his three sons and their wives" [93]; *Nemedus from Scythia with his four sons*" [95]; "*the five brothers and sons of Dela*" [96], and so on) until, finally, he reaches the group from whom the contemporary Irish are claimed to be directly descended (no previous group of settlers having persisted on the island beyond a limited number of generations). These are the Basclenses—of Spanish origin—who, Gerald tells us, were directed to Ireland by Gurguintius, the king of the Britons: "Their leaders approached [Gurguintius], and told him whence they had come and the reason for their coming, namely to settle in a country of the West. . . . Eventually the king, on the advice of his counsellors, gave them that island that is now called Ireland, and which was then either entirely uninhabited or had been settled by him. He also gave them pilots for their expedition from among his own fleet" (99). This story is invoked by Gerald as one of the reasons why "Ireland can with some right be claimed by the kings of Britain" (99). The assertion of a relationship of agreement between the ancestors of the inhabitants of the neighboring islands of Ireland and Britain, from the

"Ad Remotissimas Occidentis Insulas"   { 45 }

moment of the first sustained "impeopling" of Ireland (to borrow a phrase from Spenser), is thus important to Gerald in terms of justifying the Norman-English claim to sovereignty in the island.[14] But it is noteworthy that, having once established this historic relationship between the two populations, Gerald immediately switches focus in his text. The historical narrative is, for the moment, abandoned (it will be resumed later in the section) as Gerald turns his attention to *"the nature, customs and characteristics of the people"* (100).

What follows in this portion of the text is a deployment by Gerald of some of the most traditional strategies of colonialist analysis, as if, having admitted a historic relationship of accord between the populations of the two islands, Gerald is now at pains to separate the two groups and distribute them into a relationship of opposition. This portion of the text is heavily dependant on the deployment of what Andrew Hadfield has characterized as "signifiers of unnaturalness" (1988, 266). In one of the most conventional extended passages of the *Topographia,* Gerald writes that "this people is . . . a barbarous people, literally barbarous. Judged according to modern ideas, they are uncultivated, not only in the external appearance of their dress but also in their flowing hair and beards. All their habits are the habits of barbarians" (102).[15] In straightforwardly aligning the Irish here with the barbarian, Gerald is, of course, deploying a traditional paradigm, the roots of which, in the European tradition, date back to the Greeks.[16] Anthony Padgen has noted, in *The Fall of Natural Man,* that, as antonyms for "barbarian," the terms "civil" or "politic" derive from "the words *civis* and *polis,* both of which, in their rather different ways, apply to cities . . . and to man as a uniquely city-building, city-dwelling animal" (1982, 15). Gerald explicitly invokes this tradition in asserting that the Irish "have not progressed at all from the primitive habits of pastoral living" (101), developing his point to observe that "while man usually progresses from the woods to the fields, and from the fields to settlements and communities of citizens, this people despises work on the land, has little use for the money-making of towns, contemns the rights and privileges of citizenship, and desires neither to abandon, nor lose respect for, life which it has been accustomed to lead in the woods and countryside" (101-102).[17] In this characterization, we might say that Gerald aligns the Irish with the "sylvestres homines,"[18] "the wild men of the literary imagination, those creatures who were thought to live in the woods and the mountains far removed from the activities of rational men, which always took place in the open spaces and on the plains" (Padgen, *Fall* 1982, 21).[19] As Gerald notes again, the Irish "do not devote their lives to the processing of flax or wool, or to any kind of merchandise or mechanical art. For given only to leisure, and devoted only to laziness, they think that the greatest pleasure is not to work, and the greatest wealth is to enjoy liberty" (102).

In the wake of this long chapter on "The nature, customs, and characteristics of [the Irish]," Gerald provides a shorter chapter in which he makes his only concession to Irish culture: "It is only in the case of musical instruments," he writes," that I find any commendable diligence in the people" (103).[20] From this he returns to the historical narrative once more, taking up the issue of the number of kings who reigned in Ireland *"to the coming of Patrick"* (105).

With the mention of Patrick, Gerald's analysis arrives at the period of the dawning of Ireland's Christian history. Again, he notes in the regard the connection between Ireland and neighboring Britain, as he introduces the missionary saint as "Patricus . . . natione Britannus" (161). He tells us of Patrick that he "arrived in the island, and, finding the people given to idolatry and deluded by various errors, was the first by aid of divine grace, to preach and plant there the Christian faith. He baptized the people, whole crowds at a time, and, the entire island having been converted to the Faith of Christ, chose Armagh as his see" (104-105).

Ireland's Christian heritage represents a particularly difficult problem for Gerald, given his attempts up to this point to bring the Irish within the compass of the traditional dichotomous paradigm of civilized and barbarian. Through Patrick, Ireland is bound in a relationship with Britain, and through the faith which Patrick brings to the island, Ireland is connected to a greater European Christian realm. Furthermore, toward the end of the first millennium, with the coalescence of the concepts of *Romanitas* and *Christianitas,* the term "barbarian" had tended to become synonymous in the West specifically with the pagan, or non-Christian.[21] If Ireland's Christian tradition were fully admitted by Gerald then—virtually by definition—the Irish could not be classed as barbarian.[22]

The Irish thus had necessarily to be uncoupled from their affiliation with the Christian faith. This process was facilitated for Gerald by the fact that he was writing in a period of large-scale reformation within the Church, and Gerald himself was an enthusiastic supporter of the reform process.[23] The general perception at Rome—fostered in part by factional disputes among Irish and British churchmen—was that the Irish clergy were slow to implement reform and that the state of the Church in Ireland left much to be desired.[24] St. Bernard of Clairvaux, for instance, in his *Vita Sancti Malachiae,* had sought to emphasize the difficulties that the Irish saint, Malachy, faced in his reforming mission among his compatriots, asserting that the Irish were "shameless in their customs, uncivilized in their ways, godless in religion, barbarous in their law, obstinate as regards instruction, foul in their lives: Christians in name, pagans in fact" (quoted in Bartlett, 169).[25]

This is exactly the line that Gerald himself adopts in relation to the Irish, when he comes to discuss the question of their religious affiliation and practices. Christians they may well be, but they are so *"ignorant of the rudiments of the Faith"* (106), that the designation is virtually meaningless: "[a]lthough since the time of Patrick and through so many years the Faith has been founded in the island, and has almost continuously thrived, it is, nevertheless, remarkable that this people even still remains so uninstructed in its rudiments" (106).

We have seen that, in the case of the general historical narrative, Gerald follows up his registering of a connection between the Basclenses and the British king Gurguintius by presenting a condemnatory account of Irish culture and practices. Likewise, having admitted the connection between the Irish and the British missionary Patrick, Gerald follows up his initial assertion of the lack of genuine faith among the Irish by interrupting his discussion of religion to offer some further general observations on Irish society, commenting on *"their vices and their treacheries"* (106) and noting that "from an old and evil custom they always carry an axe in their hand as if it were a staff." In this way, he tells us, "if they have a feeling for any evil, they can the more quickly give it effect" (107). In the wake of this material, Gerald provides us with two chapters that present Irish society as being possessed of institutions of a certain primitive kind. We will remember that the possession of civic institutions is for Gerald (and for the tradition in which he was writing) one of the marks of civilization. But what Gerald locates in these chapters is a set of institutions that are perverse, virtual "parodies" of the legitimate institutions of true civilization. The first instance that Gerald cites is (appropriately, since he has been speaking of religion) a treacherous *"new way of making a treaty,"* which plays itself out as a kind of mockery of the ceremony of marriage: "Under the guise of religion and peace they assemble at some holy place with him whom they wish to kill. First they make a treaty on the basis of their common fathers. Then in turn they go around the church three times. They enter the church and, swearing a great variety of oaths before relics of saints placed on the altar, at last with the celebration of Mass and the prayers of the priests they make an indissoluble treaty as if it were a kind of betrothal" (108). "O! how often," Gerald goes on to lament, "a bloody divorce immediately follows within the same hour, or precedes, or even—and this is unheard of elsewhere—interrupts the very ceremony of the 'betrothal'!" (108).[26] In this account, we can see that the Irish have adopted no more than the trappings of religion and that they pervert religious ceremony by turning it to treacherous ends.

In the very next chapter, Gerald takes up the question of the institutions of government among some of the Irish, as he details *"a new and outlandish* [enormi] *way of confirming kingship and dominion"* (109). Here he provides an account of the ceremony of investiture of the new king in the district of Kenelcunill, in Ulster. When the people of the region have gathered, a white mare is brought forward, and then "he who is to be inaugurated, not as a chief, but as a beast, not as a king, but as an outlaw, has bestial intercourse with her before all, professing himself to be a beast also. The mare is then killed immediately, cut up in pieces, and boiled in water. A bath is prepared for the man afterwards in the same water. He sits in the bath surrounded by all his people, and all, he and they, eat of the meat of the mare which is brought to them" (110).

Here several strands of Gerald's analysis come together. As in the wonders episodes of part 2, we get a transgression of the fundamental boundary between the human and other species, as the leader-elect has intercourse with a horse. But here the identification of the human with the bestial is total, as the king, in having such intercourse, professes that he himself is also a beast. What we get in this episode is thus less a transgression of boundaries, than a defection from one oppositional pole to the other. Once again, here, the Irish are presented as being faithful to inversionary codes that amount to no more than a monstrous parody of the true instruments of civilization.[27]

Following this description, Gerald returns to the issue of religion once more. Having discounted the island's Christian tradition, he now further notes that *"many in the island have never been baptised, and have not heard of the teaching of the Faith"* (110), shifting thereby from questioning the nature of the natives' religious faith to the outright assertion that many of the Irish are literal pagans. Gerald attributes this state of affairs to "the negligence of the pastors" (110), and he devotes several chapters to attacking the Irish clergy directly.[28] This forms another important element of the maneuver to deny the validity of Ireland's Christian heritage and tradition. Gerald's line of attack of the Irish clergy is carefully chosen: they are, he tells us, contemplative rather than evangelising; monks rather than ministers: "The prelates of this land, keeping themselves according to an old custom within the enclosures of their churches, give themselves almost always to contemplation alone. They are so enamoured of the beauty of Rachel that they find the blear-eyed Leah disgusting. Whence it happens that they neither preach the word of the Lord to the people, nor tell them of their sins, nor extirpate vices from the flock committed to them, nor instil virtues" (113). Gerald even advances his analysis in this chapter to the rather astonishing claim (given Ireland's extended missionary tradition) that "all the saints of this country are confessors, and there is no martyr" (113).

Following his analysis of the state of religion in Ireland, Gerald finally resumes once more his twice-interrupted narrative of Irish history, detailing for his readers *how many kings reigned from the time of Patrick to the coming of Turgesius* [the leader of the Norwegians]" (118), and how *the Norwegians who ruled for some thirty years . . . were driven out of Ireland"* (121). Gerald notes that the Irish, from the time of the death of Turgesius "to our own times, remained free and unconquered by any attack of foreign peoples, until, invincible king, by you and your courageous daring in these our days it has at length been subjugated" (123-24). The closing chapters of the book become the occasion for Gerald's launching into a panegyric on the subject of Henry's qualities and accomplishments.

Over the span of part 3 of the *Topographia,* while Gerald acknowledges at various levels a relationship of proximity between the Irish and their neighbors in Britain and the Christian West, he also suggests various ways in which that relationship is discontinuous. Thus, insofar as the Irish are possessed of civil institutions at all, those institutions are little more than a perverse parody of the genuine instruments of civilization; insofar as the Irish are Christian, they have no real understanding of the Faith, and are therefore as bad as, if not worse than, actual pagans.

We shall see in the next section that this confident performance is not, in fact, sustained to the end of the *Topographia.* A certain note of anxiety appears at the conclusion of the book, which resurfaces again in his second Irish text, the *Expugnatio.* Before we take up this issue, however, it is worthwhile looking back to a curious episode that Gerald includes in the second part of the *Topographia,* as he is providing an account of Irish miracles and marvels. In an extended chapter in this part, he tells the story of *"a wolf that talked with a priest"* (69). In its basic form, this story is largely traditional—Solinus, in his third century *De Mirabilibus Mundi,* for instance, writes of "the country of the Neuers [where] men were transformed in the summertime into wolves" (Hodgen 1964, 42).[29] In Gerald's story, because of the imprecation of a certain Saint Natalis, two natives of the district of Ossory, "a man and a woman, are compelled to go into exile not only from their territory but also from their bodily shape. They put off the form of man completely and put on the form of wolf" (70). The period of banishment lasts for seven years. At the end of this time, the original couple returns to their natural form and homeland and another couple is transformed and banished in their place.

The novel feature of Gerald's wolf story, which makes it particularly interesting here, is an encounter that occurs in the narrative between the wolf couple and a priest who passes the night in the woods where they live. The priest is startled by the approach of the male wolf, who addresses him, exhorting, "Do not be afraid! Do not fear! Do not worry! There is nothing to fear!" (70). The male explains his predicament and tells the priest that he has been moved to approach him because his female companion, who is nearby, is seriously ill and desires "in her last hour the solace of the priesthood in bringing to her the revelation of the divine mercy" (70).

The priest follows the male to the spot where his companion is lying "grieving like a human being, even though her appearance was that of a beast" (70-71). He administers the last rites to her but balks at her request that he also grant her the sacrament of communion. At this, the male intervenes again, begging him "not to deny them in any way the gift and help of God, destined for their aid by divine providence." To ease the priest's misgivings, in a striking gesture, the male wolf pulls back "all the skin off the she-wolf from the head down to the navel, folding it back with his paw as if it were a hand. And immediately the shape of an old woman, clear to be seen, appeared. At that, the priest, more through terror than reason, communicated her as she had earnestly demanded, and she then devoutly received the sacrament. Afterwards the skin which had been removed by the he-wolf resumed its former position" (72).

On the surface, this story appears to present a collage of familiar Geraldine themes and issues: the woods serve as the location for an encounter between a priest and a monstrous liminal couple who have been transformed by a vindictive Irish saint; the priest, in what might seem like a parody of true religion, is willing to extend the most sacred rites of the church to these beasts.

What is noticeable about this story, however, is that nothing in the world of the narrative is exactly as it first appears to be. The couple encountered by the priest are, for example, oddly ambiguous — apparently neither fully lupine nor yet exactly human. But, unlike the monstrous creatures in the brief bestiary of part 2 of the *Topographia,* the wolf couple is not the product of bestial coupling across species boundaries but rather are the victims of a curse, and their state is temporary — they may be liberated from it if they survive for the period of seven years.

We might also notice here that the priest encounters the wolf couple in the forest and so they appear initially to rank among that species of incompletely human "creatures who were thought to live in the woods and the mountains far removed from the activities of rational men" (Pagden, *Fall* 1982, 21). But, once again, this is, in fact, not their real dwelling place at all — they are actually from the settled community of Ossory and have been despatched to live in the woods against their will.

Although the priest is at first greatly afraid of the talking male wolf, he is reassured by the fact that, in the wake of his initial utterance, "the wolf . . . said some things about God that seemed reasonable" (70).[30] In this sense, then, though the wolf-man may appear to be a sylvan quasi-human monstrosity, in fact his knowledge of Christian doctine serves as proof of his hidden humanity. When the priest encounters the female wolf, he is initially reluctant to grant her communion in addition to the last rites; however, he is finally convinced that it is right for her to receive the sacrament by her partner's unfolding of the outer wolf skin — to reveal her human form underneath.

Nothing in the scene as it presents itself to the priest, then, is exactly as it appears to be. The couple are not truly denizens of an outer world, beyond the range of the *civis* and *polis* but rather are the incidental victims of the curse of a cleric. They are not predatory animals but rather are vulnerable human beings. They not only understand the basic tenets of the Christian faith (and comprehend that such understanding is itself an index of their humanity and civility) but also crave the administration of its sacraments, in their fullest extent. They are, we might say, precisely everything that the *Topographia* works so hard to demonstrate that the Irish are not.

Even at the heart of this text, then, as Gerald is striving to evoke hard Manichean dichotomies that will ultimately be recruited to the task of assigning the Irish to a position of sylvan, pagan barbarity, there emerges an image of a people whose assigned role of wild, nonhuman beastliness is no more than an imposed outer construction, through which they are capable of surfacing into civil, Christian, human form. The male wolf's gesture in securing the rites of communion for his companion is, in a sense, paradigmatic of the proximate encounter: sameness partially emerges from difference in a troubling moment of doubleness that calls all assumptions of binary distance into question. The human form emergent from within the lupine body is a perfect image of the startling coalescence of sameness and difference that Ireland always presents to the writer from Britain.

V.

The *Topographia* draws to a close with a pair of short celebratory chapters that serve as a panegyric to Henry II. As we read these chapters, however, we notice a certain note of discord beginning to emerge within the narrative. Gerald is fulsome in his praise of Henry; he is "our western Alexander," who has "stretched [his] arm from the Pyrenean mountains even to these far western bounds of the northern ocean" (124). Throughout the entire penultimate chapter, emphasis is placed on the king's ability to open up territory and to press outward, in his victories, toward the very limits of the world: "As many as are the lands provided by nature in these parts, so many are your victories. If the limits of your expeditions are sought—there will be no more of the world left for you before there will be an end to your activities. A courageous heart may find no lands to conquer. Your victories can never cease. Your triumphs cannot cease, but only that over which you may triumph" (124). Gerald raises here the specter of a Henry who is capable of expanding the territory of his victories so that it becomes coterminous with the limits of the world. In this sense, there would be no periphery in which nature might "[draw] aside and [go] away . . . to [indulge] herself in . . . secret and distant freaks" (31)—no site where the anomalous and the marvelous might exist. Henry's victories would effect a single, unified realm.

In the final chapter of the *Topographia,* however, Gerald acknowledges that this global Henrician expansion is far from having been realized. Gerald ponders a projected eastern campaign by Henry that has been stymied by internal dissent and treachery: "The entrails, as it were, most unnaturally and shamefully having conspired against the belly in a plan that was evil, unjust, and most damaging to the whole Christian world, postponed your eastern victories in Asia and Spain (which you had already decided in your noble mind to add to those of the West and so to extend in a signal way the Faith of Christ)" (124). So, just as the East erupts at the end of part 1 of the *Topographia,* it intrudes here also, denying the text a triumphant closure. In an odd way we find here Same and Other once again unexpectedly and inextricably intertwined, since it is the conspiracy of the entrails against the belly—of, that is, Henry's fractious sons against their own father—that interferes with Henry's projected campaign to conquer the East as he has conquered the West. In this sense, we might say that we find the inverse here of the Irish paradigm, in that, instead of seeing sameness emerge within difference, we in fact witness difference emerging within what is presumed to be the same. The effect of this conflict is to spare the East from the projected onslaught of the West, and so, in this instance, internal dissent serves to preserve difference.

The intrusion of events relating to the East and to Henry's projected campaign there recurs in Gerald's second text about Ireland, the *Expugnatio Hibernica,* raising an equally complex set of issues. The *Expugnatio* was completed in 1189, just two years after the fall of Jerusalem, and in it Gerald provides a history of the Norman-English incursion into Ireland, consisting largely of a celebration of Gerald's own family's part in the affairs of those years. The Geraldines are represented in the *Expugnatio* as a "noble breed, each one of whom could have earned everlasting renown by his noble deeds." "Even if I had 'a hundred tongues, a hundred mouths and a voice of iron,'" Gerald writes, invoking Virgil, "I could not relate all their deeds as they deserve" (157).

The affairs of the Geraldines are eclipsed at one point in the text, however, as Gerald interrupts his narrative of their story to give an account of the events surrounding *"the arrival in England of the Patriarch Heraclius"* (201).[31] Heraclius came to England in 1185, as an emmisary of King Baldwin of Jerusalem. He was received by King Henry at Reading and "falling at the king's feet with tearful entreaties," "he humbly begged that [the king] should be moved with compassion to help the Holy Land, Christ's own particular heritage, which was now in desperate straits, hard-pressed by the enemies of the faith" (201). In a curious recognition of Britain's own peripheral status (in a sense, uniting Britain with Ireland once more), Gerald celebrates the great tribute that is afforded Henry by Heraclius's mission: "What a great honour for the king and his realm that, ignoring and bypassing all other emperors, kings and princes, someone should come to this furthest corner of the world, almost another world in the far-flung fastnesses of the Atlantic shore, to seek help in such a vital matter, as if this bid to help the Holy Land could find no place in the preoccupations of the central part of the world!" (201). In the event, however, Henry refused to lead or participate personally in the projected Crusade, offering instead to "make a generous contribution of money toward the defence of the Holy Land" (203). Henry also refused the patriarch's revised demand that the king "[give] them one of his sons as their prince, even John, the youngest, if he was unwilling to give any of the others" (203).

Prince John had, in fact, eight years previously (in 1177), been created "Lord of Ireland" by his father, and, at the time of Heraclius's visit to Britain, Henry had already settled on a plan to send his youngest son on an expedition to his appointed realm. The king announced this intention while the patriarch was still at court, overriding John's own protestations on the matter. John, Gerald tells us, "fell at his father's feet and, so men say, begged to be sent to Jerusalem instead [of Ireland], with an insistence which did him credit. However he did not get his way" (203). Before leaving Britain, Heraclius denounced Henry and prophesied that divine retribution would follow his failure to take up the Christian cause in the Holy Land.

Gerald ties this prophecy of Heraclius to the fact that, in the last five years of his life, Henry suffered "punishment, affliction and dishonour, as being an ungrateful servant who had been utterly condemned and rejected" (205). As his first piece of evidence in proof of this assertion, Gerald cites the fact that "in the second year of that five-year period . . . Henry's first enterprise within that period, one that he had prepared for with such care, namely the despatch of his son John to Ireland, came to nothing and was totally unsuccessful, so that all his careful preparation and expenditure of money was wasted" (205). In a later chapter of the text, Gerald relates this failure of John's Irish expedition directly to Henry's refusal to accede to the request for help which he received from Heraclius. In the process, Gerald comes to acknowledge, once again, Ireland's place in a Christian world distinguished from a heathen East. The most important reason for John's failure, Gerald observes, was that,

whereas his father the king should have responded to the powerful summons issued by the patriarch at this time . . . by immediately embarking on the crusade in person, or at any rate by the prompt despatch of one of his sons to serve Christ in his place, at the very time when he received this summons, and in the very presence of the distinguished emissary who had come to proclaim this important message, he sent his son not to the East, but to the West, not against the Saracens, but against Christians, to pursue their own interests rather than Christ's interests. (237)[32]

Here, once again, we see the alignment of the Irish with a positive Christian West, contradistinguished from a negative East. The attempt to forge a coherent sense of Otherness for the Irish is fractured in the text: the contradictions provoked by the combination of local and distant projects serve to undermine any efforts to assign a coherent set of colonial values to the Irish situation. Just as the human emerges unexpectedly from the lupine in *Topographia*'s story of the wolf that talked with a priest, so here the force of the failure of the crusade program is such as to drive the Irish back into alignment with their neighbors as fellow Christians. Once again, sameness is seen to emerge within difference, as Irish proximity persists.

We can begin to see the extent of the impact of these issues on Gerald if we look at another episode from the *Expugnatio,* again concerning the king's failure to take up the Christian cause in the Holy Land. Gerald tells us that, "during that period of hateful internecine strife between the king and the count of Poitou" (which is to say the familial power struggle that, we recall, was one of the factors keeping Henry from embarking on the crusade), he "was with the king at the castle of Chinon" (213). Sleeping in the castle, Gerald is disturbed by a dream. In the dream, he sees a "great crowd of men all looking towards the sky as if in amazement at some strange, new spectacle." Gerald himself looks up and sees the clouds parting to reveal the court of heaven. He discovers that the court is under attack: "All kinds of weapons were aimed at it from every direction, and it was given over to plunder and exposed to its enemies, so that they might slaughter its citizens." Gerald continues his description of the vision: "In a little while these bloodstained murderers completely vanquished all the others and then combined to attack the leader of the heavenly host, who was seated in majesty among His people. . . . They dragged Him from the throne, His right breast bared to the midriff, and pierced His right side with a spear. This was immediately followed by a terrifying voice which cried out: 'Woch, Woch, Father and Son. Woch, Woch, Holy Ghost.' . . . The terror which I experienced on hearing those words and seeing the vision finally wakened me and put an end the the dream" (213). Gerald himself provides and interpretation of the dream in his text, linking it specifically to the events taking place in the Holy Land. In Gerald's analysis, the conflict in the dream becomes a version of the conflict in the East, with Christ's suffering serving as a manifestation of the suffering of the faithful armies fighting for the Christian cause. "In that holy land which He finally hallowed by the shedding of His own blood, after it had enjoyed so many wonderful manifestations of His bodily presence, His faithful followers have been suffering, no longer on the cross, but in martial conflict" (215).

In view of the broader significance that the Holy Land assumes within Gerald's narrative and the various ways in which the East in general impinges on his representations of Ireland, we might well see something more complex at play in this dream (presented, as it is, within the context of a book that aims to provide a history of the conquest of Ireland) than simply an exalted and fearful replication of distant events. Certainly, the dream seems to have had a profound and enduring impact on Gerald:

> While I was sitting on my bed immediately afterwards and anxiously turning all this over in my mind, for the space of half an hour or more I was overcome with such a violent trembling of my body and such an agitation of spirit that I was almost beside myself, and feared that I was going out of my mind.
>
> To this very day I have never been able to bring to mind this vision without experiencing an intense feeling of dread. (215)

What exactly is at stake in Gerald's dream that provokes such intense anxiety and overwhelming sense of fear?

The dream, we note, presents an antagonistic division between the forces of Heaven and a group of opponents who overwhelm the heavenly court. The negative forces overrun the positive, even displacing Christ from His throne. What we get here, we might say, is the most extreme version of the process of displacement that Gerald elsewhere associates with Ireland. Unlike the other instances of displacement, however, in this case it is not so much that a sense of positive proximity unexpectedly emerges within the intended negative difference as that the hierarchy of positive and negative is entirely upended; the dichotomy in inverted, and Christ is swept away.

Taking the story within an Irish framework, we might say that Gerald's dream signals, again, the profound anxiety over the stability of the structures of interpretation that he evokes to engage with the Irish and their relationship with the Norman-English. The fragility of his heavenly realm points to the fragility of his own textual strategies and manuverings. But, more than this, it also points to another anxious element within the colonial situation. The dream indicates not just an Irish fracturing of the containing structures of Gerald's colonial discourse—the triumphant resurgence of the Irish beyond the limits that Gerald has sought to impose on them—but the final outcome of this fracturing is the fatal displacement of the cardinal figure of positive identity in the dethronement and wounding of Christ. This displacement can be seen as reflecting the position of the colonist in Ireland—a position articulated in the *Expugnatio* by the figure of Gerald's uncle, Maurice Fitzgerald. Gerald tells us that, in rallying his troops for battle, Maurice makes a speech to them in which he asks, "What then are we waiting for? Surely we do not look to our own people for succor? We are now constrained in our actions by this circumstance, that just as we are English as far as the Irish are concerned, likewise to the English we are Irish" (81).[33] In one sense, of course, Maurice's speech represents a typical statement of colonial deracination—the sort of thing that Aimé Césaire, for instance, registers in his adaptation of Shakespeare's *Tempest,* when his Prospero remains on the island at the end of the play, unable to return to the colonial metropolis, yet equally alienated from the island colony in which he has made his home. But such deracination takes a peculiar form in an Irish context. What we will find again and again in English texts about Ireland is that, even as Irish proximity frustrates English efforts to reduce Irish identity to form a coherent difference, so it also calls English identity itself into question in a variety of ways. The instability that proximity provokes within colonial stereotyping rebounds on the colonizer, calling the English sense of *self*-identity into question as much as the English sense of an Irish identity predicated on essential and enduring Otherness. Just as Irish proximity interrogates the stability of English structures of colonial interpretation, we might say that it also threatens to dethrone the English themselves from a sense of secure identity.

VI.

Gerald was the first person from Britain to write extensively about Ireland. The seventeenth-century Irish historian Seatrún Céitinn (Geoffrey Keating) characterized him as "the bull of the herd for [the English] for writing the false history of Ireland" (quoted in O'Meara's introduction to Gerald's *The History and Topographia of Ireland,* 13).[34] The "falseness" of Gerald's "history" was intimately bound up with his attempt to engage with and to *disengage* Ireland's relationship of proximity with Britain and with the greater European Christian realm. We have seen some of the strategies deployed in Gerald's text in pursuit of this aim. We have also seen some of the ways in which Irish proximity eluded such efforts to contain and circumvent it. A certain strand of anxiety persists throughout these texts regarding the issue of proximity. This anxiety focuses itself not only on the issue of the persistence of sameness within Irish difference but also on the potential for the redoubling of Irish identity on an English sense of self-identity such that, in an Irish context, the stability of English identity is itself at risk.

As Céitinn noted, there was a clear link between Gerald's Irish works and the texts about Ireland produced by English writers within the span of Céitinn's life. English writers of the early modern period drew on Gerald for information about Ireland and its population, and his work provided a paradigm for his successors as they wrote in support of a new phase of the English colonial project in Ireland. As we will see, these writers themselves evolved strategies for engaging the issue of Irish proximity, yet, once again, the anxiety of proximity persisted in their texts much as we have seen it persist in Gerald's.

3

"They Are All Wandred Much: That Plaine Appeares"
Spenser and the Old English

By graunting Charters of peas,
To false English withouten les,
This Land shall be mich undoo.
But Gossipred, and alterage,
And leesing of our Language,
Haue mickely holp theretoo.
Quoted in Sir John Davies, *Discoverie of the Trve Cavses*
Why Ireland Was Neuer Entirely Subdued

I.

In 1587, Gerald's *Expugnatio* appeared in print in an English translation for the first time ever—included as part of Holinshed's *Chronicles* by John Hooker. Subsequently, in 1602, William Camden included the complete Latin text of both the *Expugnatio* and the *Topographia* in his *Anglica, Normannica, Hibernica, Cambrica a Verterivus Scriptis.*[1] The renewed interest in

Gerald's work can in part be attributed to a general enthusiasm for antiquarianism in the period, but there are also other reasons that explain the increased level of attention paid to Gerald's Irish writings.[2] The sixteenth century was a period of intensive development in Anglo-Irish relations, and Gerald's texts provided a useful resource for many of those involved in theorizing about England's relationship with Ireland.[3]

To understand the nature of some of the developments that occurred over the course of the sixteenth century, it is necessary first to consider briefly the way in which the Anglo-Irish relationship had evolved over the previous three centuries or so. However one chooses to interpret the Norman-English incursion into Ireland in the late twelfth century, it is clear that it never amounted to a total and complete subjugation of the island. Perry Anderson has usefully characterized it as "a precarious military conquest that was soon awash with a Celtic reflux" (1979, 135). This "Celtic reflux" indicated both a resurgence of the native Irish population, to reclaim control over much of the territory that initially had been lost to the Norman-English and an absorption of many of the Norman-English themselves into the prevailing networks of Gaelic cultural, judicial and familial relations, so that they became, in the exaggeration of the traditional clichéd phrase, "more Irish than the Irish themselves."[4]

The 1366 Statutes of Kilkenny sought to address this gradual expansion of Gaelic Irish influence by, among other things, strictly prohibiting the settler community from intermarrying with the Irish, wearing Irish dress, and speaking the Irish language. Traditionally, nationalist Irish historians have tended to see the statutes as a virulent set of anti-Irish measures, but, in fact, as Steven Ellis has observed, "to modern historians they mark an official recognition of the partial nature of the Norman conquest" (*Tudor* 1985, 24). Brendan Bradshaw has argued that the statutes effectively indicated a certain ceding of territory in Ireland and an attempt to concentrate and consolidate power within a limited number of clearly defined areas: "The statutes of Kilkenny [indicate] that the main emphasis of crown policy in Ireland had come to centre on consolidating the colony within the area under Norman-English control, and with securing political stability in the Lordship generally. As a corollary, more grandiose notions of conquest and colonisation receded into the background, though they did not entirely disappear from view" (*Constitutional* 1979, 10). In the next century, the scope of English objectives in Ireland diminished even further. As Bradshaw again argues, over the course of the fifteenth century, "the central administration gradually abandoned the attempt to exercise active and regular jurisdiction over the whole area of the 'Englishry,' the area to which it had confined its direct jurisdiction under the system of dual government. As crown government in England became less interested in Irish affairs, and less willing to subsidise its counterpart in Dublin, the latter became less and less capable of involving itself in the administration of the outlying feudal lordships and their adjacent shires. The defence and government of these areas was perforce left to the feudal magnates while crown government confined the area of its own regular administration to the four shires in the hinterland of Dublin where the administration was centred. This Pale now became the focus of the crown's policy of consolidation" (13).

By the opening decades of the sixteenth century, however, English policy objectives had begun to shift once more, and a desire to bring Ireland more fully within the ambit of English control began to emerge. The uprising of Thomas Fitzgerald (Silken Thomas) in 1534 proved something of a catalyst for change, and several initiatives followed as a result. The most innovative of them was the one Anthony St. Leger—supported by elements of the settler community in Ireland—sought to put into effect during his period as Lord Deputy in Ireland in the 1540s. Bradshaw has dubbed St. Leger's scheme a "liberal formula" and has characterized its aims as an attempt "to transform the island's political infrastructure while leaving its superstructure intact":

> It was designed to assimilate the non-constitutional lordships to the polity of the crown, constitutionally, jurisdictionally and socially, but without disturbing the existing framework of local leadership or landownership. This required a process of political engineering at two levels. At the local level the non-constitutional lordships had to be stripped of the features of the Gaelic political system, reorganising on the English model, and provided with constitutional status. At the national level the concept of the island's inhabitants as an integral political community under the sovereignty of the crown, rather than an English colony and an alien Irishry, had to be given expression constitutionally, and in the institutions and practice of government. (*Constitutional* 1979, 195)

The new constitutional program had a number of important implications. Henry VIII's title was amended from "Lord of Ireland" to "King of Ireland," with the intention of rendering all of the inhabitants of Ireland his subjects. As part of the program, native Irish chieftains were to surrender their traditional Gaelic titles to the crown, to be regranted a new title by the king and thereby supposedly incorporated into the English aristocracy. As Ciarán Brady has observed, although the policy was "not unambiguously conciliatory" it did, nevertheless, signify "the Tudor resolution that civil society was to be established in Ireland through the instruments of government already available and by the conventional means of institutional development and reform" ("Court" 1986, 28). As we have noted above, this policy seriously complicated English perceptions of Irishness, as it offered a mechanism of incorporation in some sense predicated on proximity (the Irish were imagined as being sufficiently like the English to be gradually assimilable to an expanded sovereign English community).[5] Although it is true that the reform program of the 1540s became gradually marginalized over the course of the succeeding decades, nevertheless, as Karl Bottigheimer, Ciarán Brady, and Michael Neill have shown, even after the policy had effectively been abandoned, it continued to have an impact on the way in which Ireland and the Irish were perceived by the English. As Bottigheimer observes, Ireland "could never escape its legacy as a kingdom of the realm" ("Kingdom" 1978, 55).

This is not to deny that English policy objectives did, indeed, shift in the middle decades of the sixteenth century, and Canny is clearly correct when, in *The Elizabethan Conquest of Ireland,* he identifies this shift as a movement toward a more fully colonialist agenda. Steven Ellis observes of the rise of colonialism in the period that "of the fashionable get-rich-quick schemes for surplus capital, like alchemy and piracy, colonization alone could provide land and also appeared a pious work and a remedy for the overpopulation then worrying thinking Englishmen" (*Tudor* 1985, 266).[6] Many small-scale colonizing schemes were tried out in Ireland, including one in the Ards peninsula, undertaken by Thomas Smith and his son and intended as "an English colony around the great city of Elizabetha" (Quinn 1966, 107). Ellis's observation regarding the rationale and ideological grounding of colonial projects is borne out by a pamphlet produced in support of the Ards scheme, in which the author writes that "England was neuer that con be heard of, fuller of people than it is at this day" (Smith 1873, 409), suggesting that the Ards scheme provides a perfect answer to the problem of overpopulation, and observing that "to inhabite and reforme so barbarous a nation as [the Irish] and to bring them to the knowledge and law, were bothe a godly and commendable deede, and a sufficient worke for our age" (409).[7]

The Smiths' venture was a failure, but the collapse of the project did not deter others from embarking on even larger scale endeavors of a similar nature.[8] In the early 1580s, following the confiscation of the Earl of Desmond's lands in Munster, an ambitious new government-sponsored program was undertaken in that province. Thirty-five undertakers were granted a total of 298,653 acres of Munster land.[9] Included among their number were Sir Walter Raleigh and Edmund Spenser.

In this era of renewed colonial activity, Gerald's Irish works proved to be particularly useful. The period witnessed a great burgeoning of English texts about Ireland, and many newly arrived writer-adventurers rehearsed the catalog of barbaric Irish traits and practices that had been assembled by Gerald some four centuries before. But if negotiating Irish proximity had proved to be a complex and anxious business for Gerald, for this new generation of writers the complexities were all the more pronounced. For one thing, of course, they were writing in the wake of the (largely moribund, but never wholly abandoned) assimilationist policies of the 1540s—policies that had aimed to construct the Irish as sovereign subjects of the English monarch rather than as hostile aliens. For another, they faced, in Ireland, a population rather differently composed than the population Gerald had encountered. This new generation had to contend not just with the native Irish but with the descendants of the original Norman-English settlers, or the "Old English" as they were sometimes known (as distinct from the new arrivals, known as the "New English").[10]

The Old English were complexly positioned, being, as R.F. Foster has put it, "the element in Irish life most emblematic of the mixed polity and the uncertainty of conquest" (1989, 11). As we have already noted, some sections of this community had been to a greater or lesser extent assimilated by their Gaelic Irish neighbors. This assimilation raised the disturbing specter for the new arrivals of an attractive Irishness that might serve to collapse English identity into a seductive Irish difference, even as residual English policy objectives imagined the possibility of an Englishness capable of absorbing Irishness.[11] At the same time, of course, the Dublin administration was very largely dominated by other elements of this community. This section of the Old English had, as Nicholas Canny notes, very largely favored the assimilationist policy of surrender and regrant, "both because they were the ones who usually acted as intermediaries between the government and those Gaelic lords who agreed to surrender and because they were most active in providing for the future by bringing the designated successors of the surrendering lords into their own households to be educated after the English manner and familiarized with English legal procedures" ("Identity Formation" 1987, 162). The influx of the New English both confirmed the abandonment of this policy in favor of a more clearly colonialist agenda and signaled a further threat to Old English hegemony, as the New English began to fight for greater political control in the island in order to advance their own interests. The antagonism between the two groups increased steadily over time, with the Munster plantation scheme serving particularly to alienate the Old English. As Canny has noted elsewhere, the scheme "threatened to strengthen the position of the New English in Ireland, thus enabling them to challenge the dominant position hitherto enjoyed by the Old English in parliament and government. Thus, as the Old English saw it, their very survival as a privileged élite depended upon their ability to frustrate the intentions of the New English" ("Edmund Spenser" 1983, 12).

The New English writer on Ireland had thus, in addition to engaging with the native Irish, to tackle the topic of the Old English, who represented a threat on several counts.[12] One section of the Old English retained a high (if progressively diminishing) degree of political control in Ireland and fought tenaciously to retain this power in the face of the challenge posed by the New English. Another section of the Old English had succumbed to Irish culture, refocusing the issue of proximity in a novel way, raising the specter of an Irish attractiveness that had already consumed certain elements of English identity and that might threaten also to absorb the new generation of settlers.[13]

Edmund Spenser presents a particularly useful case study for exploring the issue of New English engagement with the Old English, since he was a direct participant in the Munster plantation and, like Gerald, wrote two texts that take up the issue of Ireland.[14] Unlike Gerald, however, Spenser's texts are in two very different genres, one a political prose tract and the other an epic poem.[15] Taken together, *A View of the Present State of Ireland* and the relevant sections of *The Faerie Queene* present a diverse and complex meditation on the question of Otherness, proximity, and Ireland, with the issue of proximity playing itself out rather differently in the political treatise and in the poem.[16]

II.

Clare Carroll has usefully observed that, in both *A View* and in the Irish sections of the *Faerie Queene*, "the moral qualities attributed to the Irish constitute a taxonomy of vice" (1990, 177). The general thrust of Spenser's portrayal of the Gaelic Irish has much in common with Gerald's efforts in the *Topographia* and the *Expugnatio*— the Irish are barbaric and lacking in the civil virtues of their English neighbors. Like Gerald, Spenser is keen to establish points of discontinuity between the two peoples. So, for instance, where Gerald attempts both to descredit Ireland's Christian heritage and, further, to suggest that many in Ireland are not possessed even of a debased form of Christianity ("many in the island have never been baptised, and have not heard of the teaching of the faith" [*Topographia,* 110]),[17] Spenser likewise observes of the Irish that "they are all Papistes by theire profession but in the same so blindelye and brutishly enformed for the most parte as that ye woulde rather thinke them *Atheists* or infidles for not one amongest a hundred knowethe anye grounde of religion or anie article of his faithe but Cane perhaps saie his pater noster or his *Ave marye* without anie knowledge or vnderstandinge what one worde thearof meanethe" (136).[18] Like Gerald's, Spenser's strategy here is to deny any relationship of continuity between the English and the Irish. They may both be Christian peoples, but the best that can be said about the Irish is that they are unreformed Christians; in truth, however, they hardly possess even a papist perversion of the true faith. We sense here an attempt to establish a fully alien identity for the Irish, as "Atheistes or Infidells."

There is, then, we might say, a certain inevitability about Spenser's engagement with the Irish—his objectives are not particularly different from those we found in Gerald's texts, some four centuries earlier. Nicholas Canny thus has argued that "the novelty of Spenser's *View* is not . . . the invective which it directed against the Gaelic institutions but rather the vicious attack which it launched against the leaders of the Old English" ("Spenser and Reform" 1979, 20). The real challenge for Spenser is the issue of how to engage with the particular set of problems that the Old English present to the New English writer on Ireland. He meets this challenge in the *View* in part by collapsing all of the Old English into a single grouping, denouncing "the entire Old English population (urban as well as rural) as a people who had lapsed from true civility" (Canny, "Debate" 1988, 205-206). Spenser thus makes no distinction between the Gaelicized Old English, who had been to a greater or lesser extent absorbed into the community of the Irish, and those segments of the Old

English who saw themselves as possessing a primary role in both the maintenance of English standards of civility and the communication of such standards to those they considered their barbarian Irish neighbors. Having reduced the Old English to a homogeneous, unregenerate grouping, Spenser then sets about disconnecting them in various ways from their New English counterparts. Adopting a strategy similar to Gerald's, he attempts, in the *View*, to set up a series of discontinuities between the Old English and the new generation of settlers.

We can see Spenser's strategy beginning to take shape if we look at the way in which he sets up the narrative of the *View* just prior to the introduction of the Old English. The text as a whole is structured as a debate between Eudoxus and Irenius. As Bruce Avery has observed, Eudoxus "represents the voice of the home authority to Irenius's colonial administrator" (1990, 263). Irenius begins his discourse on Ireland by setting out for Eudoxus an account of the origins of the native Irish population, detailing what groups settled in the island at what different time periods. For Irenius, the most significant of the original settlement groupings are the Scythians—"the Chiefest which haue firste possessed and inhabited" (82) Ireland. A number of writers have registered the significance of Spenser's alignment of the Irish with the Scythians. Peter Stallybrass and Ann Rosalind Jones, for instance, note that "the term 'Scythian' was used loosely to suggest any kind of barbarism" (1990, 159).[19]

To this extent, then, the Scythianism of the Irish conveniently facilitates the attempted establishment of their alien otherness. There is, however, something else also at stake here. Irenius notes that the Irish themselves prefer a narrative of origins that aligns them firmly with the Spanish, "whom they now see to bee a verye honorable people and nexte borderinge vnto them" (90). Irenius dismisses this claim as nothing more than "a verye desire of Newfainglenes and vanitye" (90) on the part of the Irish and he notes that there is no firm evidence to suggest a Spanish migration to Ireland.[20] He then goes on to make what may appear to be a slightly odd comment, as he argues that the Irish should rather take their descent from the Scythians, since they have a higher degree of ethnic purity than the Spanish, who "of all nacions vnder heaven . . . is the moste mingled, moste vncertaine and moste bastardlie" (91). In the complex set of alignments being offered here by Irenius, the Irish become associated with an originary barbarian "nation," but a nation that, by contrast with the Spanish, is relatively pure, relatively "unmingled." One of the functions of this set of maneuvers is to set the stage for the introduction of the Old English into the narrative. Spenser's objection to the Old English is precisely that they *are* a "mingled" grouping, having assimilated with the native Irish. Setting up this contrast between the Scythian/Irish and the Spanish is just one of the ways in which the text suggests that the Old English are, in fact, worse than the Irish themselves—whereby the Irish are relatively pure barbarians and the Old English are impure barbarians and hence are doubly savage.

Before introducing the Old English into the narrative, Spenser adds one further twist to the issue of the mingling of nations. Challenged by Eudoxus about his characterization of the Spanish, Irenius retreats somewhat, conceding that "I thinke that theare is no nacion now in Christendome nor much farther but is mingled and Compounded with others" (92). In shifting ground, he further grants that the process of mingling has its place in the divine scheme of things, "for it was a singular providence of god and a moste admirable purpose of his wisdome to drawe those Northerne heathen nacions downe into these Cristen partes wheare they mighte receaue Christianitye and to mingle nacions so remote so miraculouslye to make as it weare one kindred and bloud of all people and eache to haue knowledge of him" (92). Irenius is suggesting here that, in the narrative of European Christian expansion, the mingling of nations has been providential, because it has led to the spreading of the faith among a diverse range of populations. In this sense, ethnic interpenetration is associated with a positive and providential outcome. In the instance of Ireland, however, Irenius will indicate that the opposite has proved to be the case, with the intermingling of the Old English and the Irish having led to the loss of civility (and, of course, of true faith) on the part of the Old English.

Having set the stage, Spenser introduces the Old English. Eudoxus asks Irenius whether there was any other "generall impeoplinge of [the] Ilande" (96), and Irenius replies, "Yeas theare was another and that the laste and greatest which was by the Englishe when the Earle of Strangbowe havinge Conquered that Lande delivered vp the same vnto the handes of Henrye the Second then kinge, whoe sente ouer thither great store of gentlemen and other warlicke people amongest whom he distributed the Lande And settled suche a stronge Colonye thearein as neuer since coulde with all the subtill practises of the Irishe be roted out but abide still a mightye people of soe manye as remayne Englishe of them" (96). Irenius's qualification at the end of this observation comes as a shock to Eudoxus. "What is that ye saie of soe manye as remayne Englishe of them?" he asks. "Why? are not they that weare once Englishe abidinge Englishe still," to which Irenius responds that "the most part of them are degenerated and growen allmoste meare Irishe yea and more malitious to the Englishe then the verye Irishe themselves" (96). Irenius thus establishes for Eudoxus that the Old English are, like the Spanish, mingled people, assimilating with the Irish and in the process becoming worse than the Irish themselves. Eudoxus professes astonishment at this and asks how it is "that an Englisheman broughte vp naturallye in suche swete Civilitye as Englande affordes can finde suche likinge in that barbarous rudenes that he shoulde forgett his owne nature and forgoe his owne nacion?" (96). This is the question that will in large measure dominate the *View,* with Spenser returning to it again and again, to offer a number of different accounts of the mechanisms of Old English degeneracy, on each occasion seeking to uncouple the Old English from their New English successors.

At this point in the dialogue, Irenius offers no more than a rather vague explanation for how the Old English have come to be "allmoste meare Irishe," attributing this development to "the firste evill ordinaunce and institucion of that Comon wealthe" and telling Eudoxus that he does not wish to be distracted from the original intended plan of his discourse, observing that "heare is no fitt place to speake" (96-97) of such matters. Eventually, however, the thread of the dialogue does loop back to the Old English, as Irenius works his way systematically through the "abuses in the customs of Ireland" introduced by the various groups to have inhabited the island. As he approaches the end of his account, Eudoxus observes,

> Yee haue verye Well run thoroughe suche Customes as the Irishe haue derived from the firste olde nacions which inhabited that Lande. . . . It now remayneth that youe take in hande the Customes of the old Englishe which are amongest the Irishe of which I do not thinke that ye shall haue muche to finde faulte with anie Consideringe that by the Englishe moste of the olde badd Irishe Customes weare abolished and more Civill fashions broughte in theire steade. (113)

Irenius contradicts Eudoxus's view of the state of civility of the Old English and their successful prosecution of a civilizing mission in Ireland. In place of Eudoxus's vision, he offers an explicit statement of a hierarchy in which the Old English have, in fact, descended to a level lower than the Irish themselves:

youe thinke otherwise *Eudox:* then I doe, for the the [*sic*] Chiefest abuses which are now in that realme are growen from the Englishe and the Englishe that weare are now muche more Lawles and Licentious then the verie wilde Irishe, so that as muche Care as was then by them had to reforme the Irishe so muche and more muste now be vsed to reforme them so muche time dothe alter the manners of men. (113)

Where initially Irenius had characterized the descendants of the original settlers from Britain as having "growen *allmoste* meare Irishe," he now figures them as being *"muche more* Lawles and Licentious *then* the verie wilde Irishe" (emphasis added). From this perspective, the Old English are more in need of reform than the Irish themselves.

We are still faced with the question here of how it is that the Old English should have come to be in need of such reform. How exactly have they arrived at this state? At this point Irenius simply says, "So much time dothe alter the manners of men," as if it is purely a matter of temporal degradation—a simple example of the process of degeneracy that, as Margaret Hodgen has noted, held a central place in Renaissance thought.[21] But Eudoxus challenges this as a sufficient explanation: "That semethe verie strange which youe saie that men shoulde so muche degenerate from theire firste natures as to growe wilde" (114), and this prompts Irenius for the first time to provide a detailed historical rationale for the decline of the Old English.

The core of the historical explanation is that internecine feuding among the descendants of the original settlers weakened them and strengthened the Irish—a process exacerbated by the fact that "when either parte was weake they woulde wage and drawe in the Irishe to take theire partie by which meanes they bothe greatlie encouraged and enhabled the Irishe" (114-15). But Irenius further argues that this process occurs in the first place largely because of isolation from direct oversight by the home government and by the monarch (or the sovereign's direct representative):

> *Eudox:* That semethe verie strange which youe saie that men shoulde so muche degenerate from theire firste natures as to growe wilde.
>
> *Irenius:* Soe muche Can libertie and ill example doe.
>
> *Eudox:* What libertye had the Englishe theare more then they had heare at home? weare not the Lawes planted amongest them at the

firste and had they not Gouernours to Curbe and kepe them still in awe and obedience.

Iren: They had, but it was for the moste parte suche as did more hurte then good, for they had governours for the moste parte of themselues and Comonlie out of the Two families of the *Geraldines* and the *Butlers* bothe Aduersaries and Corrivals one againste the other, whoe thoughe for the moste parte they weare but deputies vnder some of the kinges of Englandes sonnes and Bretheren or other neare kinsemen whoe weare the kinges Lieftennantes yeat they swayed soe muche as they had all the rule and the others but the title. (113-14)

In this analysis, then, it is the failure to maintain Ireland as an extension of the English realm—its isolation from sovereign control—that has led to its anomalous development. The politics of geography thus serve as a mechanism of discontinuity for Irenius—the Old English have degenerated because they have been physically isolated from their home territory and, in their isolation, have declined into a kind of pernicious, debased autonomy.

As the section proceeds, Eudoxus continues to register his astonishment at the very possibility of such divergence. "Is it possible that anye shoulde so far growe out of frame that they shoulde in so shorte space quite forgett theire Countrie and theire owne names," he asks, noting "that is a moste daungerous *Lethargie*" (115). And again, "Coulde they euer Conceaue anye suche divilishe dislike of theire owne naturall Contries as that they woulde be ashamed of her name and bite at the dug from which they sucked liffe" (116). Irenius's response is to present as evidence the details of specific Old English families who have indeed "quite caste of theire Englishe name and Allegeaunce" (116). The accumulation of such evidence seems to satisfy Eudoxus, at least to the extent that he shifts from a sense of amazed disbelief to a state of resolved commitment to the reform process: "In truethe this which youe tell is a moste shamefull hearinge and to be reformed with moste sharpe Censures" (118). In this spirit, he seeks to draw Irenius back to the matter in hand—the question of the bad customs introduced into the island by the various segments of its population: "Hearby sure we haue made a faire waye vnto your selfe to laye open the abuses of theire evill Customes which ye haue now nexte to declare The which no doubt but are verye bad and barbarous beinge borrowed from the Irishe as theire apparrell theire language theire ridinge and manye other the like" (118). We might note, however, something of a reversal here. Where previously in the dialogue, Irenius has been detailing the pernicious customs brought to Ireland by the various groups to have settled there, here Eudoxus anticipates that Irenius will tell him of "evill Customes" "borrowed *from* the Irishe" *by* the Old English. Again, stress is being laid here on the absorption of the Old English into Irish culture. The effect of Eudoxus's structuring of the direction of influence is to maintain the alignment of the Old English with other non-English, barbarian settlers in Ireland (such as the Scythians) but to sever them from any alignment with an English historical tradition (whence evil customs might be derived) and instead to align them with the Irish as inheritors and perpetuators of Irish customs.

In answering Eudoxus here, Irenius, like Gerald in the *Topographia*, invokes a conventional scale for societal and cultural development but applies this scale chronologically to the history of Britain itself.[22] In the process, he realigns the Old English with their Norman-English progenitors in Britain but places the Norman-English collectively at close to the zero point of his developmental scale:

> Ye Cannot but thinke them sure to be verye brute and vncivill for weare they at the beste that they weare of olde when they weare broughte in they shoulde in so longe an alteracion of time seme verye straunge and vncouthe for it is to be thoughte that the vse of all Englande was in the Raigne of Henrye the Seconde when Irelande was firste planted withe Englishe verye rude and barbarous so as if the same shoulde be now vsed in Englande by anye it would seme worthie of sharpe Correccion and of new lawes for reformacion but it is but even the other daye since Englande grewe Civill. (118)[23]

Irenius's response represents an elegant solution to the problem of proximate alignment: Old English proximity is acknowledged, but on terms that effectively merge proximity with disjunction, since Irenius makes it clear that the English themselves as a civilization have advanced far beyond the crude civil state of their Norman-English ancestors.

Having thus in one and the same gesture aligned the Old English with and detached them from an extended English tradition that includes the New English, Irenius now picks up on Eudoxus's reversal of the direction of influence between the Old English and the Irish. "In Countinge the evill Customes of the Englishe theare," he tells Eudoxus, "I will not haue regarde wheather the beginninge theareof weare Englishe or Irishe but will haue respecte onelye to the inconvenience theareof" (118). By simply abandoning any attempt to establish the direction of the relationship of influence between the Old English and the Irish, Irenius effectively collapses both groups into a single community, as if, having uncoupled the backward Old English from the fully developed English stock to which Irenius and his New English contemporaries belong, they can all the more easily be incorporated with the Irish. Irenius's next move with regard to the Old English is to provide a detailed and exact account of the process whereby they have come to be assimilated by the Irish.

As Irenius produces his account of the Gaelicization of the Norman-English, we learn that the process has its roots in the twin practices of intermarriage and fosterage ("two moste dangerous infeccions" [119]). Building on this foundation, Irenius erects what we might call a psychophysiology of incorporation:

> The Childe that suckethe the milke of the nurse muste of necessitye learne his firste speache of her, the which beinge the firste that is envred to his tounge is ever after moste pleasinge vnto him In so muche as thoughe he afterwardes be taughte Englishe yeat the smacke of the firste will allwaies abide with him and not onelye of the speche but allsoe of the manners and Condicions for besides that younge Children be like Apes which will affecte and ymitate what they see done before them speciallye by theire nurses whom they love so well, they moreouer drawe into themselues togeather with theire sucke even the nature and disposicion of theire nurses ffor the minde followethe muche the Temparature of the bodye and allsoe thewordes are the Image of the minde So as they procedinge from the minde the minde must be nedes affected with the wordes So that the speache beinge Irishe the harte muste nedes be Irishe for out of the abundance of the harte the tonge speakethe. (119)

What Irenius appears to be attempting in this passage is to venture *beyond* a theory of the assimilation of the Old English to a suggestion that it is, in fact, possible — through something like an intersection of culture and nurturance — for the Old English in some literal way to have *become* Irish (as

"They Are All Wandred Much"   { 73 }

distinct from a process of assimilation, by which they would become *like* the Irish).

There are two basic strands to the argument that Spenser advances here. In the first instance, he sees the Irish wetnurse as offering the Old English child a set of linguistic and behavioral exemplars — exemplars that will ineluctably remain with the child throughout life.[24] In this way, the child receives Irish as its first language, together with a set of social and cultural "manners and Condicions," by aping its nurse. As a later English writer on Ireland, Parr Lane, puts it, "Since then they found and love their nurses best / theyl imitate them more then all the rest" (fol. 159v).[25] No subsequent linguistic or social experience can serve to erase the effects of this early encounter — as Irenius observes, "Thoughe he afterwardes be taughte Englishe yeat the smacke of the firste will allwaies abide with him and not onelye of the speche but allsoe of the manners and Condicions."

In the second half of the passage, however, we are offered a more elaborate account of the mechanisms of assimilation. Anne Laurence has noted that early modern medical authorities found the tradition of employing wetnurses to be deeply reprehensible. She observes that behind this suspicion of the figure of the wetnurse lay "the belief that the quality of an infant's milk was critical to the formation of character" (76). Thus, for example, in some medical textbooks, the wetnurse is exhorted to "refrain from sex[,] which would make her milk 'of an unsavoury taste, tasting hot, and rank, or goatish'" (76). Parr Lane again helps to make clear the significance of this in an Anglo-Irish context: "But with their milke we suck such manners in / which bred in bone will never from our skinne / as beinge rare in other partes to find / deforme the body efferate the mind" (fol. 159v). Lane's argument here is that the milk provided by the nurse very literally serves to form the body, becoming "bred in bone" and skin. The infant English body is thus "deformed," reconstituted into Irishness. This process of reconstitution extends even into the mind itself, which is thereby rendered "efferate"— fierce or wild.[26]

Lane had almost certainly read Spenser's tract, and what he offers us here is a condensed version of Spenser's own argument.[27] Irenius makes clear to Eudoxus that the assimilation of the Old English infant is more than just a matter of apelike imitation, as he says of such children that "they moreouer drawe into themselues together with theire sucke even the nature and disposicion of theire nurses." Thus, the general makeup of the child is determined by characteristics transmitted by the nurse's milk. Like Lane, Spenser sees the mind as being continuous with the body, as he observes that "the minde followethe muche the Temparature of the bodye." By "Temparature," here Irenius intends the composition of the body, its mixture of elements (such as, for example, the humours). As Irenius has made clear, one of the main constitutive components of the body is the nurse's milk, as the child's primary source of sustenance. It follows that, in the case of the child suckled by a native Irish wetnurse, a significant component of the "Temparature of the bodye" is native Irish and, as such, physically contributes an Irish component to the composition of the child's mind.

Having noted the relationship between body and mind, Irenius moves on further to posit a relationship between mind and language. "Wordes," he tells Eudoxus, "are the Image of the minde." Therefore, it follows that, in the case of the child who has been brought up speaking Irish, if "the wordes . . . procedinge from the minde" are Irish words, the mind itself must in some sense be an "Irish mind."[28] The connection between mind (or heart) and language was a commonplace of Renaissance thought and Thomas Elyot, for example, argues in *The Boke of the Governor* that he "intended to augment our Englyshe tongue, whereby men shoulde as well expresse more abundantly the thynge that they conceyved in theyre hertis (wherefore language was ordeyned) havynge wordes apte for the purpose" (quoted in Elsky 1989, 65).[29] It should be noted, however, that in Irenius's assertion that "the minde must be nedes *affected with* the wordes," the phrase "affected with" has the force of "laid hold of" (as "by a disease"), so that we might say that the strength of language in this instance is such that, rather than being an "Image of the minde," in fact it is language that morbidly *possesses* the mind, as if the mind of the foster-child is virtually appropriated by the Irish language it learns from its nurse.[30]

At the close of the passage, in observing that "out of the abundance of the harte the tonge speakethe," Spenser invokes the words of Jesus, chiding the Pharisees in Matthew 12: "O generation of vipers, how can ye, being evil, speak good things? for out of the abundance of the heart the mouth speaketh" (12:34). Here we get a negative conjunction of heart and tongue, as an evil tongue is incapable of speaking good things ("an evil man out of the evil treasure bringeth forth evil things" [12:35]). By inference, we might conclude that the inverse is also true: that an evil tongue betokens an evil heart or, in the case of the Old English, that an alien-speaking tongue speaks of an alien heart or, again, that an Irish-speaking tongue betokens an Irish heart.

Irenius essentially attempts to demonstrate in this passage that, by the dual constitutive processes of consuming Irish milk and issuing forth Irish speech, the Old English in a complex sense literally *become* Irish, and he hints that they do so in a manner that is, in fact, irreversible ("thoughe he afterwardes be taughte Englishe yeat the smacke of the firste will allwaies abide with him"). Thus, Irenius adds a further layer to his solution to the problem of Old English proximity: not only were those who undertook the initial colonialist project in Ireland civilizationally inferior relative to the advanced state of development of current English stock, but, in fact, intimate physical contact with the Irish transformed the essential nature of their physical being and rendered them virtually coidentical with the Irish themselves.

In the final section of *A View,* Irenius sets out his reform proposals for Ireland and the issue of the assimilation of the Old English by the native Irish is raised once more. Irenius begins by again pressing the need for prosecuting a more vigorous reform program among the Old English than among the Gaelic Irish: "These doe nede a sharper reformacion then the Irishe for they are muche more stubborne and disobedient to lawe and governement then the Irishe be, and more malicous againste the Englishe that dailye are sente ouer" (210). Eudoxus again registers his surprise, this time at Old English belligerence toward the New English ("Is it possible I praye youe howe comes it to passe and what maie be the reason theareof?" [210]). Irenius explains that the Old English "saie that the lande is theires only by righte beinge firste Conquered by theire ancestours and that they are wronged by the new Inglishemens intrudinge thearevnto." Out of resentment over this and of being denied the right to self-rule, "they thinke themselues greatelye indignifyed and disgraced and thearby growe bothe discontente and vndewtifull" (210). At this, Eudoxus seems to despair of the situation completely: "In truethe *Iren:* This is more then euer I harde that the englishe Irishe theare shoulde be worse then the wilde Irishe. Lorde how quicklye dothe that country alter mens natures It is not for nothinge I perceaue which I haue harde that the Councell of Englande thinke it no good policye to haue that Realme reformed or planted with englishe leaste they shoulde growe as vndewtifull as the Irishe and become muche more dangerous" (210).

We notice here that, for Eudoxus, the Old English have now acquired a new name, as he refers to them as "the englishe Irishe," as if in confirmation of Irenius's recasting of assimilation as a process whereby the English literally become Irish. But in Eudoxus's version of that "alter[ation of] mens natures" that occurs in Ireland, the agent of alteration becomes simply "that country" in the abstract. This raises the troubling possibility that—Irenius's elaborate psychophysiological theorizing notwithstanding—there may be something inherent to the realm of Ireland that necessarily leads to a transformation of identity. Such a possibility would threaten the entire ongoing colonial project, since the New English might prove, ultimately, to be just as vulnerable to assimilation as were their Old English predecessors. In his final set of manuvers in the text, Irenius attempts to foreclose this possibility, attempting to shield the New English from any prospect of assimilation.

Irenius begins his task by observing that "Noe times haue bene without bad men," and he continues,

> But as for that purpose of the Cownsell of Englande which ye spake that they shoulde kepe that Realme from reformacion I thinke they are moste lewdlie abused for their Carefullnes and erneste endevours do wittnes the Contrarye Neither is it the nature of the Countrye to alter mens manners, but the bad mindes of the man, whoe havinge bene broughte vp at home vnder a streighte rule of dutie and obedience beinge allwaies restrained by sharpe penalties from lewde behauiour, so sone as they Come thither wheare they see lawes more slacklye tended and the harde Constrainte which they weare vsed vnto now slacked, they growe more lose and Careles of theire duetie and as it is the nature of all men to loue libertye So they become Libertines and fall to all licentiousnes of the Irishe, more boldlie daringe to disobaie the lawe thoroughe presumpcion of favour and freindeshippe then anye Irishe dareth. (210-11)

Irenius thus denies here that exposure to the realm of Ireland necessarily leads to loss of civility. Instead, he suggests that degeneracy is a matter of geography only to the extent that displacement from the political center (and hence isolation from strict mechanisms of control) can sometimes lead to indiscipline. Irenius is careful to establish that such loss of discipline is not an inevitable and universal effect of displacement—rather, it is something to which "bad men," possessed of "bad mindes" are likely to be susceptible. Such individuals are held in check by the strict laws of the metropolitan center, but a slack colonial regime will give license to their faults. Thus, the solution to the problem identified here is the general imposition of a strict political regime—a regime of "harde Constrainte." Such a solution fits neatly with Spenser's greater political agenda, since the New English program in Ireland was predicated precisely on the rejection of the Old English reform strategy and the advocacy of an uncompromising military campaign, followed by a regime of close control. Thus, by a kind of neat ambidextrous political logic, the very measures that the New English propose for bringing the country to conformity and civility are conceived by Irenius as being the mechanism that will render the New English themselves secure against degeneration.

Irenius's reform plan calls ultimately for the intermingling of the communities of the English and the Irish, within certain tightly controlled conditions. Eudoxus objects to this,

> Me thinkes your late advizement was verie evill whereby youe wished the Irishe to be sowed and sprincked with englishe and in all the Irishe contries to haue Englishe planted amongest them for to bringe to Englishe fashions, since the Englishe sonner drawe to the Irishe then the Irishe to the Englishe. for as youe saide before they muste rvn with the Streames the greater nomber will Carrye awaie the lesse, therefore me semes by this reason it shoulde be better to parte the Irishe and Englishe then to mingle them togeather. (211)

But Irenius replies,

> Not soe *Eudox:* but wheare theare is no good staie of gouernement and stronge ordinaunces to houlde them theare indede the fewer will followe the more: but wheare theare is due order of discipline and good rule there the better shall goe formoste and the worste shall followe. (211)

Irenius thus places his faith here in government, law, and discipline not only to counter the effects of incipient degeneracy but also to effect a general reform of the country. As the text draws to a close, Irenius projects forward to a future in which the effects of assimilation will be reversed to the extent that the closely controlled Irish will be drawn to English civility and the two communities will live in harmony:

> I thinke it best by an vnion of manners and Conformitye of mindes to bringe them to be one people, and to put awaie the dislikefull Conceite

bothe of thone and thother which wilbe by no meanes better then by there enterminglinge of them, that neither all the Irishe maye dwell togeather, nor all the Englishe, but by translatinge of them and scatteringe them in smalle nombers amonge the Englishe, not onely to bringe them by dailye Conuersacion vnto better likinge of eache other but allsoe to make bothe of them lesse hable to hurte. (211-12)

In one sense, we might say that the vision of the future that Spenser offers does not differ so radically from the vision offered by the Old English reformers, who imagined that the Irish could be brought to surrender their identity in order to be granted English culture. The distinction is that where the Old English considered that this objective could be achieved for the most part peacefully, Spenser's New English program called for the Irish first to be broken through a campaign of starvation and conquest.[31] In this sense, Spenser believed that if the Irish were once destroyed militarily and politically, the mechanism of proximity might well be recruited to the cancellation of Irish difference and the absorption of the Irish within the community of the English, reversing the troubling paradigm presented by the Old English. As we will see, this vision of Spenser's has much in common with the view of the erasability of Irish difference proposed by writers such as Ben Jonson and Sir John Davies, once the Irish had, indeed, been defeated in the opening years of the seventeenth century.

Ciarán Brady has observed of the *View* that it is "riddled with ambiguity" and that "internal contradictions . . . may be seen to operate on a number of levels in the text" ("Crisis" 1986, 33). In offering an opposing reading of the *View,* Nicholas Canny refutes this claim.[32] In one sense, we might say that both views of the work are correct. Spenser's text is troubled by the same issues that disturb the tranquility of all English writing about Ireland. As we have seen to some extent here, Spenser is driven to a kind of explicatory excess in the text, offering a multilayered account of the mechanisms of Old English degeneracy and assimilation. In this way, the tract does attain a certain form of surety and closure.[33] I maintain that the *Faerie Queene,* by contrast, offers us a much more obviously conflicted text, as it negotiates what Richard McCabe has termed "the complex process whereby the blunt recommendations of the prose [are] transformed into the idealised vision of the poem" (1989, 110). As we will see below, as Andrew Hadfield notes, ultimately "the master trope of the *View* have no privileged status in [the] world" of the poem ("Spenser, Ireland" 1964, 18).[34]

III.

Book 5 of *The Faerie Queene* is dedicated to "the legend of Artegall," whose appointed quest is "to succour a distressed Dame, / Whom a strong tyrant did vniustly thrall" (V i 3 6-7).[35] The "Dame" in question is Irena, a figure, as the name suggests, for Ireland. Irena is subjugated by Grantorto ("great wrong")—a composite figure of Catholic oppression. In the section of the narrative dedicated to the liberation of Irena, Artegall assumes the allegorized identity of Arthur Lord Grey de Wilton, as Spenser seeks to vindicate Grey's actions during his period of tenure of the Lord Deputyship in Ireland.[36]

These are the specific allegorical connections between Ireland and *The Faerie Queene,* but, as Lisa Jardine has argued, the presence of Ireland in the text seems more generally pervasive than this. Spenser, Jardine suggests, "consistently takes his cultural bearings from Ireland, and . . . Ireland and Irish history are an intrinsic part of his epic narrative" ("Mastering the Uncouth" 1993, 70).[37] Certainly as far as book 5 is concerned, the entire text seems to be supersaturated with images of Ireland.[38] We might note, for instance, that the remorseless and unremitting violence of Artegall's "yron man" companion, Talus, is reminiscent of the campaigns of such English military commanders as Humphrey Gilbert, Essex, and Grey, who gave no quarter in their pursuit of the Irish.[39] Likewise, canto 9's shape-changing, wily, flitting Malengin seems a version of the English image of the Gaelic Irish, whose glibs and mantles made them indistinguishable one from the other and whose military strategy was always the guerrilla raid: emerging from and disappearing back into the fastness of the island's abundant woods.[40]

While book 5 as a whole is informed by Spenser's experience in Ireland generally, the opening of the book seems darkly colored by an issue that is particularly relevant to his attitude to the Old English—the question of degeneracy. Artegall's story is attached by Spenser to a prior classical legend: the myth of Astraea, the goddess of Justice who flees the earth when it grows to be too wicked: "Now when the world with sinne gan to abound, / *Astræa* loathing lenger here to space / Mongst wicked men, in whom no truth she found, / Return'd to heauen, whence she deriu'd her race" (V i 11 1-4). The myth invoked here serves to provide a classical frame for the story of Artegall. Artegall is styled as Astraea's "apprentice" and successor in the realm of earthly justice—in token of which she makes him a present of "Chrysaor," the sword of justice. But the sense of the world evoked in this passage—of a realm falling progressively into greater wickedness—accords well with the general tone of book V as it gets underway. The Proem to the book dwells broodingly on images of a world (indeed an entire cosmos) falling evermore away from its appointed orbit:

> So oft as I with state of present time,
> The image of the antique world compare,
> When as mans age was in his freshest prime,
> And the first blossome of faire vertue bare,
> Such oddes I find twixt those, and these which are,
> As that, through long continuance of his course,
> Me seemes the world is runne quite out of square,
> From the first point of his appointed sourse,
> And being once amisse growe daily wourse and wourse.
>
> (V Proem 1)

In this introduction, Spenser is summoning up a long-standing convention of the progressive degeneration of the world—one that is common to classical, Judaic, and Christian thought.[41] For all his invocation of the trope of humanity's inevitable and ineluctable descent "from the golden age" to "a stonie one" (V Proem 2 1-2), however, we have already seen that, in the case of the *View,* Spenser suggests that, at least as far as the Old English are concerned, degeneracy involves more complex mechanisms than a simple matter of degradation over time.[42] We will remember that Irenius argues in *A View* for a specific link between degeneracy and the intimate nurturing relationship between the Old English infant and the child's Gaelic Irish nurse or foster mother. In this instance, the mechanism of degeneration for Spenser appears to be intimately tied to the issue of gender, in that the source of degeneration is traced by Irenius specifically to the female caregiver.

A number of commentators have noted that gender and degeneracy are linked elsewhere in the *View* also. For instance, Irenius recounts the story of how the loss of the necessary markers of gender identity can lead to a profound transformation and general diminishment of identity:

> It is written by *Aristotle* that when *Cirus* had ouercome the Lidians that weare a warlike nacion and devised to bringe them to a more peaceable liffe he Chaunged theire Apparrell and musicke And in steade of theire shorte

"They Are All Wandred Much" { 81 }

warlike Coate cloathed them in longe garmentes like weomen and in steade of theire warlike musicke appointed to them certaine Lascivious layes and loose gigs by which in shorte space theire mindes weare so mollified and abated that they forgate theire former firesnes and became moste tender and effeminate wheareby it appeareth that theare is not a little in the garment to the fashioninge of the minde and Condicions. (121)

Irenius's parable here clearly resonates with one of the central episodes of book 5, the Herculean narrative of Artegall's sojourn in the Amazon kingdom of Radegone.[43] Artegall first comes across the Amazon warriors when, en route to liberate Irena, he digresses to save Sir Terpin from "a troupe of women warlike dight" (V iv 21 8). Terpin, once rescued, explains to Artegall that it is the policy of Radigund, the leader of the Amazon band, that:

> For all those Knights, the which by force or guile
> She doth subdue, she fowly doth entreate.
> First she doth them of warlike armes despoile,
> And cloth in womens weedes: And then with threat
> Doth them compell to worke, to earne their meat,
> To spin, to card, to sew, to wash, to wring;
> Ne doth she giue them other thing to eat,
> But bread and water, or like feeble thing,
> Them to disable from reuenge aduenturing.
>
> (V iv 31)

Artegall continues on to fight with Radigund herself, but he is defeated by her and so duly yields himself to the conditions to which he has agreed prior to their encounter—to become her prisoner and to render her service. Like Aristotle's Lidians in *A View,* and like the other defeated knights in Radegone, he is stripped of the markers of his masculine gender identity and submits to having new markers substituted in their place. Radigund, we learn,

> caused him to be disarmed quight,
> Of all the ornaments of knightly name,
> With which whylome he gotten had great fame:
> In stead whereof she made him to be dight
> In womans weedes, that is to manhood shame,

And put before his lap a napron white,
In stead of Curiets and bases fit for fight.

(V v 20)

Clare Carroll (in "The Construction of Gender" [1990]) and Ann Rosalind Jones and Peter Stallybrass have noted the extent to which, in Spenser's writings, narratives of Irish degeneracy are folded into narratives of degendering and effeminization. Thus, writing of the mechanisms that Spenser maps out for the hibernicizing of the Old English in the *View*, Jones and Stallybrass note that "What Spenser conjures up . . . is a parody (for him, grotesque) of the colonial enterprise, a parody in which the domestic triumphs over the state, female over male, Irish over English. Pandora's box, Circe's cup — these insistent figures of female misrule are embodied in the very homes of the English elite in the Irish wet-nurse and the Irish mother" (1992, 164).[44] Likewise, Carroll directly relates Spenser's conception of Old English degeneracy to the narrative of the Radigund episode.[45] Certainly, the parallels between Spenser's resentation of the assimilation of the Old English and of Artegall's defeat are compelling. We might note, for example, that a certain element of complicity inheres in Artegall's defeat at Radigund's hands. In fact, *he* initially has effectively defeated *her* in combat, reducing her to a "sencelesse swoune" (V v 11 4). As she lies "before his foote prostrated" (6), he is prepared to decapitate her, but he first stops to unlace her helmet, in the process revealing her face. The effect of seeing her visage "bath'd in bloud and sweat together ment" (V v 12 5) is such that Artegall discards his sword, rendering himself vulnerable to Radigund when she recovers. It is thus, we are told, that Artegall was

ouercome, not ouercome,
But to her yeelded of his owne accord;
Yet was he iustly damned by the doome
Of his owne mouth, that spake so warelesse word,
To be her thrall, and seruice her afford.
For though that he first victorie obtaynèd,
Yet after by abandoning his sword,
He wilfull lost, that he before attaynèd.
No fayrer conquest, then that with goodwill is gaynèd.

(V v 17)

The analogy with the Old English should be clear. On their first arrival in Ireland, the Norman-English achieved a high degree of military success against the Irish. However, they failed to sustain their campaign and, ultimately, succumbed to a certain Irish attractiveness, in the process losing what they had previously gained. Like the Old English in this respect, Artegall is "ouercome, not ouercome / But . . . [yields] of his owne accord."[46] Similarly, just as the Old English abandoned their Norman-English names and traditions and adopted Irish dress styles and practices, so Artegall submits to being "disarmed quight, / Of all the ornaments of knightly name, / With which whylome he gotten had great fame" and puts on "womans weedes."[47] As Clare Carroll observes: "Artegall is degenerated according to his gender role as well as his political role. Made to do women's work and wear women's clothes by Radigund, Artegall is like the Old English in their adoption of Irish customs" (1990, 182). Thus, though in the allegorical code of the poem it is the Irena episode that is tied specifically to Irish affairs, we can nevertheless see in the Amazon narrative the emergence of Spenser's prose version of the Old English into the poetic text in the figure of Artegall. By extension, we find in Radigund a figuring of the Gaelic Irish.[48]

If, in one sense, the Radigund episode seems to offer a relatively clear representation of the degeneration of the Old English as they surrender to the feminized seductiveness of the native Irish, there are, nevertheless, certain strands of the narrative that trouble any easy evocation within the episode of a field of stable, binary differences. The figure of Radigund herself, in particular, indicates a certain odd uncertainty and instability of identity. When Britomart overthrows Radigund and repeals "the liberty of women . . . / Which they had long vsurpt; . . . restoring [them] / To mens subiection" (V vii 42 5-7), we may be put in mind of Spenser's anxious negotiation of the issue of female power in canto 5 of the same book: "Vertuous women wisely vnderstand, / That they were borne to base humilitie, / Vnlesse the heauens them lift to lawfull soueraintie" (V v 25 7-9), where Spenser seeks to discount female rule, while at the same time being careful to exempt Elizabeth from his critique. Radigund herself is presented as a powerful woman whose rule is illegitimate and so she must be distinguished from Elizabeth as another powerful female ruler who *is* legitimate. The problem is that, as Andrew Hadfield has pointed out, almost all female figures in the poem seem to offer the possibility of being read at some level as analogs of Elizabeth.[49] This possibility is particularly strong in the case of Radigund, since one of Elizabeth's specified equivalents in the poem, Belphoebe, is at one point in the narrative directly figured precisely as an Amazonian leader. In her encounter with Braggadocchio, she is likened to Penthesilea, "that famous Queene / Of *Amazons,* whom *Pyrrhus* did destroy, / The day that first of *Priame* she was seene, / Did shew her selfe in great triumphant ioy, / To succor the weake state of sad afflicted *Troy*" (II iii 31 5-9). And, indeed, in the iconographic world beyond the *Faerie Queene,* Elizabeth was sometimes directly figured as an Amazon in the wake of the armada victory. Thus, in James Aske's *Elizabetha Triumphans* (1588), Elizabeth herself is imagined as Penthesilea — in his description of Tilbury, Aske presents her as "In nought vnlike the *Amazonian Queene,* / Who beating downe amaine the bloodie *Greekes,* / Thereby to grapple with *Achilles* stout, / Euen at the time when *Troy* was sore besieg'd" (Schleiner 1978, 170).[50]

Within Radigund, then, we find the possibility of reading at least an iconographic or metaphorical trace of Elizabeth, so a troubling ambiguity haunts the whole Radegone episode. Artegall, I have suggested, appears there as a projection of the Old English, seduced into a demotic otherness by a Radigund who can be seen as emblematic of the native Irish. But, as ever, this presentation of Irishness cannot be sustained as wholly alien; difference always threatens to coalesce with identity, as the image of Elizabeth shimmers within the figure of Radigund. We will find the same problem of potential coalescence and collapse in the text's presentation of Artegall, as we continue to trace the trajectory of his narrative throughout the remainder of book 5.

We can see this process of coalescence at play if we consider the segment of the poem in which Ireland is explicitly figured in the allegory — the episode in which Artegall liberates Irena from Grantorto.[51] As we have already noted, the reading of the allegory of the poem at this point traditionally casts Artegall as a figure for Arthur Lord Grey de Wilton and reads the Grantorto episode and its aftermath as an allegorical record of Grey's Lord Deputyship in Ireland.[52] Beneath this specific layer of the allegory, however, a further and more general correspondence can be discerned in the text. If the Artegall of the Radigund encounter figures the emergence into the poem of the Old English, I would argue that the Artegall of the Grantorto episode is representative of not just one specific New English official — Lord Grey — but of the New English as a group. Thus, Artegall becomes something like a composite figure through whom the extended history of English intervention in Ireland is written into the poem.

One problematic effect of this identification of both groups in a single character is, of course, that it suggests again a clear continuity between the Old and New English. The section of the poem in which the issue of this potential continuity is most clearly taken up is the encounter between Artegall and Sir Sergis. If we take Irena as representative of Ireland itself (the realm, as opposed to any particular segment of the population), we can say that Sir Sergis implicitly admonishes Artegall for his failure to recover the realm within the timeframe to which he originally made a commitment.[53] Irena, Sir Sergis tells Artegall, is by Grantorto "in wretched thraldome bound"

> For she presuming on th'appointed tyde,
> In which ye promist, as ye were a Knight,
> To meete her at the saluage Ilands syde,
> And then and there for triall of her right
> With her vnrigteous enemy to fight,
> Did thither come, where she afrayd of nought,
> By guilefull treason and by subtill slight
> Surprized was, and to *Grantorto* brought,
> Who her imprisond hath, and her life often sought.
>
> (V xi 39)

Sir Sergis's complaint here is that Artegall—like the Old English—has made a commitment to the recovery of the realm and has failed to make good on it, with the result that Irena is further away from deliverance than ever. Artegall acknowledges his culpability in this (he "grieued sore, that through his fault she had / Fallen into that Tyrants hand and vsage bad" [V xi 40 8-9]) but offers the following excuse for his long delay: "Witnesse vnto me, ye heauens, that know / How cleare I am from blame of this vpbraide: / For ye into like thraldome me did throw, / And kept from complishing the faith, which I did owe" (V xi 41 6-9). In suggesting that he and Irena have suffered "like thralldome," so that the land of the Amazons and the realm of Irena become continuous with each other, Artegall establishes a link here between Grantorto and Radigund. The responsibility for Artegall's delay is, however, here shifted from "his fault" to heaven's blame, as Artegall essentially argues that he cannot be held responsible for the mistakes of the past. In this sense, we might say that Artegall attempts to disengage himself from past history, as if endeavoring to shed his Old English skin and take on the cloak of a New English champion.

This he succeeds in doing, at least to the extent that he is able to kill the monster Grantorto and thereby liberate Irena. Allegorically, then, Artegall apparently succeeds in fulfilling the New English goal of taming and reforming the realm. Thus, Tom Healy observes that "Artegall's final encounter with Grantorto, . . . organised as a formal chivalric contest, shows Artegall as intensely self-composed and controlled as opposed to the giant's enraged but chaotic behaviour. Artegall keeps control and this allows victory over a savage force which appears much larger and more powerful than the knight" (*New Latitudes* 1992, 96). Artegall's victory ultimately proves to be imperfect, however, as he is recalled to the Faerie Court and is, as he departs, assailed by Envy, Detraction, and the Blatant Beast. This is conventionally read as a figuring of the outbreak of scorn and criticism that accompanied Lord Grey's recall to London, but the implications of the episode run much deeper.

For one thing, the nature of Artegall's victory is itself somewhat suspect, as we can see by examining more closely the circumstances surrounding the victory and the manner in which it is achieved. We should first note that Artegall's determination to make amends for his delay in coming to Irena's aid does not preclude his first engaging in one more digression along the way. Coming on "a Knight in daungerous distresse / Of a rude rout him chasing to and fro," Artegall sends Talus to intervene. The knight, Sir Burbon, is rescued and explains to his saviors how the cause of the trouble is his mission to recover his love who "by force is still fro me detayned, / And with corruptfull brybes is to vntruth mistrayned" (V xi 54 8-9). Artegall takes the time to find Burbon's love, rebuke her, and bring the couple to reconciliation.

One of the most heavily marked incidents of the Burbon episode is Artegall's calling on Burbon to account for the loss of his shield. As Artegall notes, "That is the greatest shame and foulest scorne, / Which vnto any knight behappen may / To loose the badge, that should his deedes display" (V xi 52 3-5). Burbon explains that, although the shield has brought him much honor and success, since "many did that shield enuie, / And cruell enemies increased more" (V xi 54 2-3), he considered it to his advantage to set the shield aside. Artegall, however, takes his fellow knight severely to task for abandoning

that which doth containe
Your honours stile, that is your warlike shield.
All perill ought be lesse, and lesse all paine
Then losse of fame in disauentrous field;
Dye rather, then doe ought, that mote dishonour yield.

(55 2-3, 5-9)

The potency of this issue is such that it persists into the argument to the following canto, even though it has, in fact, no place there. Spenser writes: "Artegall doth Sir Burbon aide, / And blames for changing shield," but this summary applies to the preceding canto and is not pertinent to canto 12.

What does happen in canto 12 is that Artegall, in spite of his so very recent great remonstrances to Burbon, relinquishes his own shield—in the process of defeating Grantorto.[54] The giant strikes Artegall's shield so hard with his battleaxe that he cannot extricate his weapon from it, much as he draws Artegall "all about" "Which *Artegall* perceiving, strooke no more, / But loosing soone his shield, did it forgoe, / And whiles he combred was therewith so sore, / He gan at him let driue more fiercely then afore" (V xii 22 6-9).

In the standard reading of the allegory of the Burbon incident, Burbon himself is taken for Henri de Navarre and his surrendering of his shield is seen as an allegorical rendering of Henri's repudiation of his Protestant faith and his embracing of Catholicism in order to attain the crown of France (famously observing that *"Paris vaut bien une messe"*). We have already noted in chapter 1 that the issue of religion and of how religious differences were perceived in sixteenth-century Ireland was complex. At its most basic level, however, the broad fidelity of the majority of the Old English to the unreformed church provided New English writers such Spenser with ammunition in their struggle for control in Ireland, as it signaled another way in which the Old English could be conflated with the native Irish as a single grouping in need of the kind of rigorous reform that only the New English could provide. This being the case, Artegall's replication of Burbon's "Catholic gesture" is particularly surprising, because it appears to figure a collapsing (indeed, on Artegall's part, an abandonment) of precisely those distinctions that Spenser is elsewhere so very anxious to maintain. The "Old English" Artegall and the "New English" Artegall no longer appear so coherently distinguishable from each other. The surrender of the shield is also reminiscent of Artegall's submission to Radigund's stripping away of his markers of knightly identity, as she "caused him to be disarmed quight, / Of all the ornaments of knightly name" (V v 20 4-5), so the loss of the shield reflects again not only a failure to sustain a rigid hierarchy of distinction, but, indeed, an active complicity in the disruption of such a hierarchy.

In spite of having surrendered his shield, Artegall is, of course, presented as taking the offensive against Grantorto and so defeating him:

> So well he him pursew'd, that at the last,
> He stroke him with *Chrysaor* on the hed,
> That with the souse thereof full sore aghast,
> He staggered to and fro in doubtfull sted.
> Againe whiles he him saw so ill bested,
> He did him smite with all his might and maine,
> That falling on his mother earth he fed:
> Whom when he saw prostrated on the plaine,
> He lightly reft his head, to ease him of his paine.
> (V xii 23)

Artegall thus achieves his victory over Grantorto by striking him with "Chrysaor"— the sword of justice given to him by Astraea before she departed from the earth. But what we are witnessing here is an odd failure of memory within the text, since in the Radigund episode we have been told that, following Artegall's submission and degendering, Radigund "causd his warlike armes / Be hang'd on high, that mote his shame bewray; / And broke his sword, for feare of further harmes, / With which he wont to stirre vp battailous alarmes" (V v 21 6-9). So, in effect, we discover here that, from the perspective of the complete narrative of Artegall's quest, the rendering of his victory is curiously compromised, because the symbol of his judicial and martial power has already been presented as having been destroyed in his encounter with the potent, seductive Otherness figured in Radigund.[55] In this sense, the emergence of Envy and Detraction may simply serve to confirm the emptiness of Artegall's victory as another figuring of the narrative's inability to achieve secure closure.

What the Artegall narrative in book 5 offers us is, we might say, a sustained consideration of Anglo-Irish relations. This consideration contrasts with the relatively controlled program of Spenser's prose text, which is designed with the intention that, as Andrew Hadfield has put it, the reader should "follow Irenius's arguments, so that at the end of the dialogue, like Eudoxus, s/he is convinced of the necessity of sending over a huge army to conquer Ireland, making it ready for [New English] reformation and the establishment of proper laws" ("Spenser, Ireland" 1994, 9). The allegorical and fantastical world of the poem allows an altogether more conflicted picture to emerge. The distinction between Old and New English that the prose text strives so hard to effect and maintain does not hold here, as the composite Artegall is seen to be continuous across both versions of Ireland that the text can be seen to provide.

But more than this, we find that, in both the Radigund episode and the fight with Grantorto, Artegall seems complicit in his own failure. Thus, if Spenser's attempt to disjoin the New English from proximity with their Old English counterparts unravels here, so too does his attempt to separate the English from the Irish. On the one hand, the suppressed proximity of the English and Irish simply resurfaces, as certain equivalences between the two cultures emerge, and, on the other, Ireland itself emerges as a site of profound and undeniable desire—a desire deeply interwoven with the wish to engage with and submit to the ambiguous identity of the Other.

By the end of book 5, the elaborate ideological fabric of difference that Spenser attempts to construct has almost completely unraveled. In the final stanza of the book, the most basic element of Spenser's plan for the reformation of Ireland also comes to be repudiated. Irenius's modest proposal for the island involves deploying the twin strategy of vigorous military campaigning and induced famine.[56] Talus, throughout book 5, has been the embodiment of such extreme measures, and, as Artegall's enemies multiply, it appears as if only the remorseless and unremitting violence of his iron companion can restore him to the anticipated successful conclusion of his knightly quest. Artegall, however, rejects this option also. As Envy mocks Artegall, Talus offers to intervene:

> But *Talus* hearing her so lewdly raile,
> And speake so ill of him, that well deserued,
> Would her haue chastiz'd with his yron flaile,
> If her Sir *Artegall* had not preserued,
> And him forbidden, who his heast obserued.
> (V xii 43 1-5)

At the end of book 5, Artegall balks at imposing the kind of solution to the Irish problem that Irenius endorses in the closing pages of *A View.*

David Norbrook has observed that "it is with a sigh of relief that Spenser turns in the Proem to Book VI from Justice to Courtesy, and critics sometimes write of Book VI as if the cruel atmosphere of Book V has passed" (1984, 143). However, as Norbrook himself goes on to argue, "we are not long into Book VI before it becomes clear that the concerns of the previous book have not disappeared" (143).[57] Norbrook lists some of the bloody incidents that disturb the intended graceful world of Calidore, the knight of Courtesy:

> By stanza 23 Calidore has despatched a churl by cleaving his head asunder to the chin; the carcass, a "lumpe of sin," blocks the door. When Calidore fights Crudor, the knight's sides gush forth blood like a purple lake (VI i 37). In canto iii Serena is given a gory wound and Turpine wounds Calepine till the blood gushes forth like a well gushing out of a hill. The Salvage Man avenges this attack by laying about him until he is "steeming red" with the blood of Turpine's servants. . . . Courtesy, it turns out, needs to be supplemented by violence in the chaotic landscape of Book VI in which brigands and wicked churls are constant menaces. This setting has much in common with the Irish landscape Spenser would have known, where brigands would suddenly emerge from forests. . . . (143-44)

A number of other critics have noticed that this reeruption of the violence of book 5 within book 6 is accompanied by a general waning of purpose within the narrative. Thus, Tom Healy writes of "a failure of resolve" in the book, amounting to "an internal lethargy" (*New Latitudes* 1992, 103), and Andrew Hadfield describes it as "a book lacking both a narrative core and a central authority" (*Spenser's Irish Experience* 1997, 177). Calidore wanders out of his own book and absents himself for canto after canto, as a cast of extras is marshaled to improvise a set of narratives during his absence.[58] When he does return, in canto 9, he quickly loses sight of (and interest in) his appointed quest—the capture of the Blatant Beast—choosing instead to linger in the pastoral world. Richard Rambuss notes that "this movement of retreat—and often outright retirement—is repeated in a number of career narratives throughout Book 6 as a pattern of withdrawal to a variety of hiding places" (1993, 115).[59] Calidore's turn to the pastoral appears also as a version of Artegall's surrender to

Radigund's degendering, as he too exchanges his armor for a style of dress that figures a different identity: "Doffing his bright armes, himselfe addrest / In shepheards weed, and in his hand he tooke, / In stead of steelehead speare, a shepheards hooke" (VI ix 36 3-5).

Spenser himself seems to sponsor this move, as his pastoral poetic alter ego Colin Clout puts in an appearance in canto 10 of book 6. In his prior incarnation, in *Colin Cloutes Come Home Againe,* this figure for the poet had also indicated a turning away from the court toward a pastoral alternative. In the earlier poem, this rejection had figured also a certain rejection of Spenser's native England in favor of his adopted colonial home in Ireland.[60] As Rambuss argues, Spenser, disillusioned by his visit to Elizabeth's court, "recasts his relative lack of success at court as self-remove above the fray, implying by the second half of *Colin Clout* that he now can find poetic inspiration only at a distance from Elizabeth's court. Irish pastoral thus figures as another place to go, another space in which to write poetry" (1993, 99).

In book 6, Colin's pastoral dance of the Graces, with his own "countrey lasse" advanced (even momentarily above Gloriana herself) to be "another Grace," represents an attempt to retrieve the world of the poem, by again seeking to establish "another place," free from political and allegorical interweavings—a space reduced to the personal.[61] As Julia Reinhard Lupton has argued, in this scene, "Spenser draws most heavily on the tradition of pastoral as an elevated, isolated, private world of literary self-reflection and self-confection. Here, Spenser's created 'home' is not 'Ireland' or 'distance from the court' so much as poetry itself, a *locus amoenus* established as both compensation for and critique of the public world" (1990, 140).[62] That the attempt to evoke such a space is doomed to failure is apparent even from the very fact that we are provided with the identification of the personal center of the vision only *after* the vision itself has been dispelled and after Colin has broken his pipes "for fell despight / Of that displeasure" (VI x 18 4-5) of being interrupted by Calidore.[63] Eventually, the pastoral world is itself in its turn swept away, overrun by a group of brigants, who appear strikingly similar to Spenser's prose version of the Irish (they "neuer vsde to liue by plough nor spade, / But fed on spoile and booty, which they made / Vpon their neighbors, which did nigh them border" [VI x 39 4-6]).[64] It is almost as if Ireland again erupts into the text here to emphasize further the denial of any possibility even of some kind of consolatory retreat to what is constructed as the purely personal.

{ 92 }   But the Irish Sea Betwixt Us

Finally, Calidore does return to his appointed quest and does succeed in capturing and muzzling the Blatant Beast. But, like Artegall's, Calidore's victory is also imperfect and short lived. The Beast's escape at the end of the book figures the failure of the poet either to control (as *A View* attempts) or to contain the issues of proximity and desire that Ireland raises, or even adequately to evoke any alternative space—even a generic space (say, pastoral rather than epic)—in which solace might be found. Finally, even the text itself falls victim to this irruption, as it too is consumed by the very issues raised in the poem. We learn of the Blatant Beast in the final canto of book VI: "Ne spareth he the gentle Poets rime, / But rends without regard of person or of time" (VI xii 40 8-9). The beast's rending of "the gentle Poets rime" serves as an image of the text's effectively consuming itself at the last, unable to sustain itself under the weight of its own ideological contradictions.[65]

It should come as no surprise, then, that the final surviving fragment of the poem returns us to Ireland.[66] As Harry Berger notes, the Mutabilitie Cantos offer a "return to the present and to the nearness, the actuality, of the dark 'state of present time' in Ireland" (1988, 257). In his brilliant readings of the Mutabilitie Cantos, Andrew Hadfield has focused on an often neglected episode in the text—the segment of the narrative in which a naked Diana is secretly observed by the "Foolish God *Faunus*" (VI 42 7) as she bathes in an Irish river ("Molanna"—the Behanagh, in county Cork). The hidden Faunus reveals himself by "breaking forth in laughter" (VI 46 5) at the sight of Diana. She sets her nymphs to chase him with their hounds, but he evades them, and Diana, "full of indignation" (VI 54 1), lays upon the land "an heauy haplesse curse" (VI 55 3) and abandons the island. Constructing a subtle political reading of the episode that takes Diana as a figure for the English queen, Hadfield suggests that, at this juncture in the cantos, "Ireland is the place where Elizabeth/Diana is seen naked, exposed like Serena before the salvage nation, the mysterious power of her regal body rendered helpless" (*Spenser's Irish Experience* 1997, 195). In a development of this theme, he argues that this exposure betokens a figuring of Ireland as "the place where both the political stability of the British Isles is threatened and the religious certainties outlined in the earlier books of the poem are rendered problematic" ("Spenser's Savage Religion" 1995, 42).

The Faunus episode can thus be read as effectively anticipating much of what follows in the Mutabilitie Cantos, as political stabilities and identities begin to fracture. Like the Radigund episode, the Mutabilitie Cantos present a strong female character whose intention is to overthrow the existing order of things. Mutability begins her campaign of rebellion by attacking Cynthia, who is, of course, another one of the poem's figures for Elizabeth I. As Richard Rambuss has noted, there is a certain resonant irony in the fact that Mutability here should displace an allegorical figuration of the monarch whose motto was "*semper eadem*" ("always the same"), and, indeed, the anxieties indicated by the episode might well remind us of the apprehensions regarding displacement that are registered in Gerald's *Expugnatio* nightmare vision of the heavenly court overrun and the deity cast from his throne.[67] Again, like the proximate Irish (and like Faunus in Hadfield's reading), Mutability appears in the poem as a principle of instability, threatening to collapse the certainties of English power and identity.

Dame Nature is presented in the poem as the last line of defence against this attempted inversion, and her judgement on Arlo Hill appears to guarantee the present order and to dispel the threat that Mutability poses. As Hadfield makes clear, however, "Nature's argument against Mutabilitie" is finally no "more than a neat trick" ("Spenser, Ireland" 1994, 15), and Berger clarifies the implications of the unconvincing dismissal of Mutabilitie's claims offered by Nature:

Although she is conveniently defeated and "whist" in the single action of the trial, this is the classic Spenserian feint: the defeat of an externalized and localized enemy diverts attention from the continuing and deepening effectiveness of the enemy within; Mutabilitie is limited mainly by the rigid qualities and archaic personification to which "she" lays claim, and the disappearance of the titanesse corresponds to the infiltration of all nature by mutability. (259-60)

The poem finally offers no possibility of arresting this general permeation of mutability, which we might figure in terms of the present study as a final dispersal of any stable or fixed sense of identity. The fiction of the assurance Nature provides seems to evaporate in the final canto, as the first person speaker appears unconvinced by the resolution that has been offered:

When I bethinke me on that speech whyleare,
Of *Mutability,* and well it way:
Me seemes, that though she all vnworthy were

Of the Heav'ns Rule; yet very sooth to say,
In all things else she beares the greatest sway.
                                    (VIII 1 1-5)

The final turn of the poem is away from the earthly realm entirely, toward the transcendent, imagined as the only source of consolation. But even here, as Berger again indicates, there is no certainty to be found:

> The final line is not a great leap through faith; it is a slow and guarded turning *toward* prayer and faith, moving from mere indication ("Him that is . . . ") through half-apostrophe ("O *that* great Sabbaoth God") to the final direct exhortation. It is as if, should he turn too quickly, too hopefully, too unguardedly, nothing would be there. (270)

What *is* there, finally, for the speaker in the poem, is, we might say, only change, uncertaintly, and instability; ultimately there is no defence against this. As Tom Healy has observed, "Change haunts Spenser, even when he acknowledges that a providential order is operating" (*New Latitudes* 1992, 87).

IV.

Ireland emerges in the text of the *Faerie Queene* as a site of contention — a site so potent that it brings about the premature ending of the very text itself. As the poem closes with the appended Cantos of Mutabilitie we get a sense, in the treatment of Mutabilitie herself, of the presence of a looming ominous figure who seeks to overthrow everything, threatening not just the text but even the very speaker himself. If we remember that, while Spenser was writing his poem in Ireland throughout the 1590s, the country was drifting ever closer to an islandwide war, the personal relevance to the poet of the potent figure of Mutabilitie will become all the more clear. In the fictional world of the *Faerie Queene,* the force of Mutability is just barely contained. But just as the solutions of the *View* prove ineffective in the world of the epic poem, so too the constraints imposed on the forces of change in canto 7 of "Mutabilitie" would prove ineffective in what Anthony Sheehan has called Munster's "archipelago of little islands of Englishness" (1982-83, 11), as the southern plantation was overrun by the rebels in 1598.

Mutabilitie based her claim to rule in part on her ancestral connections with the gods themselves (VI 26-27). The closing decades of the sixteenth century saw the rise in Ireland of a Gaelic Irish leader who had been cultivated by the English. Where Spenser's concern in his Irish texts was primarily with the issue of Old English proximity to the New English, the rise of Hugh O'Neill—at one and the same time second Earl of Tyrone and inheritor of the traditional Gaelic title "The O'Neill"—marks the return of the issue of Anglo-*Irish* proximity as a pressing and urgent concern.

4

"The Remarkablest Story of Ireland"
Shakespeare and the Irish War

What intricate confusion haue we heere?
Not two houres since, we apprehended one
In habit Irish, but in speech not so;
And now you bring another, that in speech is Irish,
But in habit, English.
Anonymous, *The Life of Sir John Old-castle*

I.

We have seen that a primary concern of Spenser's in *A View of the Present State of Ireland* lay with the problem of the Old English. Spenser's prose tract can thus be said to provide a concerted engagement with a novel version of the problem of proximity—the existence in Ireland of a population of settlers who have adopted certain aspects of Irish culture and practice. Even as Spenser engages with the issue of Old English proximity, however, there is a rising sense in the *View* as it draws to a close that the situation with regard to the Gaelic Irish is shifting in a way that demands renewed attention. As Irenius outlines his plans for pacifying Ireland, Eudoxus asks him, "Now touchinge the Arch-Rebel himselfe I meane the Earle of Tyrone if he in all the time of these warrs shoulde offer to Come in and submitt himselfe to her maiestie woulde ye not haue him receaued givinge good hostages and sufficiente assurance of himselfe" (166), to which Irenius replies, "No marrye, for theare is no doubte but he will offer to Come in as he hathe done diuerse times allreadie, but it is without anie intente of trewe submission as theffecte hathe well shewed" (166). Hugh O'Neill, the Earl of Tyrone referred to here, is thus to be treated no differently from the other Irish leaders currently in rebellion, and yet his very title as "Arch-Rebel" points to his special status in the affairs of the island.[1]

At the time of Spenser's writing of *A View*, in 1596, O'Neill was the most powerful local ruler among the Irish and was in the process of extending his influence throughout the island as a whole by means of his domination of a loose confederacy of Gaelic Irish leaders. It was at O'Neill's instigation that the Munster plantation was overrun in 1598, sweeping the English settlers — Spenser and his family among them — from the land. A witness to the event (possibly Spenser himself) described the overwhelming of the settlements as follows:[2]

> There came vpp latelie of the Rebells not past 2000. being sent by the said Traitour E: of Tyreone vpon whose ariveall all the Irish rose vpp in Armes against the english which were lately planted theire . . . And going straight vppon the English as they dwelt disparsed before they could assemble themselues spoiled them all, there howses sacked and them selues forced to flie away for safetye, so many as they could catch they hewed and massacred miserablie the rest leaving all behinde them fledd with their wives and Children to such porte townes as were next them . . . (Spenser, *A Brief Note* 1949, 238)

The image of O'Neill that emerges here — the Irish Arch-Rebel inciting and directing an islandwide Gaelic alliance — is, however, incomplete. When we examine a further exchange between Irenius and Eudoxus in *A View* we realize that O'Neill's situation in Ireland and, specifically, his relationship to both Irish *and* English centers of power and sources of identity were much more complex than his characterization as the "Arch Rebel" suggests. Detailing the origins of O'Neill's ascendancy, Irenius explains,

When as the laste Oneale Called Terlagh Lenagh, beganne to stande vppon tickle terme this fellowe [Hugh O'Neill] then called Baro[n] of Du[n]gano[n] was sett vp as it weare to bearde him, and Countenaunced and strengthened by the Quene so farr as that he is now hable to kepe her selfe playe. muche like vnto a gamster that havinge loste all borrowethe of his nexte fellowe gamster that is the moste winner somwhat to mayntaine playe which he settinge vppon him againe shortlie therby winnethe all from the winner. (167)

In response, Eudoxus asks, with his characteristic sense of wonder, "Was this Rebell then sett vp firste by the Quene as yowe saie and now become so vndewtifull" (167), to which Irenius replies,

He was I assure youe the moste outcaste of all the Oneals then, and lifted vp by her maiestie out of the duste to that he nowe hathe wraughte himselfe vnto, And now he playeth like the frozen Snake whoe beinge for Compassion releived by the husbandman sone after he was warme, begane to hisse and threaten daunger even to him and his. (168)

It is clear from this exchange that O'Neill does not easily fit into what should be his expected category in the standard tripartite division of the population of Ireland (meer—i.e., Gaelic—Irish; Old English; New English) so readily delineated by Spenser and his fellow writers. In Spenser's text, O'Neill appears as a member of a powerful Gaelic Irish family who has been fostered by the queen and her ministers in an effort on their part to gain an opening into the political world of Gaelic Ulster and who, as the beneficiary of such fosterage and intrigue, becomes the bearer of English titles (initially Baron of Dungannon, then Earl of Tyrone). Being, in Spenser's words, "verye subtillye headed" (166), O'Neill proves ultimately not to be so pliable as the English would wish, and he finally plays a key role in leading a rebellion against his erstwhile sponsors and allies.

The extent and seriousness of the general uprising that O'Neill directed—the "Nine Years' War"—served to spur renewed attention to the specifically Gaelic Irish dimension of the situation in Ireland in the closing years of the sixteenth century. With O'Neill at the head of this uprising, the question of Irish proximity was intensified and complicated, since, as we have seen from Spenser's text, O'Neill himself occupies a curiously intermediate position, straddling markers of English and Irish identities. In Spenser's account, we see him moving effectively here between two worlds—the realm of Gaelic Ulster and the world of the English gaming table, at which he can borrow a stake from the queen herself. His presence on the Irish scene on the one hand raises new questions about the issue of Irish identity in that his ambiguous nature serves to destabilize and call into question the validity of traditional English views of the Irish. On the other hand, however, the rise of O'Neill has also, again, profound implications for the issue of *English* national identity, since O'Neill demonstrated throughout his career a keen eye for manipulating and inverting the symbolism and icons of that identity, thereby disrupting the very foundations of its certainty and stability. As R.F. Foster has observed, O'Neill represents "the Janus-face of Ireland, whose ambivalence and elusiveness exhausted contemporaries and historians alike" (1989, 4). As a contemporary of O'Neill's, Nicholas Dawtry, put it in writing to the queen, "And yet if I shall deliver unto Your Highness the outward show of the man: I never saw an Irishman of more plausible behaviour to content all men."[3]

We can see some of these issues of identity and ambiguity at play in Shakespeare's *Henry the Fift,* which was likely written at the height of the Nine Years' War. The play is very much concerned with the issue of forging a sense of national identity, and in the play we can clearly see the way in which that process of national imagining is put under pressure by the concurrent events in Ireland. Before examining the issue of the impact of O'Neill on Shakespeare's engagement with the construction of national identity, however, it is worthwhile first to trace the outline of O'Neill's career and the way it was represented by contemporary writers.

II.

Hugh O'Neill was born in Ireland, probably in 1550; he fled the country in 1607 and died an exile in Rome in 1616.[4] In the words of Thomas Gainsford, an English writer who published a pamphlet entitled *The Trve Exemplary, and Remarkable History of the Earle of Tirone* in 1619 (intending thereby to "set [Tyrone] . . . on the Stage of fearefull admiration" [6]), O'Neill's was "the remarkeablest Story of Ireland" (A2 v). He was grandson to Con O'Neill, who had been granted the title of "Earl of Tyrone" in 1542 by Henry VIII.[5] Hugh's father Matthew was ousted from succession within the family (and murdered) by his half-brother Shane,[6] who, in a colorful visit to the English court in 1562,

Being gently asked, by what right he had excluded *Hugh,* his brother *Mathews* sonne, out of his forefathers inheritance, he answered fiercely, (as he had done before already in *Ireland,*) By very good right; to wit, that he being the certaine and lawfull sonne and heire of *Con,* as borne of his lawfull wife, had entred vpon his fathers inheritance: that *Matthew* was the sonne of a Blacksmith of *Dundalke,* begotten by a Smith, borne after his marriage with his wife *Alison,* but by his mother cunningly obtruded vpon *Con* for his sonne, to bereaue him of his inheritance and dignity of *O-Neal:* which though he endured, yet none other of the house of the *O-Neals* would euer suffer it. (Camden I, 62)[7]

Thus, within the world of Gaelic familial politics, Hugh's position was ambiguous before he was ever born, being, in Shane's account, the son of a claimant to a position of ascendancy whose legitimacy (or legitimate illegitimacy, perhaps) was entirely spurious.

The anomalousness of Hugh's position with regard to his Gaelic heritage was further compounded by the details of his early upbringing. Until relatively recently, it was believed that as a child O'Neill had been taken into the care of Sir Henry Sidney (father of the poet Sir Philip Sidney), who served two terms as Lord Deputy in Ireland, and that he had been raised in England by the Sidney family.[8] This belief was in part prompted by Sidney's own reference in his *Memoir* of 1583 to "the young baron of Dungannnon, Shane's eldest brother's son, whom I had bred in my house from a little boy, then very poor of goods and full feebly friended" (1583, 92). Hiram Morgan has, however, challenged this belief, stating bluntly that "Hugh O'Neill did not spend his youth in England" ("Making History" 1990, 61) and charting an alternative account of O'Neill's boyhood. According to Morgan, O'Neill became a ward of the crown on the death of his father and was raised by Giles Hovenden, a "New English" settler with property in Laois. In Morgan's view, O'Neill received an English education in the Pale — the English administrative region, centered on Dublin.[9]

Morgan does not deny, however, that O'Neill did make several trips to England and to Elizabeth's Court — there is clear evidence that he visited the Court in 1567/68, 1587, and 1590. It is probably the first of these visits that Gainsford refers to when he writes of O'Neill as "in his yonger time . . . troop[ing] in the streets of *London* with sufficient equipage, and orderly respect" (1619, 14). The significance of these visits is registered by Morgan when he writes that they "permitted the establishment of links with the earl of Leicester (Sidney's brother-in-law) and then with his political successor, the second earl of Essex. Another connection at Court is suggested by the fact that O'Neill wore armor given to him by Sir Christopher Hatton, the lord chancellor, at the battle of Clontibret. These connections with the English establishment in both Ireland and England were to stand Hugh O'Neill in good stead throughout his long and eventful career" (*Tyrone's Rebellion* 1993, 97).

In his early career, O'Neill appears as an Anglicized Irishman who has been groomed by the English to act as an instrument of their policy in the intractable territory of Ulster. Elizabeth herself described O'Neill as "a creature of our own" (Morgan, *Tyrone's Rebellion* 1993, 85). In his earliest years in Ulster, O'Neill became Baron of Dungannon and appeared loyal to the crown. As Margaret Mac-Curtain notes in *Tudor and Stuart Ireland,* "to all appearances he became English . . . He joined the earl of Essex in his futile effort to colonise Antrim and Down in 1573 and when Sir Henry Sidney was [re]appointed deputy in 1575, Hugh O'Neill hurried to the support of his patron" (1972, 83).

Soon enough, however, O'Neill began to pursue his own independent expansionist goals in Ulster, attempting in the process to consolidate his power within both the Gaelic and the English realms. It is a testament to his capacity to straddle *both* worlds (and to achieve his ends within those worlds) that he contrived to succeed to the English title of "Earl of Tyrone" and subsequently also to the traditional Gaelic title of "The O'Neill" (signifying his overlordship of the entire sept of the O'Neills, together with their dependents and clients).[10] Camden, in his history of Elizabeth's reign, reports O'Neill's accession to the Gaelic title as follows: "watching his aduantage, *Turlogh Leinigh* being dead, who had borne the title of *O-Neal,* [he] arrogated the same title to himselfe (in comparison whereof the very title of *Cæsar* is contemptible in *Ireland,*) contrary to what he had sworne, and was prouided against by a statute of treason. Yet he excused it, saying, that he did it, lest others of the house of *O-Neal* should inuade the same: But he promised to renounce it, yet hee earnestly besought that hee might not be bound thereto by oath" (IV, 54). Such intricate evasiveness as this is typical of the kinds of strategies O'Neill adopted in his dealings with the crown—claiming that the Gaelic title was assumed not as a self-serving end in itself but was rather a factional move undertaken in the greater interests of English policy; assuring his English sponsors that the Gaelic title would eventually be renounced; pleading that the promise of renunciation be taken at face value and not be formalized into a legal commitment. His proceedings with them appeared as a seemingly endless series of challenges, submissions, and evasions: "*Tyrone* hitherto with all subtilty and a thousand sleights abusing the State, when he saw any danger hanging ouer him, by fained countenance and false words pretended humblest submission, and hearty sorrow for his villanies; but as soone as opportunity of pursuing him was omitted, or the forces were of necessity to be drawne from his Countrey, with the terror of them all his loyalty vanished, yea, he failed not to mingle secretly the greatest Counsels of mischiefe with his humblest submissions" (Moryson 1617, 2:20).

As O'Neill contrived to temporize with his English sponsors while he expanded his power in Ulster, he also drew on his formative experience among the English in manipulating to his advantage the sign system of English civility. He ended one visit to the court in England (undertaken to protest—successfully—his innocence of charges laid against him) by conspicuously ordering some costly furnishings to be sent into Ulster with him on his return journey: "At his departure the more to make this state secuer of his good intentions, that he ment to leive civilie and honorable accordinge to the English manner, he bought riche furniture for his howse, of beddinge, arras, carpettes and the lyke, wherof he would not have the State here to be ignorant, in soemuch that the Lord Burley, Lord Treasorer of England, sayd he was glade to see such furniture goe into Ulster as a good hope conceved that the Erle would reduce this contrie unto civilitie" (Perrot 1993, 67-68).[11] Even as the Lord Treasurer was impressed with his civilizing initiative, however, O'Neill was reportedly putting other such exports from England to an altogether different use: "Pretending to build a faire house (which our State thinkes a tye of ciuilitie) he got license to transport to *Dungannon* a great quantitie of Lead to couer the Battlements of his house: but ere long imployed the same only to make bullets for the warre" (Moryson 1617, 2:12). Where in his earlier gesture O'Neill used the trappings of English civility to secure an English sense of his alignment with the crown's interests, in this second instance he takes other tokens of civility and empties them of their intended meaning, refashioning them literally as ammunition to be used *against* the English. This must surely be the ultimate instance of Jonathan Dollimore's "transgressive reinscription"—"a *turning back* upon something and a perverting of it typically if not exclusively through inversion and displacement" (1991, 323)—or of what David Baker has usefully characterized as "subversive re-interpretation from within" ("Some Quirk" 1986, 157). A passage from Foucault, which

Dollimore points to, is relevant to O'Neill's situation here: "Rules are empty in themselves, violent and unfinalized; they are impersonal and can be bent to any purpose. The successes of history belong to those who are capable of seizing these rules, to replace those who had used them, to disguise themselves so as to pervert them, invert their meaning, and redirect them against those who had initially imposed them . . . so as to overcome the rulers through their own rules" (*Language* 1977, 151). Such reinscription and "overcom[ing] of the rulers through their own rules" would be entirely characteristic of O'Neill's mode of operation for much of the rest of his career.[12]

We can see these tactics being deployed if we look in greater detail at the onset and unfolding of the Nine Years' War. As the 1590s progressed and O'Neill continued to consolidate and expand his position of power in Ulster, the fragile working equilibrium of relations with the crown became increasingly difficult to maintain. Throughout this time, O'Neill organized his forces in Ulster against the prospect of open conflict. As Steven Ellis notes, "Exploiting a previous concession which allowed him to maintain a peace-keeping force, he began militarizing his lordship, buying arms, ammunition and equipment in lowland Scotland, and later English and Irish towns, and hiring redshanks [Scots mercenaries]. By 1595 he was reputedly maintaining 1,000 pikemen, 4,000 musketeers, and 1,000 cavalry" (*Tudor* 1985, 300).[13]

In June of 1595, O'Neill's forces defeated the English at Clontibret. The details of the encounter greatly surprised O'Neill's opponents. As Hiram Morgan notes in *Tyrone's Rebellion,*

> The battle of Clontibret shocked the Dublin government. . . . In the engagement, the earl of Tyrone had deployed combinations of cavalry and shot to telling effect. English commanders with continental experience compared his ability with that of the Prince of Parma. In assessing the new situation, the Irish council declared that "these traitors are increased to a greater strength in numbers and wonderfully altered from their Irish manner of arms and weapons, and the use thereof, besides their order and discipline in governing their men." (179)

G.A. Hayes-McCoy has observed of this same encounter that

> When Hugh O'Neill, Earl of Tyrone, won his first victory at Clontibret in 1595 he astonished his opponents by bringing a force of musketeers clad

"in red coats like English soldiers" into action against them. In the days of his seeming loyalty he had secured the services of six English captains to train six companies of Tyrone men for action, as was supposed, against the Queen's enemies in the north. (1949-53, 105)[14]

In his military strategy, then, O'Neill once again drew on his experience among the English and turned their own tactics against them. He organized his forces along English lines: drilling them, issuing many of them with uniforms, and arming them with muskets in addition to the traditional pike. In establishing what amounted to a standing army in Ulster, trained and equipped according to the English manner, O'Neill surprised his opponents by confronting them in battle with forces trained, armed, and garbed like themsleves.

O'Neill's greatest success came in the battle of the Yellow Ford in 1598, a year that, according to Fynes Moryson, together with "the next following, became so disasterous to the English, and successefull in action to the Irish, as they shaked the English gouernement in this kingdome, till it tottered, and wanted little of fatall ruine" (1617, 2:24).

The issues of identity and reinscription that we have been tracking here are brought to an interesting convergence in that "next [year] following" to which Moryson refers, in one of the most striking episodes of the Nine Years' War—the campaign conducted against O'Neill by Robert Devereux, Earl of Essex, in 1599, when Essex briefly held the appointment as Lord Lieutenant in Ireland. Essex was exactly the governor that Spenser had wanted sent to Ireland and David Norbrook has suggested that Spenser's controversial advocacy of Essex was one of the reasons that led to the *View*'s not being granted a license for publication in 1598.[15]

Essex set off for Ireland in an atmosphere of great expectation, "accompanied," Camden tells us, "with a gallant traine of the flower of the Nobility, and saluted by the people with ioyfull acclamations" (1630, 4:139). Before leaving, he wrote to John Harington, inviting him to join the campaign. Essex informed Harington that he had secured the Irish commission despite opposition from certain members of the Privy Council: "I have beaten Knollys and Montjoye in the councele, and by G—d I will beat Tyr-Owen in the feilde" (Harington, *Nugæ* 1804, 246). For the purpose of the campaign, "he had," Moryson informs us, "an Army assigned him, as great as himselfe required, and such for number and strength, as *Ireland* had neuer yet seene" (2:27).[16]

Essex began his stint as Lord Lieutenant by conducting several ineffectual forays into the southern parts of the island, before finally riding northward in search of O'Neill. The two armies eventually made contact with each other at Bellaclinthe and, during the standoff that followed, O'Neill requested a private conference with Essex at a nearby river. The meeting is chronicled in a contemporary diary of the Essex campaign: "Knowing the foorde, [O'Neill] found a place, where he, standing up to the horsses belly, might be neere enough to be heard by the L. Liuetenant, though he kept the harde grownde; upon which notice the L. Liuetenant drew a troupe of horsse to the hill above the foord, and seing Tirone theare alone, went doune alone: at whose comming Tirone saluted his Lop. with a greate deale of reverence, and they talked neere half an houre, and after went ether of them up to their compagnies on the hills" (Harington, *Nugæ* 1804, 299).[17] Over the course of the encounter, O'Neill provides Essex with what amounts almost to a parodic reinscription of English courtly behavior—from another contemporary account we learn that "before the Lord Lieutenant was fully aryved at the foarde Tyrone tooke of his hatt and enclyninge his body did his duty unto his Lordship with very humble ceremony, contynewynge the same observancy the whole tyme of the parlye" (Dymmok 1843, 50).[18] From this position, and deploying these tactics, O'Neill succeeds in wresting a truce from Essex that is much to his own advantage, in the process effectively setting Essex on a trajectory that would ultimately lead to his execution for treason.[19]

We can see this process of inversion and reinscription at work all the more clearly in the events that unfolded after the initial private meeting between Essex and O'Neill. In order to finalize the arrangements for the truce between the two sides, an English party led by Sir William Constable visited O'Neill's camp. Constable invited John Harington to attend.[20] In a report on the visit, Harington notes his surprise at the reception afforded him by O'Neill:

Sir William had told him of me, and given such a report of me above my desert, that next day, when I came, the earl used far greater respect to me than I expected; and began debasing his own manner of hard life, comparing himself to wolves, that fill their bellies sometime, and fast as long for it; then excused himself to me that he could no better call to mind myself, and some of my friends that had done him some courtesy in England. (*Nugæ* 1804, 248)

Harington's surprise is all the greater when he meets with O'Neill's sons, in an encounter that serves to contradict their father's description of his manner of living in the field:

> [I] took occasion the while to entertain [O'Neill's] two sons, by posing them in their learning, and their tutors, which were one Fryar Nangle, a Franciscan; and a younger scholer, whose name I know not; and finding the two children of good towardly spirit, their age between thirteen and fifteen, in English cloths like a nobleman's sons; with velvet gerkins and gold lace; of a good chearful aspect, freckle-faced, not tall of stature, but strong, and well set; both of them [learning] the English tongue. (*Nugæ*, 249)

O'Neill's characterization of his community as living like wolves is (much like his wading midway into the ford to meet Essex or his importing of English furniture) a calculated gesture, touching as it does on well-worn English visions of the native Irish and playing on what Andrew Hadfield has called a "signifier of unnaturalness" ("Materialist" 1988, 266).[21] The gesture serves to heighten Harington's sense that this is precisely how O'Neill's community does *not* live, as he finds the younger O'Neills exhibiting all the trappings of English civility (private tutors, English clothes of velvet and gold lace, proficiency in the English language) even as they are camped in the field in mid-campaign.

This process of inversion is further emphasized by a moment of interaction between Harington and O'Neill himself, as Harington presents the younger O'Neills with a gift of his translation of Ariosto (his *Orlando Furioso in English Heroical Verse* had been published in 1591): "I gave them (not without the advice of Sir William Warren) my English translation of 'Ariosto,' which I got at Dublin; which their teachers took very thankfully, and soon after shewed it to the earl, who call'd to see it openly, and would needs hear some part of it read. I turn'd (as it had been by chance) to the beginning of the 45th canto and some other passages of the book, which he seemed to like so well, that he solemnly swore his boys should read all the book over to him" (149-50).[22] On O'Neill's asking to hear some of the work, Harington affects choosing a passage at random but, in fact, is quite calculating in his selection as he turns "as it had been by chance" to the forty-fifth canto and reads the opening lines. These lines appear as follows in Harington's text:

Looke, how much higher Fortune doth erect
The clyming wight, on her unstable wheele,
So much the nigher may a man expect
To see his head where late he saw his heele:
On t'other side, the more man is oppressed,
And utterly ov'rthrowne by Fortune's lowre,
The sooner comes his state to be redressed,
When wheele shal turne and bring the happy houre.

(*Nugæ*, 249)

There is a sly suggestion on Harington's part here that his quotation is predictive of the future course of Anglo-Irish relations. Where now O'Neill is in the ascendant (having effectively blocked the threat represented by Essex's army), he will, Harington intimates, soon enough suffer a reversal—at Fortune's hands, if not at those of the English. O'Neill apparently chooses simply to ignore the veiled prediction of Harington's supposedly random selection, professing unperturbedly to like the poem so well "that he solemnly swore his boys should read all the book over to him" (or perhaps he chooses to see Essex rather than himself as Fate's potential victim).

Harington's choice of passage is, however, revealing in a way that he himself perhaps does not envisage. Where he apparently conceives of the image of Fortune's wheel as anticipatory (of a reversal in O'Neill's fortunes), in fact, the double inversion indicated by the complete image implies a certain kind of circularity and exchange entirely consonant with the intense, complementary inversions prompted by the trajectory of O'Neill's career in Ireland. In these circumstances no sense of identity seems stable. The picture of the Irish traditionally cultivated by the English cannot hold. Because O'Neill, his sons, and his soldiers appear on the scene bearing the trappings of English identity, yet asserting fidelity in other respects and at other times to their Gaelic lineage and yet apparently not truly faithful to that identity either, they seem to beg a question as to what exactly *is* their identity, rather as if Spenser, in turning from his meditation on the Old English, were compelled to address a new question: not "are not they that weare once Englishe abidinge Englishe still" (*A View* 1949, 96) but rather "are not they that were once *Irish* abiding *Irish* still?"[23] But if the nature of "Irishness" is called into question by the ambiguity inherent in O'Neill's position, his ability to manipulate the counters of English civility seems to raise questions also about the nature of *English* identity. In the uncertainty of O'Neill's Ireland, where signs of identity are traded and manipulated, the loss of stable identity emerges, again, as a threat to the English themselves.

We can get a further sense of this anxiety from a poem written to Henry Wotton by John Donne while Wotton was serving with Essex in Ireland.[24] Donne's "H. W. in Hiber. belligeranti" takes Wotton to task for his failure to maintain his friendly correspondence with Donne since Wotton's journey into Ireland. Ireland appears in the poem as a dangerous place, where death "gleanes . . . many of our friends away" (1967, 7).[25] But Donne seems almost accepting of such physical hazards as these—the chance consequences of war:

> Lett shotts, and boggs, and skeines
> With bodies deale, as fate bidds or restreynes;
> Ere sicknesses attack, yong death is best,
> Who payes before his death doth scape arrest.
> (9-12)

The more serious potential threat that Ireland poses, Donne suggests, is not to the body, but is rather to the core of one's identity. The poem opens:

> Went you to conquer? and have so much lost
> Your self, that what in you was best and most,
> Respective frendship, should so quickly dye?
> In publique gaine my share'is not such that I
> Would loose your love for Ireland: better cheap
> I pardon death (who though he do not reap
> Yet gleanes hee many of our frends away)
> Then that your waking mind should bee a pray
> To lethargies.
> (1-9)

As the opening line of the poem unfolds, intended conquest is reversed, becoming loss. The poem thus begins with a statement of inversion. But the enjambment reveals the nature (or, keeping open both readings, the consequence) of that inversion: what is lost is not the vaunted conquest but in fact Wotton's very "self." With that loss of self goes loss (now figured as death) of "respective frendship"—the connection between Wotton in Ireland and Donne at home in England. *Physical* death, the poem seems to suggest, is preferable to this loss of connectedness. Donne himself is unwilling to entertain the loss for the sake of the public benefits that may accrue from the Irish campaign: "In publique gaine my share'is not such that I / Would loose your love for Ireland." But these lines are, we notice, ambiguous. Conceivably—at least before we read the entire sentence through—it may be Wotton's "love for Ireland" rather than the mutual love of their "respective friendship" that Donne would not "loose." What the text seems to raise here is the specter of a certain potential attractiveness in Ireland. The double reading thus sets up a troubling equivalence between the two realms.

Donne's fear is openly articulated in his anxiety that Wotton's "waking mind" may "bee a pray / To lethargies." It might be suggested, thus, that it is not finally an Irish *seductiveness* that seems to lie at the root of Donne's fear, so much as an anxiety over a certain kind of Irish stasis (or *lethargy*): of a decline into something like a state of suspension, where identity is eroded.[26] This becomes clear when the poem returns to the issue in lines 13-16: "Lett not your soule (at first with graces filld / And since and thorough crooked lymbecks, stild / In many schooles and courts, which quicken it,) / It self unto the Irish negligence submit." Here Donne presents a Wotton who is naturally possessed of certain "graces" and whose soul has been meticulously refined in the institutions (the "many schooles and courts") of English civility. But this identity is threatened by an Ireland whose "negligence"—again a kind of passive suspension rather than an active seduction—would strip away the effects of such careful distillation.

The poem ends—in a move reminiscent of Spenser's introduction of Colin Clout and his "countrey lasse" in VI.x of the *Faerie Queene*—by consciously turning away from the tokens of public identity, with an appeal to the private realm of personal friendship: "I aske not labour'd letters which should weare / Long papers out: nor letters which should feare / Dishonest cariage: or a seers art: / Nor such as from the brayne come, but the hart" (17-20). The overdue letters that Donne finally calls for from Wotton are those that include no political or cryptic content (which need not "feare / Dishonest cariage" nor require "a seers art") but that are rather an expression only of personal friendship. It is almost as if Donne is willing finally to cede the public realm in the hope that it might somehow be possible to construct a realm of personal identity founded on friendship alone that might survive intact the disruption of other identities that takes place in Ireland.

O'Neill's career thus serves to raise in a new light the issue of the Gaelic dimension of Anglo-Irish relations, compounding the question of Irish prox-

imity and, in the process, challenging the English sense of national
Having sketched the outlines of O'Neill's career and some of the tra〈
impact, I will next examine the way in which certain of the issues r〈
that career can be charted through Shakespeare's *Life of Henry the F*
Nine Years' War and, specifically, the Essex campaign form the backdrop for
this play, which was likely written in 1599, just after Essex's departure for
Ireland.[27] Shakespeare's patron Southampton was one of those who em-
barked for Ireland with Essex, and a direct reference to the Essex expedition
is made in the opening lines of the final act of the play.[28] "But now behold,"
declares the Chorus at the opening to act five, "how London doth powre out
her Citizens"

> As by a lower, but by louing likelyhood,
> Were now the Generall of our gracious Empresse,
> As in good time he may, from Ireland comming,
> Bringing Rebellion broached on his Sword;
> How many would the peacefull Citie quit,
> To welcome him?[29]
>
> (TLN 2872-84)

This reference to Ireland is part of a general array of direct and indirect allu-
sions to the country and to things Irish that occur throughout the play.[30]
Henry the Fift also includes Shakespeare's only Irish character, the irascible and
enigmatic Captain Mackmorrice.

III.

Like *A View of the Present State of Ireland* and the *Faerie Queene*, *Henry the Fift*
shows an interest not just in the question of contemporary colonization but
also in the issue of the consequences and implications of a prior period of conquest and colonization. We see this initially in the protracted discussion of the
"Law *Salike*" in the first act of the play. Canterbury is at pains to distinguish
the Salike land from the kingdom of France and attempts to clarify the exact
historical rationale of the provisions of the Salike Law:

> *Charles* the Great hauing subdu'd the Saxons,
> There left behind and settled certaine French:
> Who holding in disdaine the German Women,

For some dishonest manners of their life,
Establisht then this Law: to wit, No Female
Should be Inheritrix in *Salike* Land.
(TLN 193-98)

Properly understood, therefore, the purpose of the Salike Law (in Canterbury's historicist view) is to prevent the very assimilation of the colonizer by the colonized (through intermarriage) that Spenser decries in *A View*. Canterbury argues that the law should thus be no bar to the English claim to the French crown, since it is in no way applicable either to the territory of France or to the realm of Anglo-French relations.

The play returns to this issue at a later point, however, in a manner that suggests that England and the lands "'twixt Elue and Sala" (TLN 199) are not entirely disconnected from each other. Angry at the extent of the gains made by Henry's army, the French council fulminate against the English:

Const. And if he be not fought withall, my Lord,
Let vs not liue in France: let vs quit all,
And giue our Vineyards to a barbarous People.
Dolph. O Dieu viuant: Shall a few Sprayes of vs,
The emptying of our Fathers Luxurie,
Our Syens, put in wilde and sauage Stock,
Spirt vp so suddenly into the Clouds,
And ouer-looke their Grafters?
Brit. Normans, but bastard Normans, Norman bastards.
(TLN 1381-89)

This French outburst raises an issue touched on briefly in Spenser's *View:* the question of England's *own* colonial past.[31] England becomes itself something like a version of the Salike Land here, where the Salike Law has *not* held and the Norman conquerors, much like their fellows in Ireland, have indeed inter-bred with the locals like "Syens, put in wilde and sauage Stock." The French disdain for such "bastard Normans" is similar to Spenser's contempt for the Old English.

This raising of England's own colonial past as figured in the Norman con-quest touches on the very center of Shakespeare's concerns in *Henry the Fift,* for *Henry the Fift* is a play that first and foremost addresses itself to the issue of

English national identity.[32] As such, it takes its place within the process of "the Elizabethan writing of England" that Richard Helgerson traces in *Forms of Nationhood*. As Helgerson notes, in sixteenth-century England, "a unique set of conditions . . . gave men of middling status and humanist education, men born at or shortly following the midcentury, the task of laying the discursive foundations both for the nation-state and for a whole array of more specialized communities that based their identity on their relation to the nation and the state" (1992, 299). A play such as *Henry the Fift* sits comfortably with Helgerson's model of an English quest for national identity in the period. But his thesis fails to register the extent to which English self-imagining in such a play is significantly informed by the English experience in Ireland during these years.[33]

The extent of this informing becomes apparent when we notice the difference between *Henry the Fift* and an earlier play of Shakespeare's such as *The Life and Death of King Richard the Second*, written probably in 1595, just as the Nine Years' War was getting underway.[34] In the earlier play, Ireland appears (in a description reminiscent of Gerald) as a land of "rough rug-headed Kernes, / Which liue like venom, where no venom else / But onely they, haue priuiledge to liue" (TLN 803-805). The Irish wars are simply the occasion for Richard's cynical raising of taxes and seizure of Gaunt's "plate, coine, reuennewes, and mouables" (TLN 808).

Ireland itself functions in the play as an unseen realm to which Richard ventures, with his voyage there serving as a marker of a turning point in his fortunes. With Richard's journey into Ireland thus intertwined with the demise of his power, we get something akin to the consuming of a discordant element within the English polity by the discordant realm that lies adjacent to (but outside of) it, almost as if Richard and Ireland negate each other.

In the same play, Gaunt, in his speech to York, provides one of the most celebrated images of the English national unit in his "sceptred isle" speech. As we read through Gaunt's description, however, we note that his England has a strange quality to it:

This royall Throne of Kings, this sceptred Isle,
. . . .

This precious stone, set in the siluer sea,
Which serues it in the office of a wall,
Or as a Moate defensiue to a house,

Against the enuy of lesse happier Lands,
This blessed plot, this earth, this Realme, this England

. . . .

England bound in with the triumphant sea,
Whose rocky shore beates backe the enuious siedge
Of watery Neptune. . . .

(TLN 681, 687-91, 702-704)

As Philip Edwards pointed out many years ago in *Threshold of a Nation* (1979, 74), Gaunt's reference to *England* as a sceptred *isle* is rather telling. Gaunt's England extends here westward and northward, to obliterate Scotland and Wales, becoming an entire island unto itself, "bound in with the triumphant sea."[35] In this account of the nation, the problematic territory of Ireland is essentially excluded, as if simply abandoned to its venomous kern. The definition of national identity offered is simple (albeit in very obvious ways flagrantly false, ignoring, as it does, the existence of Scotland and Wales as distinct political and cultural entities): the nation coincides with a certain bounded geographic space.

As we progress through the subsequent three plays of the second Henriad over the course of the four years following the composition of *Richard the Second,* the question of the construction of national identity deepens and becomes increasingly more complex. In the Henry IV plays, the nation splinters, and dissident northern and Welsh voices (indeed, even the Welsh language) are heard on the stage.[36] In *Henry the Fift,* Shakespeare's most complex meditation on the nature of national identity, the question of what constitutes such identity is staged on several levels simultaneously. As David Cairns and Shaun Richards have noted in *Writing Ireland: Colonialism, Nationalism and Culture, Henry the Fift* presents "a dramatization of the process involved in the constitution of the unified nation, particularly as the process is expressed in the constitution of the unified and ordered subject who, to emphasise the power of the process, is the monarch himself" (1988, 8). The construction of the image of the nation is, then, in the first instance intimately bound up with the construction of Henry himself as a unified subject. Out of the dissonance and dissidence of Prince Hal arises the appearance of unitary coherence of the King. As Canterbury notes in the opening scene of the play, "Neuer came Reformation in a Flood, / With such a heady currance scowring faults: / Nor neuer *Hidra*-headed Wilfulnesse / So soone did loose his Seat; and all at once; / As in this King" (TLN 73-77). The reformation of "*Hidra*-headed Wilfulnesse" within the king himself is paradigmatic of a larger endeavor within the world of the play to reduce other such "*Hidra*-headed" elements within the body politic to coherence and uniformity.

Jonathan Dollimore and Alan Sinfield have noted in their analysis of *Henry the Fift* that "the play circles obsessively around the inseparable issues of unity and division, inclusion and exclusion" ("History and Ideology" 1985, 218). The exclusion of certain discordant elements is, as we have noted, first staged within Henry's own constitution: "The breath no sooner left his Fathers body, / But that his wildnesse, mortify'd in him, / Seem'd to dye too" (TLN 64-66), and that exclusion is subsequently staged within the greater realm of England presented in the play as the King's former Eastcheap associates are pushed to the margins of the play's world and killed off one by one, with only the discredited figure of Pistol surviving. This purging of the lower class comic characters from the world of the tetralogy is accompanied by and associated with a concommitant purging of the dissonant element within the nobility, with the dispatching of the treasonous Cambridge, Scrope, and Grey.[37] The play's grappling with issues of class in this way can be characterized as an effort to explore the question of what constitutes the nation *internally*, as it were, rather as if Gaunt, having erected his "Moate defensiue" around his island England, were to turn inward and contemplate who within those boundaries was eligible for citizenship. As we have noted, the Henry IV plays differ from *Richard the Second* in that they register in some measure the reinscription of the boundaries of those *cultural* and *political* differences within the realm of the island of Britain that are erased in Gaunt's speech. *Henry the Fift* tackles these issues in greater depth. The second scene of the play touches on the adversarial relationship that exists between England and its northern neighbor, as Henry warns his council, "We must not onely arme t'inuade the French, / But lay downe our proportions, to defend / Against the Scot, who will make roade vpon vs, / With all aduantages" (TLN 283-86). Canterbury and Exeter seek to reassure Henry that the Scots present no real threat to the integrity of England, that his northern English loyalists "Shall be a Wall sufficient to defend / Our in-land from the pilfering Borderers" (TLN 288-89). We get a sense here of England's being drawn in behind its northern borders, which are marked now not by "the triumphant sea, / Whose rocky shore beates backe the enuious siedge / Of watery Neptune" but rather by a Hadrianesque defensive wall that serves to keep the alien element at bay (as if Gaunt's English island has now shrunk to Canterbury's "in-land" England).[38] Canterbury concludes with a piece of confident advice:

> Diuide your happy England into foure,
> Whereof, take you one quarter into France,
> And you withall shall make all Gallia shake.
> If we with thrice such powers left at home,
> Cannot defend our owne doores from the dogge,
> Let vs be worried, and our Nation lose
> The name of hardinesse and policie.
>
> (TLN 361-67)

The play is finally, however, unwilling to settle for such ceding of territory as this and such retrenchment on firmer ground (perhaps because, as we have seen in the treatment of the Eastcheap group and the trio of traitorous nobility, that ground is, in fact, itself not quite so firm).[39] Where Canterbury calls on Henry to "diuide [his] happy England into foure," the play as a whole shows a willingness to explore the fact that the greater British realm is *already* divided into four distinct units and the play struggles to make sense of the relationship that exists among the four elements.

We see this four-part division in the "four captains" scene of the play, where Shakespeare presents an army that is, as Cairns and Richards (1988, 12) suggest, paradigmatic of the nation as a whole. It is a mark of the extent to which the Nine Years' War has heightened awareness of the importance of the Irish situation that Shakespeare includes an *Irish* captain here side by side with his counterparts from Scotland, Wales, and England.[40] Whereas, in *Richard the Second,* Ireland was a dangerous realm adjacent to (but not continuous with) Gaunt's island England, here Ireland takes its place with those other realms *within* the boundaries of the island that require to be accommodated in some way to a conception of national identity.

Many contemporary critics have regarded the four captains scene as something like a calculated (and none-too-subtle) exercise on Shakespeare's part to enact a bogus vision of unity within the British realm, with the playwright taking great care to include markers of *exclusion* in his characterization of the three Celtic captains, even as they are incorporated into the larger institution of the English army. Cairns and Richards, for instance, write, "[The three] Celts are united in their service to the English Crown. Their use of the English language, however, reveals that 'service' is the operative word, for in rank, in dramatic importance, and in linguistic competence, they are comical second-order citizens. They are, moreover, disputatious, and the argument between Fluellen and Macmorris, which is resolved by Gower's admonition, is further dramatic evidence of the harmony that England has brought to the fractious occupants of the Celtic fringe" (10). Taking a similar line, Dollimore and Sinfield conclude that "the Irish, Welsh and Scottish soldiers manifest not their countries' centrifugal relationship to England but an ideal subservience of margin to centre" ("History and Ideology" 1985, 217). Support for this view can be found in the way in which the Celtic characters appear in the F1 text of the play. The three Celtic captains are only ever referred to in the speech prefixes for the scene as "Welch," "Irish," and "Scot," respectively.[41] By contrast, the English captain is always assigned the personal name "Gower" in the scene's prefixes. It is clear, thus, that the Celtic captains are conceived of primarily as ethnic types rather than as individuated characters.[42]

At the same time, however, there is something rather more complex happening here with the character of "Irish" (named in the dialogue variously as "Makmorrice" and "Mackmorrice") than most critics have acknowledged. Discussions of Irish have tended to focus in particular on his explosive outburst when the Welsh captain begins to talk about the Irishman's "nation":

> *Welch.* Captaine *Mackmorrice,* I thinke, looke you, vnder your correction, there is not many of your Nation.
>
> *Irish.* Of my Nation? What ish my Nation? Ish a Villaine, and a Basterd, and a Knaue, and a Rascall. What ish my Nation? Who talkes of my Nation? (TLN 1237-42)[43]

Irish's response is obscure and has given rise to a number of different interpretations. In an influential commentary on the passage, Philip Edwards has suggested that

> The paraphrase should run something like this. "What is this separate race you're implying by using the phrase 'your nation'? Who are you, a Welshman, to talk of the Irish as though they were a separate nation from you? I belong in this family as much as you do." This is the essence of it—

indignation that a Welshman should think of Ireland as a separate nation from the great (British) nation to which the Welshman apparently thought he belonged. (75-76)

Most subsequent critics have adopted Edwards's interpretation of the exchange, with Gary Taylor, for instance, quoting Edwards's proffered paraphrase as his gloss on the line "What ish my nation" in his introduction to the Oxford edition of the play.

One of the problems with Edwards's interpretation is that it seeks to produce a single meaning from what is, in fact, a profoundly ambiguous passage. In the process, Edwards misses the deeper resonances of Irish's response. In addition, we should note that Edwards essentially treats his interrogative not as a question but as a statement — "a furious repudiation of difference," as he calls it (76). But in so doing, he disregards the possibility that Irish's question may be just that — a genuine question: "What ish my nation?"[44]

Taken as a question, Irish's interrogative opens up a variety of issues pertinent to the play in the context of the particular historical moment in which it was written. In the first instance, we note that Irish's remark represents a challenge, because it effectively makes explicit the question raised by O'Neill in, for example, his encounter with Harington. O'Neill's presentation of a set of overlaid markers of national and cultural identities — toying with the codes and expectations of ethnic identity — throws into doubt the issue of how the Irish can properly be classified and identified. Irish's question is a blunt expression of this uncertainty, an interrogation of what *constitutes* the Irish nation.[45]

Viewed in this light, the question is further intensified by the fact that O'Neill, in 1599, appeared on the Irish scene as the first Irish leader since the eleventh century to attempt to forge an islandwide coalition, with some ambitions toward uniting the country as a whole and creating from it a single national unit. As O'Neill's nineteenth-century nationalist biographer, John Mitchell, put it, O'Neill was "the first, for many a century, to conceive and almost to realize the grand thought of creating a new Irish nation" (1845, viii).[46] Delcan Kiberd, we will remember, has suggested that "the English did not invade Ireland — rather, they seized a neighbouring island and invented the idea of 'Ireland'" ("Anglo-Irish Attitudes" 1986, 83), but here in the 1590s it is the Irish themselves who seem to be grasping the opportunity to seize the island and to invent the idea of an Ireland for themselves. In this sense, then, again, the question of "what ish [that] nation" seems entirely pertinent to the moment in which Irish asks it.[47]

Even as Irish raises the specter of a self-defined Irish identity here, he also, of course, simultaneously highlights a certain Irish proximate liminality, for, like O'Neill, he is an oddly ambiguous figure. Appearing here as virtually the first "stage Irishman," his speech betokens a stereotypical Irish identity, yet he nevertheless takes his place within the English army, fighting for the English imperial cause. And like O'Neill's own soldiers, he appears, we presume, as an Irishman garbed in the redcoated uniform of an English soldier. To the extent, then, that Irish, like O'Neill himself, ambiguously and mercurially indicates a kind of hyphenated "Anglo-Irish" identity, the question "What ish my nation?" may emerge as being directed both at and from that very condition of liminal uncertainty itself.[48] In this sense, we might say that Edwards's assessment of the passage as "a furious repudiation of difference" is exactly right, at least in the sense that what Irish's questioning serves to effect is an interrogation of difference itself—of the bases on which difference is erected and achieved. As David Baker has observed of this exchange in general, "Mac-Morris' questions have the effect of preventing any final meaning—any discursive end 'point'—from emerging at all. Here, the voicing of imperial power gives way to a discursive heterogeneity, interrogates itself, and finds itself unable to sustain the distinctions on which it rests" ("Wildehirissheman" 1992, 46).[49]

But if Irish's question can be related both to the condition of "Irishness" and to that ambiguous state at which distinctive national identities fail to be sustained, we should note that the question is also pertinent to the issue of the evocation of an *English* national identity. This is the task, of course, that Richard Helgerson assigns to Shakespeare and his generation, to whose lot, in his view, fell the responsibility for "laying the discursive foundations both for the nation-state and for a whole array of more specialized communities that based their identity on their relation to the nation and the state" (1992, 209). Viewed from this perspective, the question "What ish my nation?" has as much force for Shakespeare the English writer as it has for Shakespeare's Irish soldier.

Given the coming together of these related issues in Irish's speech, we might say that the processes of evoking an English national identity and of engaging with the question of the identity of the Irish seem to become deeply intertwined projects in the play. When the English council debate the danger

"The Remarkablest Story of Ireland" { 119 }

of Scottish cross-border incursions into England while the French campaign will be underway, one of the king's advisers recites "a saying very old and true, / *If that you will France win, then with Scotland first begin*" (TLN 313-14). The saying is conventional and occurs in a variety of different forms, including that reproduced as an "old prophesie" by Fynes Moryson in his *Itinerary*: "He that will England winne, / Must with Ireland first beginne" (2:3). The relevance of this latter version of the old adage to the period of the Nine Years' War—when Spain repeatedly tried to establish a foothold in Ireland in order to secure a launching point for an invasion of Britain—is obvious. But we might also say, in the context of the current discussion, that the "prophesie" seems to ring true in a less literal way also. With Irish asking a question that is simultaneously relevant to both the situation in Ireland *and* the English situation, it almost appears as though the construction of an English identity has somehow become contingent on some kind of working through of the Irish question—as if a sense of England cannot be won (if it can be won at all), without first beginning with some kind of engagement with Ireland.

This raises once again the issue of proximity in a way that becomes more apparent when we turn to the final scene of the play. Here the military conflict between England and France has been resolved and the royal parties of French and English come together in an effort to secure the peace. The scene is the occasion for what seems like a curious error in the text. As the scene opens, Henry extends a welcome to the French party and his courtesy is returned by the French king, Charles: "Right ioyous are we to behold your face, / Most worthy brother England, fairely met. / So are you, Princes (English) euery one" (TLN 2996-98). King Charles thus iterates here two of the most commonly used words in the play, "England" and "English." Queen Isabel then moves to second her husband's sentiment, but, addressing Henry, she makes a revealing substitution. "So happy be the Issue Brother *Ireland*" (TLN 2999), she greets him, rather than, as we might expect, "So happy be the issue brother *England*."[50]

This "error" in the text could be recruited in support of the view of the ending of *Henry the Fift* put forward by Dollimore and Sinfield. Taking their cue from Edwards, they "see the attempt to conquer France and the union in peace at the end of the play as a re-presentation of the attempt to conquer Ireland and the hoped-for unity of Britain . . . The play offers a displaced, imaginary resolution of one of the state's most intractable problems" ("History and

Ideology" 1985, 225). It should be noted, however, that it is not the conquered France that gets confused with Ireland here but rather the conquering England. Again, this overlapping seems to point less to what Dollimore and Sinfield have traced in the play as "the ideal subservience" of Ireland to England than to the deep interconnectedness of the two national groups and to the intense difficulty of the task of distinguishing discrete, coherent (and hierarchically organized) separate national identities from among them.

Henry the Fift appears to end in a grand gesture of unity, as Henry, in wooing Katherine, tells her that "England is thine, Ireland is thine, France is thine, and *Henry Plantaginet* is thine" (TLN 3226-28), holding out the possibility of a great union of thrones, nations, and bodies. Seen in this light, Cairns and Richards may well be right when they see the play as presenting "a piece of dramatic wish-fulfilment: that a contemporary cause of discord, namely Ireland, should come to [a] satisfactory conclusion" (1988, 9). For all that, however, we must also say that the play finally fails to effect its ambitious project of maintaining a certain Gauntean sense of a coherent England, while somehow simultaneously (through the attempted incorporation/subordination/unification of the diverse national elements within the realm) accommodating to that sense of England the very boundaries and differences that Gaunt ignored.[51] Ireland is crucially at the center of that failure, as it raises issues of equivalence, proximity, and identity that the play is finally unable to assimilate to its grand unifying ambition. As Michael Neill has astutely noted, the epilogue serves as a focal point for the failure of the play's ambitious optimism:

The tone of the Epilogue marks a surprising collapse in the rhetorical confidence of the Chorus: in the Epilogue he wanly confesses that the dramatist *can* take the story no further because, beyond the celebratory-marriage ending, which gives the play its satisfying sense of formal completeness, lies the debacle of Henry VI's reign. Only upon the stage can *The Life of Henry V* end with the hero at the height of his achievement, his betrothal to the French princess apparently sealing his claim to the throne of France; and the Chorus's disconcerting reminder of the disintegration of Henry's empire after his death emphasizes the arbitrary nature of such closure. Where the French Queen has invited us to see Henry's "incorporate league" of kingdoms as a harmonious resolution instituted by divine providence . . . , the Chorus finally recognizes only the erratic violence of "Fortune." ("A Modern Perspective" 1995, 261)

IV.

Essex was succeeded in Ireland by Charles Blount, Lord Mountjoy.[52] The style of Mountjoy's departure from England was in marked contrast to that of his predecessor: "Without any publique ostentation, or great attendancy, in the month of February 1600. he tooke his iourney toward *Ireland*" (Gainsford 1619, 28). Richard Vennard published a poem entitled *St. George for England* in honor of Mountjoy, after he had left for Ireland, exhorting

> Saint George's Knight, goe noble Mountjoy on,
> Bearing thy Saviour's badge within they breast:
> Quell that Hell's shape of divellish proud Tirone,
> And cover with the dust his stubborne crest:
> That our deere Princesse and hir land be safe
> Such power to him, Oh Jesus Christ vouchsafe.
> (quoted in F.M. Jones 1958, 45)

Where Shakespeare in 1599 had drawn a parallel between Henry V and Essex, in 1601 it was Mountjoy who found himself in a position much like Henry's at Agincourt. Spain had finally succeeded in landing a substantial force at the harbor town of Kinsale in the south of Ireland, and O'Neill and his northern confederates rode to make contact with them. Mountjoy and his forces were lodged in between the two, laying siege to the town, in hostile territory in the midst of one of the harshest winters the region had experienced for decades. Reinforcements from England barely served to make up for the huge English losses from starvation, exposure, and disease. Moryson, in his memoir of the campaign writes, "Our men dailie died by dozens, so as the sicke and runnawaies considered, wee were growne as weake as at our first setting downe" (2:176).

But, like Henry, Mountjoy succeeded in winning an extraordinary victory against the odds. O'Neill, at the urging of his confederates and much against his better judgment, sought to meet the English forces in battle formation on the open plain. The Irish contingent were unequal to the task of executing the necessary complex maneuvers and were routed by the English, suffering heavy losses.[53] Striking a note familiar from Shakespeare's Henry, Mountjoy wrote to the Lords in England, "It pleased God in his goodnesse to giue vs a gracious victory, with a handfull of men in respect of [O'Neill's] Army." In the same letter, he was able to report that O'Neill's "reputation by this last ouerthrow, is both with the forraigne enemy, and his owne followers, very much blemished" (quoted in Moryson 2:180). O'Neill never recovered from the defeat, becoming in Gainsford's evocative phrase "the tennis-ball of fortune" (37). Although he remained in the field with his dwindling band of supporters, he made persistent overtures to be allowed to come in and surrender, and finally, in March 1603, Mountjoy accepted his submission.

O'Neill did, in fact, contrive to receive yet another pardon from the crown, and he returned to Ulster once more as Earl of Tyrone. He even accompanied Mountjoy on a visit to the English court (much to Sir John Harington's annoyance: "I have lived to see that damnable rebel Tir-Owen broughte to Englande, curteouslie favourede, honourede, and well likede" [*Nugæ* 1804, 340]).[54] But for all of O'Neill's ability to negotiate his way back into favor with the English and to salvage one last period of local autonomy in Ulster, the situation in Ireland had, in the wake of Kinsale, changed drastically. It is a measure of this change that O'Neill's restoration was short lived: by 1607 he was forced to leave Ulster under cover of darkness, sailing into continental exile with his family and supporters and living the last decade of his life in Rome, the recipient of a Papal pension.[55]

Mountjoy's campaign effectively brought the entire island of Ireland under English control for the first time in history. The breaking of Irish power signaled an assuaging of the anxiety prompted among Elizabethan writers by the disturbing proximate Otherness of the Irish. Early seventeenth-century English texts about Ireland, by contrast, have a rather different cast and thrust to them. In them, the power of Irish identity is conceived of as being so fatally weakened as to be capable simply of being banished. In an odd way, the expectation of such writers is that English-Irish proximity will become absolute, in the sense that the Irish will be brought so much to approximate the English that there will finally be no difference between the two peoples. As we shall see, this ideology of assimilation was fostered by the ideal of union that resulted from James VI's accession to the throne of England in 1603.

5
"The Irish Game Turned Again"
Jonson and the Union

*God bring it once to passe, that wee might all ioyne together as
well English as Irish, in the true acknowledgement of one God,
of one Religion, of one King, of one Law, and of one Loue.*
Barnabe Rich, *A New Description of Ireland*

I.

Fynes Moryson, in his *Itinerary,* describes the scene of O'Neill's surrender to
Mountjoy on March 30, 1603: "They came altogether to *Mellifant* in the af-
ternoon, where *Tyrone* being admitted to the Lord Deputies chamber, kneeled
at the doore humbly on his knees for a long space, making his penitent submission to her Maiesty, and after being required to come neerer to the Lord
Deputie, performed the same ceremony in all humblenesse, the space of one
houre or there abouts" (1617, 2:279). In Thomas Gainsford's account of the
surrender, O'Neill confesses "to offending God and her Maiesty," acknowledging "how hee had abused her fauours, disturbed her Kingdome, disobeyed
her lawes, wronged her subiects, abandoned all ciuility, and wrapped himselfe

in the very tarriers of destruction; so that nothing remained, but to flie to the refuge of her Princely clemency, which had so often restored both his life and honour" (1619, 41).

The irony of O'Neill's abject surrender to Elizabeth was, of course, as Mountjoy well knew, that the queen to whom he was surrendering had, as Gainsford puts it, already "gone to take possession" of "a better Kingdome" (42): she had died six days before, on March 24. Elizabeth was succeeded on the throne of England by James VI of Scotland, and thus, as John Davies noted in his *Discoverie of the Trve Cavses,* "the Warre which finished the Conquest of *Ireland,* was ended almost in the instant when the crown descended vpon his Maiesty" (1612 [1969], Ll1r).

On James's accession to the English throne Scotland, England and Wales were for the first time united under a single monarch. As Francis Bacon wrote in the year of the accession, "It dooth not appeare by the recordes and memories, of any true history, nor scarcly by the fiction and pleasure of any fabulous narration, or tradition: that euer, of any antiquity, this Iland of great *Brittaine* was vnited vnder one King, before this day" ("A Briefe Discovrse" 1603, A7r). In acceding to the throne of England, James simultaneously acceded to the title King of Ireland. Mountjoy's victory had, of course, brought that entire realm securely within the monarch's power, also for the first time ever in its history. The coincidence of Elizabeth's death and O'Neill's surrender thus allowed of the possibility of rethinking the way in which the national unit was constituted and of how the relationships among the communities who made up the nation were to be conceived.

Where Scotland and England were concerned, James immediately set about initiating a program that he envisioned would effect a complete union of both kingdoms.[1] As Brian P. Levack has observed, "No British king or statesman of the seventeenth or eighteenth century was as thorough, imaginative, or genuinely dedicated to the creation of a united national community or British people as James" (1987, 180). In addition to setting in train a debate on the issue in both the Scottish and the English parliaments, James also assumed the style "Kinge of Great Brittaine" and ordered the issuing of coins with emblems and inscriptions celebrating the union, including a gold piece inscribed "Faciamus eos in gentem unam" ("Let us make ourselves into one people").[2]

Several questions arise at this point as we contemplate James's golden motto. In the first instance, we might ask who exactly are the "us" and "ourselves" of the tag's "faciamus eos."[3] James was motivated to circulate the coin as part of a general campaign to attract support for the union of the crowns of Scotland and England, so in this sense, the "us" is the Scots and the English.[4] But where exactly do the inhabitants of his other kingdom—the realm of Ireland—fit into this program? Are they also to be part of the "gentem unam," whose self-making James solicits? And we might also ask, What precisely is involved in this same process of self-making? How is union to be effected, and what, finally, is meant by the notion of "union"?

This last question is particularly important, especially where Ireland is concerned, because of the relationship between union and proximity. The possibility of union necessarily presumes some sort of prior common connection between those who would be united. Thus, in the tracts supporting the Anglo-Scottish union published in the years immediately following James's accession, the various links between the English and the Scots are stressed again and again.[5] John Hayward, for instance, writing as I.H. in *A Treatise of Vnion of the Two Realmes of England and Scotland*, states, "If we compare together the English and the Scots, in regard of habit (as *Sofia* said in *Plautus*) *non lac lactis magis est simile; milke is not liker to milke than one of them is to the other.* . . . And as for language, euen in *Zetland*, and in the most distant ilands inhabited by Scots, English preachers are well understood of the common people" (E4r-v).[6] Union itself (or at least certain forms of union) anticipates the expansion of such commonality, so that residual difference is cancelled, leading to an equality of identity among those whose identities had originally been similar but distinct.[7] Thus, Hayward continues, "it seemeth, that if the two nations were reduced vnder one common name, there should remaine betweene them very little generall, either note of difference, or prouocation of dislike" (E4v).

The relevance of this to the Irish situation lies in the connection between this paradigm and proximity. In the case of so many of the texts we have examined so far, a paradigm of anticipated difference is disrupted by the unexpected emergence of sameness within difference—the emergence, in other words, of a proximate relationship where a dichotomous relationship is required. But the union paradigm is predicated, in fact, on just such an immanent sameness. Union requires that commonality be there to be uncovered and that such commonality be foregrounded to the point where approximation becomes so close that difference is entirely elided. Union thus intensifies proximity to the point at which proximate others become, in fact, coidentical with the self. To see how exactly the narrative of Jamesian union plays itself out in the Irish context, we must first look at the way in which the image of the nation shifted in the wake of James's accession.

II.

Among the coins James ordered minted in celebration of his accession to the English throne was one bearing the inscription "Quae Deus coniunxit nemo separet"—"what God has joined, let no one separate."[8] This motto serves to bring together the union and the marriage service, and the deployment of the metaphor of marriage became a standard trope in prounion texts.[9] As D.J. Gordon has observed, "the comparison between the union and marriage was a very obvious one, and came easily to the king's lips" (1975, 169). James certainly used the figure again and again. In his first speech to the English parliament, he repeated the tag from the wedding service and made its political meaning explicit: "What God hath conioyned then, let no man separate. I am the Husband, and all the whole Isle is my lawfull Wife" (272). In a later parliamentary speech, in 1607, James sees the two realms themselves as the bride and groom, telling the English parliament "you are to be the husband, they the wife" (294).[10]

Like many other writers associated with James's court, Ben Jonson also employed the trope of marriage in his writings in support of the union. In his 1604 epigram "On the Union," Jonson sees James as the celebrant at the wedding of the kingdoms: "When was there contract better driuen by *Fate?* / Or celebrated with more truth of state? / The world the temple was, the priest a king, / The spoused paire two realmes, the sea the ring" (*Complete Works* 1616, 770).[11] Likewise, Jonson's wedding masque for the marriage of the Earl of Essex and Frances Howard in January of 1606 also provides an intertwining of the themes of union and marriage. The presiding deity of Jonson's masque is Juno, the patroness of marriage, and Jonson exploits a fortuitous wordplay between *Ivno* and *Vnio,* or union:

> And see, where IVNO, whose great name
> Is VNIO, in the *anagram,*
> Displayes her glistering state, and chaire,
> As she enlightned all the *ayre!*
> Harke how the charming tunes doe beate
> In sacred concords 'bout her seate!
>   (917)

As D.J. Gordon indicates in his analysis of this masque, Jonson plays repeatedly throughout with the various significances of the notion of union, and the political dimension of the masque was readily apparent to the assembled audience. Gordon quotes from one spectator, John Pory, who wrote of the performance that "the concert or soul of the Mask was Hymen bringing in a bride, and Juno Pronuba's priest a bridegroom, proclaiming that these two should be sacrificed to Nuptial Union. And here the Poet made an apostrophe to the Union of the Kingdoms" (1975, 169).

One rather obvious fact that we might note of the "union as marriage" paradigm is, of course, that in all of its variations, it necessarily serves to exclude the realm of Ireland from the new relationship among territories and monarch being proposed.[12] In the same parliamentary speech in which he declares "I am the Husband, and all the whole Isle is my lawfull Wife," James goes on to express the hope that "no man will be so vnreasonable as to thinke that I that am a Christian King vnder the Gospel, should be a Polygamist and husband to two wiues" (272). If James is married to "the whole Isle" of Britain and is insistent on his own monogamous fidelity, we might well wonder how exactly Ireland is to be incorporated into the new national framework.

Where Benedict Anderson (1991) has famously referred to the construction of a sense of national identity as a process of communal "imagining," we might say that in this particular version of Jamesian imagining—this mapping of the metaphor of domestic union onto the reconstitued national unit—Ireland is excluded from what the nation is imagined to be. The same might also be said for some of the other images of the nation deployed in the texts that appear in the wake of James's accession. In his *Panegyrike Congratvlatorie to the Kings Maiestie,* published in the year of James's accession (1603), for example, Samuel Daniel writes:

> Shake hands with Vnion, O thou mightie State,
> Now thou art all great *Brittaine,* and no more,
> No Scot, no English now, nor no debate:
> No Borders but the Ocean, and the Shore,
> No wall of *Adrian* serues to seperate
> Our mutuall loue, nor our obedience,
> All Subiects now to one imperiall Prince.
>
> (A1r)

Here, as difference is abolished between Scot and English, we find something like a revival of the Gauntean image of what constitutes the nation. For both Gaunt and Daniel the national unit has "No Borders but the Ocean, and the Shore" and thus the boundaries of the nation are coterminous with the island of Britain's geographic extent.

James himself deploys a similar set of images as Daniel in his first address to the English parliament, when he asks whether God

hath . . . not made vs all in one Island, compassed with one Sea, and of it selfe by nature so indiuisible, as almost those that were borderers themselues on the late Borders, cannot distinguish, nor know, or discerne their owne limits? These two Countries being separated neither by Sea, nor great Riuer, Mountaine, nor other strength of nature, but onely by little small brookes, or demolished little walles, so as rather they were diuided in apprehension then in effect; And now in the end and fulnesse of time vnited, the right and title of both in my Person, alike lineally descended of both Crownes, whereby it is now become like a little World within it selfe. (271-72)

Again the image of the nation presented here is of a realm defined by nature, whose limits are established by certain hard geographical realities. For Gaunt, the "sceptred Isle" of England was "this little world, / This precious stone, set in the siluer sea" (TLN 686-87); for James, likewise, the nation is "like a little World within it selfe." Where Daniel effectively abolishes the borders mapped onto the island space by fiat, declaring that "No wall of *Adrian* serues to seper-ate" the two communities, James considers what it is that constitutes those borders and finds that it is merely "little small brookes, or demolished little walles." Though there is a boundary between the two territories, it is a perme-able boundary, whose contours are incomplete and hardly perceptible.

For Benedict Anderson, one of the defining characteristics of the "imag-ined community" that constitutes the nation is that it is "imagined as both in-herently limited and sovereign" (1991, 6). As Anderson explains, "the nation is imagined as *limited* because even the largest [nation] . . . has finite, if elastic boundaries, beyond which lie other nations" (7). In imagining the border be-tween England and Scotland as being sufficiently "elastic" to be stretched from its original site at the "little small brookes, or demolished little walls" to the shoreline of the island of Britain, James is able to unite his joint kingdoms into a single realm. What lies beyond this entity is not, however, in Anderson's terms, another nation, itself imagined as limited and sovereign and lying securely outside the national limits of a united Britain, but rather an Ireland that needs to be accommodated in some way to the British national unit. The question that arises, then, is just how elastic are the limits of the nation. If these limits can, in the Anglo-Irish situation, be stretched to include Ireland, how exactly is that accommodation figured and what will be its consequences?

III.

Although the metaphors and iconography of union could often, as we have seen, serve to exclude Ireland from the newly emerging conceptions of the national entity, numerous contemporary writers were nevertheless alert to the relevance of the union debate to Ireland's situation. Included among the state papers for Ireland for the year 1604, we find a short text entitled "Questions and Answers concerning the State of Ireland," in which the following exchange occurs:

> Ques.—What likelihood of rebellion is now in Ireland?

> Ans.—Little within the land, for the settled estate of England, His Majesty's most royal issue, and the union of Great Britain are barricadoes in that way. (*Calendar* 1872, 229)

Here the possibilities of peace in Ireland are weighed against the background of the union that James has effected in acceding to the English throne. In much the same vein, John Hayward, in his 1604 treatise in support of the Anglo-Scottish union, noting that union "hath in a short course of time altogether appeased the cruell and inueterate, not onely butcheries but hate, betweene the English and the Welsh," wonders "wether the want of this hath made all other appliances, whether of clemencie, or of iustice, or of armes, if not vnprofitable, yet insufficient, to represse the riotous rebellions in *Ireland*" (B2r). Hayward thus somewhat hesitantly suggests the extension of union as a potential force for securing the end of rebellion in Ireland. In another text included among the 1604 Irish state papers, a certain Richard Hudson offers a more positive version of the same argument when he suggests that "if His Majesty would be also pleased in the happy union of England and Scotland to unite His Highness's realm of Ireland in amity, being a land so fertile as wanteth nothing, serving for the necessity, use, or pleasure of man, in few years of a peaceable good government it would become the land of plenty" (*Calendar* 1872, 238). Clearly, then, the possibility that somehow the mechanism of union might be usefully extended to Ireland was contemplated by a number of contemporary commentators on the Anglo-Irish situation. But how exactly was that process of incorporation to be conceived?

John Ford provides us with one answer to this question in a text entitled *Fames Memoriall, or The Earle of Deuonshire Deceased,* published shortly after the death of Mountjoy (who had by then been created Earl of Devonshire), in 1606. One section of the poem is given over to Mountjoy's succession to Essex in Ireland and his subsequent successful prosecution of the Irish war:

> When fickle chance and deaths blindfold decree,
> From the tribunall seat of awfull state,
> Had hurried downe in black calamity
> Renowned *Deuoreux,* whose aukward fate,
> Was misconceited by fowle enemies hate:
>> Back was he cal'd from *Ireland* to come home,
>> And noble *Mountioy* must supply his roome.
>
> (C3r)

Ford goes on to outline Mountjoy's victory over Tyrone and the Irish, noting that "A land of Barbarous inhumanitye / He hath reduc't to blessed piety" (D1r). Ford celebrates Mountjoy's victory by linking it directly with the union of England and Scotland:

> As oft as *Iames* the monarch of our peace,
> Shall be in after chronicles recited,
> In that to heau'ns applause and subiects ease
> *England* and *Scotland* he in one vnited,
> A sight with which true *Britans* were delighted:
>> So oft shalt thou [Devonshire] eternall fauour gaine,
>> Who recollected'st *Ireland* to them twaine.
>
> (E1r)

We notice here that James unites England and Scotland in the first five lines that constitute the main part of the stanza, whereas Mountjoy brings Ireland into alignment with them in the offset final couplet. Ford's choice of verb to characterize the assimilation of Ireland is very suggestive—Devonshire *recollects* Ireland to the other territories. This both implies a gathering in of the neighboring island and glances at a process of remembering—as if, with the successful conclusion of the war, Ireland's proximate relatedness is recalled, bringing the island back into a prior alignment.

If we turn to the next stanza of the poem, we can begin to get a sense of how Ford sees Ireland as being integrated within the realm of the recently united kingdom once Mountjoy's "recollection" has been effected:

> A worke of thankes in strengthening the force
> Of such an entire Empire now secure,
> A world within it selfe which whiles the course
> Of heauen continueth lasting wil endure
> Fearless of forraign power, strong and sure
> A bulwarke intermur'd with walls of Brasse,
> A like can neuer bee, nor euer was.
>
> (E1r)

Where Gaunt's greater England is protected by a "sea . . . in the office of a wall . . . against the envy of less happier lands," we notice here that, in a similar image, Ford's "entire Empire" appears as "A bulwarke intermur'd with walls of Brasse," "Fearless of forraign power." Indeed, we might say that what we get in Ford is something like a further revision of the kind of image of Britain advanced by Gaunt. Where Gaunt saw Britain as an islandwide England, and where Daniel and James produced a similar image of Britain consisting of a union of the island's individual national communities, Ford presents "an entire Empire" of Britain and Ireland together as his single coherent unit. Where James speaks of a Britain that is "a little world within itself," Ford drops the "little" and gives us an extended realm of Britain and Ireland that constitutes "a world within it selfe." Ford's vision was to some extent confirmed in John Speed's *Theatre of the Empire of Great Britaine* of 1611. As Bernhard Klein has observed of this volume, it is "a sign of the changing political climate of James's reign and . . . an expression of the new king's political agenda [that] it includes, for the first time in a 'British' atlas, maps of Scotland and Ireland" (1995, 117).[13]

Ben Jonson had, in fact, produced a somewhat similiar reading of the union of the British isles three years prior to Ford, when he contributed his

"Ode. allhgorikh" to Hugh Holland's *Pancharis* in the watershed year of 1603.[14] Jonson's poem begins with a question: "Who saith our Times nor haue, nor can / Produce vs a blacke Swan?" with the poet denying such a proposition by noting the existence of just such a bird "dint[ing] the breast of *Tamisis*" (1-2; 8). Jonson addresses this black swan of the Thames and urges him not to "let one Riuer boast / Thy tunes alone; / But proue the Aire" (35-37), and the body of the poem consists of Jonson's charting out for the swan a voyage that will take it "from coast to coast" (37) in a circular journey surveying the kingdom.

The imagined journey has a double beginning, as Jonson urges the bird to "Salute old *Mône*, / But first to *Cluid* stoope low, / The Vale, that bred thee pure, as her Hills Snow" (38-40). Jonson thus begins the journey with Anglesey (*Môna*), a small island lying off the coast of Wales.[15] We might feel here that Jonson wishes to make the first stop of the swan's journey a neutral point located outside the island of Britain.[16] From this intermediate point, Jonson has the bird redouble his tracks, to visit mainland Wales. Hugh Holland, the author of *Pancharis*, was a native of Denbigh, and so the reference to Clwyd as the "Vale, that bred thee pure" is clearly a reference to Holland himself, but Wales was also, of course, in 1603, the territory most fully united with England.[17] So the revised first destination of the imaginary flight becomes the place that is in some sense the most secure center of British union.

From Wales, Jonson proposes to send the swan directly across the Irish sea:

From thence, display thy wing againe
Ouer *I'rna* maine,
To the *Eugenian* dale;
There charm the rout
With thy soft notes, and hold them within Pale
That late were out.
"Musicke hath power to draw,
"Where neither Force can bend, nor Feare can awe.

Be proofe, the glory of his hand,
(*Charles Mountioy*) whose command
Hath all beene Harmony:
And more hath wonne

"The Irish Game Turned Again"   { 133 }

Vpon the *Kerne,* and wildest *Irishry,*
Then Time hath donne,
Whose strength is aboue strength;
And conquers all things, yea it selfe, at length.

(41-56)

Here Jonson engages with the Mountjoy victory. Writing three years before
Ford, the issue is much more immediate for him (the Irish, he tells us, "late
were out"), but he produces an image of Mountjoy's accomplishment that has
much in common with Ford's "recollection." Jonson also recasts Mountjoy's
military achievement in more pacific terms. In Jonson, this manuver is accomplished across the boundary of the two stanzas just quoted. In the first
stanza, Jonson calls on the swan to "charme" the Irish with his "soft notes."
In the second stanza, the swan's musical power is conflated with Mountjoy's
power as military commander and governor so that, in Jonson's account,
Mountjoy's real achievement is to have made his period of tenure in Ireland
"all . . . Harmony." By proposing in relation to the bird's song that "Musicke
hath power to draw, / Where neither Force can bend, nor Feare can awe,"
and by then associating Mountjoy's accomplishment with that music through
the category of Harmony, Jonson succeeds in disassociating Mountjoy from
those very things that yielded success in his Irish campaign, namely, force
and fear.

Continuing to chart a flightpath for the swan, Jonson imagines the bird as
already having left Ireland, traveling on an arc that takes it first over the Scottish islands and then on over mainland Scotland. "Our Swan's on wing,"
writes Jonson,

Who (see) already hath ore-flowne
The *Hebrid* Isles, and knowne
The scatter'd *Orcades;*
From thence is gon
To vtmost *Thule:* whence, he backes the Seas
To *Caledon,*
And ouer *Grampius* mountaine,
To *Loumond* lake, and *Twedes* blacke-springing
fountaine.

(65-72)

We have had two stanzas of the poem dedicated to Ireland, and now we have one complete stanza dedicated to Scotland. Where Jonson began with Wales, as the Celtic country most securely legally bound to England, before moving on to Ireland, whose attachment is most tentative and complex, he now moves back from Ireland to Scotland, the territory so recently brought into union with England by the accession of James to the English throne. As with the opening description of the swan's imagined flight path, we begin here with an intermediate island space (or rather, series of spaces) between the two main territories of Britain and Ireland, before moving back onto the British mainland. The end of the stanza here marks the end of Celtic territory, and Jonson hurries the swan back over England to return to its point of departure:

> Haste, Haste, sweete Singer: Nor to *Tine,*
> *Humber,* or *Owse,* decline;
> But ouer Land to *Trent:*
> There coole thy Plumes,
> And vp againe, in skies, and aire to vent
> Their reeking fumes;
> Till thou at *Tames* alight,
> From whose prowde bosome, thou began'st thy flight.
> (73-80)

The swan thus ends where it began, at the metropolitan center of London. It has completed a circuit of the British isles, uniting the entire territory in its journey.

In analyzing *Fames Memoriall,* we noted that, having once attached Ireland to Britain in a union of kingdoms, Ford presents the integration of the newly united kingdom as being total and enduring. He does this in part by producing the united kingdom as an "entire Empire" secure against the threat of "forraign power." Much the same manuver occurs next in Jonson's ode. In the concluding lines of the stanza quoted above, we see the swan "at *Tames* alight, / From whose prowde bosome, thou began'st thy flight," and in the next stanza of the poem we are given some of the reasons for Thames's pride. The river is "prowde of thee, and of his Fate / In entertaining late / The choice of *Europes* pride" (81-83). As the stanza continues, Jonson sets up a division between, on the one hand, a greater Britain united by the circuit of the swan's flight, on the other, and the rest of Europe.[18] And where Britain appears in the poem as what we might call a whole assembled from its constituent parts (the individual places included within the uniting ambit of the bird's flight path), that "Europe" from which it is distinguished appears, by contrast, to be little more than a convenient collective noun for a group of distinctive and diverse nationalities. Jonson's mention of "the choice of *Europes* pride" is followed immediately by an ironic list of discreet items that breaks Europe down into its constituent nationalities:

The nimble *French;*
The *Dutch* whom Wealth (not Hatred) doth diuide;
The *Danes* that drench
Their cares in wine; with sure
Though slower *Spaine;* and *Italy* mature.
                                                    (84-88)

These assembled representatives of the diverse nationalities of Europe react with fear when they first hear the song of the British swan, but that fear soon enough turns to envy as they look on the bird:

All which, when they but heare a straine
Of thine, shall thinke the *Maine*
Hath sent her *Mermaides* in,
To hold them here:
Yet, looking in thy face, they shall begin
To loose that feare;
And (in the place) enuie
So blacke a Bird, so bright a Qualitie.
                                                    (89-96)

This theme of European envy, now turned to regret, is picked up again in the closing stanza of the poem:

It is inough, their griefe shall know
At their returne, nor *Po,*
Iberus, Tagus, Rheine,
Scheldt, not the *Maas,*

Slow *Arar,* nor swift *Rhone;* the *Loyre,* nor *Seine,*
With all the race
Of *Europes* waters can
Set out a like, or second to our Swan.

(113-20)

Again, where the early stanzas of the poem provide a list of place names that accrete to the unified entity of a greater Britain, here Jonson once more presents us with a stanza in which Europe, by contrast, is disassembled into a set of constituent elements, this time the major rivers of the various individual countries. None of these elements individually, nor in combination with all other elements under the unifying label of "Europe" ("With all the race / Of *Europes* waters"), can provide any adequate rival to the British swan.

Just as in Ford's *Fames Memoriall,* where we find that Ireland is incorporated into a greater "entire Empire" distinguished in its security from hostile "forraign power," so too does Jonson incorporate Ireland into a greater united British domain, distinguished from a fragmented Europe.

What we have been discovering thus far in our analysis of the "Ode. allhgorikh" is Jonson's account of how Ireland can be accommodated to what we might call the "geography" of union. Through the journey of the black swan, the island of Ireland is included within the sphere of the "British isles" to become part of a greater united realm—what Ford calls "an entire Empire." But a greater question yet to be answered here is how exactly the communities that make up this geographically united kingdom are to be brought into a relationship of union with each other—specifically, how the Irish are to be included within the newly expanded imagined national entity.

If we return to the Irish stanzas of Jonson's "Ode," we can begin to explore this question further. We will recall that, in sending his black swan to Ireland, Jonson exhorts the bird to "charm the rout / With thy soft notes, and hold them within Pale / That late were out. / 'Musicke hath power to draw, / 'Where neither Force can bend, nor Feare can awe.'" Jonson's urging of the swan to hold the Irish "within Pale" has the general sense of keeping the Irish within bounds or limits. But we should note, of course, that the term "Pale" also has a much more resonant political meaning in an Irish context. The Pale was that irreducible zone in which English government and control had persisted throughout the centuries since the advent of the Norman-English to Ireland, weathering all uprisings and political shifts within the country.

Viewed in this light, Jonson's exhorting of the swan to hold the Irish within Pale would seem to imply another version of Ford's "recollection," as the Irish are gathered within the metaphorical confines of the Pale. Looking at it another way, we might say that what Jonson envisions has, again, a certain Gauntean cast to it, since to keep the Irish "within Pale" implies, in effect, an extension of the area of English jurisdiction and influence such that its limits become coterminous with the Irish shoreline. Where Gaunt would write "England" large across the island of Britain, here Jonson seems to imagine that Britain can be writ large across the neighboring island of Ireland. As we shall see, what this ultimately implies is that, for Jonson as for other English writers, the assimilation of Ireland to the union involves not a discovery of commonality and merging of identities among the neighboring populations (the sort of process imagined by a number of the supporters of the Anglo-Scottish union) but rather the imagined imposition of an English identity and English codes on the Irish. We can see this more clearly if we turn to Jonson's longest text about Ireland—his *Irish Masque at Court*. The occasion of this masque, which was performed at court twice—once on December 29, 1613, and again on January 4, 1614—was once again an aristocratic wedding.

In view of the mobilization of the metaphor of marriage in support of the union project and the general exclusion of Ireland from this trope, it is worth taking a moment here to rehearse the marital history that lies behind the *Irish Masque*. Jonson's *Hymenæi*, which, as we have seen, was intended in part as a celebration of the Anglo-Scottish union was written for the marriage of Frances Howard to the Earl of Essex. Howard was thirteen at the time and Essex was fifteen and, as D.J. Gordon notes, the "marriage was dynastic," being "calculated to tie together the political and family interests of great powers, to effect a new grouping of great houses" (1975, 157). Gordon speculates that Robert Cecil himself may have taken a hand in arranging the marriage, being anxious to effect a reconciliation with the younger Essex, having been instrumental in bringing about the downfall of his father on the elder Essex's return from his disasterous Irish campaign. To this extent, we might say that the 1606 marriage was multiply embedded in the politics of union. These deep political resonances notwithstanding, however, the marriage was famously and scandalously unsuccessful. David Lindley provides a summary of the much recounted story of the relationship:

After the 1606 marriage, Essex was dispatched on foreign travels, returning to claim his bride in 1609. He got a dusty welcome, and for the next three years the marriage remained unconsummated, no doubt because Frances had, during her husband's absence, become enamored of Robert Carr, the rising favorite of the King. In 1613 Frances sued for divorce, on the grounds that her husband was impotent towards her. The case was tried before commissioners appointed by James I. When they divided evenly, he promptly nominated two more commissioners sure to vote in favor. ("Embarrassing Ben" 1986, 346)

Following her divorce, Howard went on to marry Carr, and it was for this second marriage that the *Irish Masque* was written. Thus, where the Anglo-Scottish union was celebrated in the context of a dynastic marriage between two young aristocrats, Ireland's place in the union was taken up by Jonson almost a decade later in the context of a controversial and scandalous alliance.[19] We might well feel here that the coincidence of the two marriages resonates in a peculiar way with James's own question to his English parliament as to how, as a Christian king, he might be thought to be "a Polygamist and husband to two wiues."[20]

Turning to the text of the masque itself, we find that, like most such court entertainments (at least of the Jonsonian kind), the *Irish Masque* is divided into two broad sections: the antimasque and the masque proper. The antimasque provides the occasion for much clowning and broad comedy, whereas the masque is reserved for more serious-minded matters of cultural and political consequence. In the antimasque, the king is assailed by four comic footmen, Dennis, Donnell, Dermock, and Patrick, each from one of the four provinces of Ireland ("Of Connough, Leymster, Vlster, Munster" [1001]). The footmen's speech is heavily accented, and much play is made of their self-contradictory prattling nature, as first they jostle with each other to speak with the king and then huffily refuse, one by one, the task of being spokesman for the group:

Pat. . . . Vill shome body shpeake?

Don. By my fayt I vill not.

Der. By my goships hand I vill not.

Pat. Speake DENNISH ten.

Den. If I speake, te diuell tayke me. I vill giue tee leaue to cram my mout phit shamrokes and butter, and vayter creshes instead of pearsh and peepsh. (1001)

The antimasque culminates in a dance of the footmen *"to the bag-pipe, and other rude musique"* (1003), after which they concede the floor to their Irish masters, a group of gentlemen in traditional Irish dress who, in contrast to the footmen, dance *"to a solemne musique of harpes"* (1003). Following this dance, the footmen begin to assail the king once again, but they are banished by the character Gentleman, who comes forth and bids them: "Hold your tongues. / And let your courser manners seeke some place, / Fit for their wildnesse. This is none, be gone" (1003).

With the departure of the footmen, the performance settles down to the serious business of the masque proper. As a token of this shift into seriousness, the piece moves from prose to verse. This second section of the masque concerns a different set of groupings from Irish society. The Gentleman who banishes the footmen is himself Irish (*"a ciuil gentleman of the nation"* [1003]) and, having despatched the footmen, he leads forth an Irish bard, calling on him to "come vp and view / The glad,ding [*sic*] face of that great king, in whom / So many prophecies of thine are knit" (1003). The Gentleman then requests of the poet that he "Sing . . . some charme, made of [the king's] present lookes, / That may assure thy former prophecies" (1003). The bard duly obliges by singing two songs to the accompaniment of the harps.[21] During the first song, he exhorts the Irish gentlemen present to "BOw both [their] heads at once, and hearts" (1003). Having himself been asked to come and view the king and to sing a charm made of the king's looks, the bard advises the gentlemen of the king's power, noting that "It is but standing in his eye, / You'll feele your selues chang'd by and by, / Few liue that know, how quick a spring / Workes in the presence of a king" (1003-1004). As the poet sings this song, the Irish gentlemen "let fall their mantles; and discouer their masquing apparell. Then dance forth" (1004).[22] The piece then ends with the poet's second song, again in celebration of the power of the king's gaze, concluding "all get vigour, youth, and spright, / That are but look'd on by his light" (1004).

What we appear to see in the *Irish Masque* is, thus, the incorporation of the Irish fully within the circle of the British king's subjects. Again, the union paradigm seems to mimic the mechanism of proximity, in that sameness is specifically conceived of here as being immanent within difference. The implication drawn from this in the masque is that an underlying English identity can be brought out by the force of the British king's gaze, to the extent that the outer shell that constitutes Irish difference can be broken and dispersed, to be entirely replaced by the markers of a true English identity, through a process that Ann Jones and Peter Stallybrass have neatly termed "rehabilitation" (167). Much as Spenser, in his *View of the Present State of Ireland,* imagines the Old English as literally becoming Irish, Jonson imagines the Irish here as emerging from their cocoon of difference actually to become English. The mechanism of proximity thus, in a sense, serves as the agent of union.

There are, however, several points we might make about this process of transformation. In the first instance, we notice a difference between this version of Irish incorporation and Jonson's earlier version in the "Ode. allhgorikh." In the 1603 poem, we will recall that Jonson anticipated something like an expansion of the Pale, such that all of the Irish were brought within its boundaries. To this extent, the entire island of Ireland would in essence become "English." Ten years later, in the *Irish Masque,* however, Jonson presents this process of transformation as being available only to a limited constituency. As Paul Brown has noted, following the antimasque, the "indecorous stage-Irish plebeians are banished from the stage" (63)—"Hold your tongues. / And let your courser manners seeke some place, / Fit for their wildnesse. This is none, be gone."

In part, what we are confronted with here is, of course, the inscription of class issues within the narrative. And certainly, the issue of class in the colonial situation has often tended to be overlooked. Karen Kupperman makes the rather overstated claim in respect of New World colonialism that "status, not race was the category which counted for English people in the early years of colonization" (122) and that "the care with which English writers distinguished between Indians of the 'better sort' and the ordinary is . . . central to their response to the challenge of describing Indian society and culture" (1980, 3). Perhaps this is precisely what Jonson is doing here: distinguishing between Irish "of the better sort," who will be transformed to become English, and "the ordinary" Irish, who will simply be banished from the world of the court and the world of English identity. There are, however, other factors at play within the text that complicate this issue.

We can begin to trace some of these elements if we examine the framing narrative of the masque. The function of the four footmen in the first half of the piece is to introduce the gentlemen (their Irish masters) who have come to

England, so the footmen tell the king, on hearing "a great newsh in Ireland of a great Brideall of one o'ty lords here" (1001). Their masters have come to join in the celebration "and daunsh a fading at te vedding" (1001). Their company has, however, met with a mishap during the course of their journey from Ireland: "tey vere leeke to daunsh naked, ant pleash ty mayesty; for te villanous vild Irish sheas haue casht away all ter fine cloysh, as many ash cosht a towsand cowes and garraue, I varrant tee" (1001).[23] The Irish gentlemen thus are actually well provided with the couture of English civility, before they ever leave Ireland. It is only because of having lost their better garments at sea that they are forced to come into the king's presence "and daunch i'teur mantels" (1002)—a form of dress adopted entirely as a last resort.

Several issues are raised by this aspect of the narrative of the masque. On the one hand, we seem to find an echo here of some of the anxieties over Irish proximity that we discovered in those texts written before the Irish had been defeated in the early years of the seventeenth century. We might feel that Jonson's Irish have, once again, a certain familiar dual quality to them: possessed of the trappings, the "fine cloysh," of English civility, yet reverting also to that most traditional marker of Gaelic Irish identity—the mantle. We might well be reminded here of Hugh O'Neill with his "riche furniture [of] beddinge, arras, and carpettes and the lyke," dressing his sons "in English cloths like a nobleman's sons; with velvet gerkins and gold lace."[24]

But the revelation that the Irish gentlemen are already possessed of the trappings of English civility should also prompt us to wonder just who exactly Jonson imagined these gentlemen to be. To which of the various groups living on the island of Ireland do they belong? By 1613, O'Neill had been in exile in Rome for some six years. Most of the Gaelic Irish nobility had gone into exile with him as part of the "flight of the Earls" in 1607. This departure signaled the final breaking of Gaelic Irish power in the island. No Gaelic Irish leader could thus be imagined as possessing such fine clothes "ash cosht a towsand cowes and garraue" (even allowing for the comic exaggerations of the stage-Irish footmen) or indeed as being the recipients of an invitation to come to the English court and attend an aristocratic wedding. Once again, we find a process of exclusion at work here. Like the Irish footmen—indeed, most likely *figured by* the Irish footmen—the Gaelic Irish are allowed no plausible place within the scene of transformation and incorporation.

This still leaves us, however, wondering just exactly whom Jonson wishes to signal through his Irish masquers. We can no doubt presume that no self-respecting New English gentleman—certainly none familiar with tracts such as Spenser's *View*—could be imagined resorting to so obvious and obviously charged a marker of Irish identity as the infamous mantle. In any case, the New English community in Ireland, so cautious to distinguish itself from both native Irish communities, could hardly be thought of as being in need of such a transformation as the *Irish Masque* envisions.[25]

By a process of elimination, then, we may be lead to identify Jonson's gentlemen with the remnants of the Old English aristocracy. If this is the case, Jonson's imagined transformation is predicated on a very narrow base, being offered only to a very restricted segment of the Irish population. But even this seems implausible. The Old English were, in this period, locked in a struggle with the New English for control of the Irish parliament, and the Old English ambassadors who had, in 1613, come to London to James to report on the dispute had in fact been imprisoned by the king. Included among the Irish state papers for 1614 is a letter from John Chamberlain to Sir Dudley Carleton in which he notes that, though the masque was popular enough to warrant a second performance, "yet theyre deuise wch was a mimicall imitation of t[he] Irish was not so pleasing to many."[26] Whether this indicates the presence at the masque some sort of faction sympathetic to the Old English who were offended by the performance is not clear. What does seem clear is that the masque was not conceived as anything other than a charade intended to amuse a non-Irish audience. As Lindley has astutely observed, "the masque was performed, at James's request, by his 'own men' indeed, the 'Gentlemen the King's Servants' mentioned in the work's published title. Far from insisting upon the power of masques to *transform* the masquers, to image their ideal potential, everything in this masque points toward the *fiction* of the masque, the fact that it is merely a dressing up for a party. The Gentlemen are not Irish at all; they have themselves learned nothing from the experience, and for the audience the revelation that is offered by their 'transformation' is only to confirm that they are what we knew they were all along, the English servants of the King" ("Embarrassing Ben" 1986, 357).

In fact, if we return for a moment to the "Ode. allhgorikh," we will find further evidence in support of Lindley's claim. We will recall that the point of departure for Jonson's poem is the question "Who saith our Times nor haue, nor can / Produce vs a blacke Swan?" with Jonson claiming that just such a bird is to be seen "dint[ing] the breast of *Tamisis*." Jonson explains the bird's black color by telling us that "Phœbus loue cause of his blacknesse is."

"The Irish Game Turned Again" { 143 }

Phœbus, we learn, "shew'd him first the hoofe-cleft Spring,"

> Neere which, the Thespiad's sing;
> The cleare Dircæan Fount
> Where Pindar swamme;
> The pale Pyrene, and the forked Mount:
> And, when they came
> To brookes, and broader streames,
> From Zephyr's rape would close him with his beames.
>
> This change'd his Downe; till this, as white
> As a whole heard in sight,
> And still is in the Brest:
> That part nor Winde,
> Nor Sunne could make to vary from the rest,
> Or alter kinde.
> "So much doth Virtue hate,
> "For stile of rarenesse, to degenerate.
>
> (17-32)

The black swan of the Thames is thus actually a white swan whose feathers have been darkened by the sun's rays in the act of Phœbus's enclosing him to protect him from harm. But the swan retains a white spot on his breast as a token of that purity of virtue that can never be entirely effaced. The black, then, is essentially an "overlay" on the natural white coat, rather as the mantle is a covering worn over the courtly garments that are revealed as, in the act of the dance, the mantle is let fall.[27] In each case, a predetermined sameness always lies beneath the superimposed marker of difference.

The mechanism of union is predicated on something like a positive version of the mechanism of the paradigm of proximity. Where proximity leads to the unexpected recognition of sameness within presumed difference, union actively seeks for sameness within difference and purports to promote the fostering of that commonality so that difference is finally elided. What we have found, however, in the case of Jonson's texts on the potential union of Ireland with Britain, is that the commonality that is sought, engaged with, and fostered is entirely bogus. The poet's engagement is not with the difficult and anxious proximity of the Other but rather with a projected mirror image of the Self, behind which the proximate Other is entirely occluded or absented. In his seminal work on the Jonsonian masque, Stephen Orgel details a 1377 court entertainment in which "a group of mummers appeared before the court and the young prince who was to be Richard II, and offered to play dice." The prince takes part in the performance, but "the dice were 'subtilly made so that when the prince shold cast he shold winne'" (*Jonsonian Masque* 1981, 19). Orgel comments that "there is [a] kind of rudimentary drama here: the fiction is that a game of chance is taking place, and the work thus contains adversaries and a central action. But chance has been defeated—the dice are loaded, and the prince always wins" (19). Much the same might be said of Jonson's court entertainment: there are no real adversaries, and the outcome is predetermined; the characters simply become what they already are.

IV.

We can see the implications of this loaded game more clearly if we turn finally to the way in which the fiction of union was deployed in the field of jurisprudence in Ireland and examine briefly the career of Sir John Davies. Davies successively held the posts of Solicitor General (1603-1606) and Attorney General (1606-19) in Ireland, and in the year prior to the performance of Jonson's *Irish Masque at Court,* he published a commentary on the Irish situation entitled *A Discoverie of the Trve Cavses Why Ireland Was Neuer Entirely Subdued.*

Davies's analysis of Ireland's relationship with the newly united Britain has much in common with Jonson's.[28] Like Jonson, Davies imagined that an English sameness might be located within Irish difference and that such an English identity might be brought to supplant entirely the Irish exterior that enclosed and circumscribed it. Thus, he confidently predicts in the *Discoverie* that, in the long term, "we may conceiue an hope, that the next generation, will in tongue & heart, and euery way else, becom *English;* so as there will bee no difference or distinction, but the Irish Sea betwixt vs" (Mm2v). Jonson imagines that the process of transformation will be brought about through the power of the king's gaze and, as Michael Neill has noted in "Broken English," Davies too imagines a process of change conceived "as dependent on ocular control" (1994, 27). Davies offers his reader a kind of Foucauldian relationship between power and surveillance:[29]

whereas the greatest aduantage that the Irish had of vs in all their Rebellions, was, *Our Ignorance of their Countries, their Persons, and their Actions:*

Since the Law and her Ministers haue had a passage among them, all their places of Fastnesse haue been discoured and laide open; all their paces cleard; & notice taken of euery person that is able to do either good or hurt. It is knowne, not only how they liue, and what they doe, but it is foreseen what they purpose or intend to do: Insomuch, as *Tirone* hath been heard to complaine, that he hadde so many eyes watching ouer him, as he coulde not drinke a full Carouse of Sacke, but the State was aduertised thereof, within few houres after. (Mm1v-2r [original emphasis])[30]

Where Jonson centralizes the king as the agent of change, for Davies the instrument of change is the law, which stands in place for the king in his necessary absence. The English legal system serves, Davies tells us, to "supply the Defect of the kings absence in euery part of the Realme; In that euery Iudge sitting in the seat of Iustice, dooth represent the person of the King himselfe" (Mm2v-3r). In noting the achievements of the first decade of James's rule, Davies stresses the importance of the fact that English law has been extended to the island as a whole.[31] "The number of the Iudges in euery Bench was increased, which do now euery halfe yeare (like good *Plannets* in their seuerall *spheares* or *Circles*) carry the light and influence of Iustice, round about the *Kingdom;* whereas the Circuits in former times, went but round about the *Pale,* like the Circuit of the *Cinosura* about the *Pole*" (Ll4r). Jonson, we will recall, envisaged a Gauntean expansion of the Pale so that it would become coterminous with the boundaries of the island as a whole. Here, Davies proposes that the extension of the English legal system within Ireland has, in effect, provided just such an expansion, since the law circuit that previously confined its remit to the Pale now includes the entire island.

Throughout his text, Davies stresses the importance of this extension of the writ of English law to the island as a whole and, more particularly, to the entire population of Ireland. He sees the failure of previous administrations to extend the benefits of English law to the Irish as having been a critical element in the perpetuation of Irish incivility, since, in Davies's view, the crucial factor in the persistence of Irish barbarity has been their recourse to the native (*brehon*) law system:

If the English Magistrates would not rule them by the Law which doth punish *Treason,* and Murder, & Theft with death; . . . why shoulde they not embrace their owne *Brehon* Lawe, which punnisheth no offence, but with a Fine or *Ericke*? If the Irish bee not permitted to purchase estates of Freeholds or Inheritance, which might discend to their Children, according to the course of our Common Lawe, must they not continue their custome of *Tanistrie*? which makes all their possessions vncertaine, and brings Confusion, Barbarisme, and Inciuility? (Q2r-v)[32]

Davies thus emphasizes as an important achievement of the previous decade the fact that "the streams of the publicke Iustice were deriued into euery part of the Kingdome; and the benefit and protection of the law of England communicated to all, aswell Irish as English, without distinction or respect of persons" (Ll3v-4r). The ultimate effect of this universal extension of the English legal franchise within Ireland will be, Davies argues, to provide a comprehensive solution to the problems presented by Gaelic Irish and also by the Old English, since where "heeretofore, the neglect of the Lawe, made the English degenerate, and become Jrish . . . now, on the other side, the execution of the Law, doth make the Irish grow ciuil, and become English" (Mm2v). For Davies, then, the power of the law is such that it can reverse the prior history of the colony. Like Spenser, Davies suggests that the Old English had been drawn into so close a relationship of proximity with the Irish that they literally became Irish; the effect of the universal extension of English law to the island is, by contrast, to cancel Irish difference completely so that the Irish can finally "become English."

The benefits of this extension of the English legal franchise, of this union of the English and Irish under the law, turn out on examination, however, to be just as illusory as the imagined incorporation of the Irish within the English courtly community portrayed in Jonson's *Irish Masque*. In fact, the extension of the English legal system into the Gaelic areas of Ulster was originally undertaken by Davies as a strategy to undermine the position of O'Neill and his northern Irish neighbor, Rory O'Donnell of Tyrconnell, after they had been restored to much of their lands by James, following O'Neill's surrender to Mountjoy in 1603. Aidan Clarke and R. Dudley Edwards note that, in an effort to contain the restored northern Irish leaders, Davies had "a proclamation issued in March 1605, which assured all persons in the realm that they were the 'free natural and immediate subjects' of the king, wholly independent of lords and chiefs, and declared that the pre-existing rights of freeholders were unaffected by the letters patent issued in connection with the post-war settlement" (1976, 193). Hans Pawlisch has observed in his analysis of Davies's career in Ireland that Davies's legal maneuverings were intended as a constitutional mechanism to facilitate the surrender of Gaelic holdings in return for common law estates. In turn, these common law tenures would strengthen the tenancies of tribal underlings as freeholders against the claims of superior chiefs like O'Neill (1985, 69).[33] In this way, Davies was instrumental in exerting pressure on the northern Irish leaders so that they and their supporters were eventually forced to flee from Ireland into exile on the continent. Once the earls had abandoned Ulster, Davies then turned the exact same legal instruments against the very landholders so recently granted the "benefits" of the English legal system. As Pawlisch notes,

> the flight of the earls left a vacuum so vast as to open up the whole of Ulster to confiscation and plantation. Davies had been instrumental in assimilating Gaelic tenures into the new state system ruled only by the sovereignty of the common law. The judicial resolutions against tanistry and gavelkind, previously employed as a constitutional mechanism to absorb an alien system of law and land tenure, were now to be transformed into a tool of confiscation that paved the way for one of the biggest plantations in Irish history. (73-74)

The legal rights extended to the Irish — heralded by Davies as the mechanism whereby they would become fully English — turn out, then, like Jonson's theatrical transformations, in the end to be entirely chimeral. Far from being a mechanism of union, they are an instrument for breaking the last vestiges of Gaelic power in Ulster and for the subsequent dispossession of the northern Irish landholders and the large-scale plantation of the province.[34] The English "identity" extended to the Irish turns out to be little more than a strategic ploy, a legal sleight of hand.

V.

The closing decade of Elizabeth's reign was a time of profound anxiety as far as England's relationship with Ireland was concerned. Ireland absorbed an enormous amount of English resources, and O'Neill's presence on the Irish scene prompted a complex web of anxieties about English and Irish identities and the connections and interstices between them — anxieties registered, as we have seen, in the work of writers such as Harington, Donne, and Shakespeare.[35] By contrast, the first decade of the seventeenth century was a time of great success for the English in Ireland, beginning with the effective defeat of O'Neill in 1601. The shift in English fortunes is registered in Captain Josias Bodley's account of his journey into the erstwhile northern Irish stronghold of Ulster in 1602-1603: "I remember . . . that we conversed profoundly about things political, economical, philosophical, and much else; and amongst other things we said that the time was now happily different from when we were before Kinsale at Christmas of last year, when we suffered intolerable cold, dreadful labour, and a want of almost everything, drinking the very worst whiskey. We compared events, till lately unhoped for, with the past, and with those now hoped for" (1843, 337).[36] In the short term, at least, the hopes of Bodley and his compatriots were easily realized, with O'Neill being admitted to surrender in 1603 and coerced into exile in 1607. The optimism of those years was intensified by the coincidence of James's accession just days before O'Neill's surrender, thus raising the possibility that the complex of relations between the various communities inhabiting the islands of Britain and Ireland could be conceived anew. The paradigm of union that arose from this confluence of events seemed to establish the basis for a novel engagement with the issue of Anglo-Irish proximity, not least because the mechanism of union provides a mirroring of the structure of proximity itself. However, what we have seen in the work of Jonson is that this English engagement with Irish proximity is, literally, a self-regarding exercise—a vacuous dream of transformation untroubled by the intense anxieties that haunt, say, Shakespeare's fragile fantasy of union in the four captains scene of *Henry the Fift*. In Davies, we see the paradigm of union in its legal aspect cynically deployed as a mechanism for furthering colonial dispossession and displacement.

Stephen Orgel, commenting on the masque form in *The Illusion of Power*, has noted that, "Viewed from outside the Banqueting House, the masque could be seen to provide the monarchy chiefly with an impenetrable insulation against the attitudes of the governed. Year after year designer and poet recreated an ideal commonwealth, all of its forces under rational control, its people uniquely happy and endlessly grateful" (1975, 88). The post-1603 era was, as we have noted, a propitious time for the recreation of "ideal commonwealths." But as the first period of Stuart rule in Britain drew on toward its disastrous climax, the insulation of the images served up to that monarchy began to appear more and more flimsy. As Roy Strong has observed in *Art and Power*, "the mirage of peace and power" (1984, 153), and "the illusion of control manifested in these spectacles was unable to bring with it any corresponding reality" (157).

Where Ireland was concerned, we will recall that Davies had confidently prophesized that within one generation there would "be no difference or distinction but the Irish sea betwixt vs" and that "thus we see a good conuersion, & the *Irish Game turned againe.*" In bringing the *Discoverie* to a conclusion, Davies expresses the hope "that *Ireland* (which heertofore might properly be called the *Land of Ire,* because the I*rascible* power was predominant there, for the space of 400. yeares together) will from henceforth prooue a Land of *Peace* and *Concorde*" (Nn4v). But for all Davies's confidence, and whatever "good conuersion" might have been effected within Anglo-Irish discourse during the Stuarts' first decades, one thing was certain: if the "Irish Game" was "turned againe," it would soon enough be for turning yet once more.

Conclusion
1641 and After

I.

Spenser's *View of the Present State of Ireland* appeared in print for the first time in 1633, included in a volume entitled *The Historie of Ireland collected by three learned authors,* compiled by the historian and antiquary Sir James Ware.[1] Ware's *Historie* was an eclectic volume, combining the *View* with works by Edmund Campion, an English-born Jesuit who spent some two years in Dublin and who was tortured and executed in London in 1581, and Meredith Hanmer, a Protestant English clergyman who served in various offices in the Irish church.[2] In placing the *View* in such mixed company, Ware expressed certain reservations about the tone and thrust of Spenser's tract, noting in his preface that "as for his worke now published, although it sufficiently testifieth his learning and deepe judgement, yet we may wish that in some passages it had bin tempered with more moderation" (2). Ware goes on to offer an analysis of the difference between his own historical moment and that of Spenser's 1590s: "The troubles and miseries of the time when he wrote . . . doe partly excuse him, And surely wee may conceive, that if hee had lived to see these times, and the good effects which the last 30 yeares of peace have produced in this land, both for obedience to the lawes, as also in traffique, husbandry, civility, & learning, he would have omitted those passage which may seeme to lay either any particular asperity upon some families, or generall upon the Nation" (2). Ware was so confident that, had Spenser lived on through the early decades of the seventeenth century his views on Ireland would have moderated, that he took on himself the task of adjusting the tone of the tract accordingly—as Ciarán Brady notes, he "silently but systematically purged Spenser's text of all its more offensive blemishes, omitting whole sections in places and changing the sense of argument in others."[3] The cumulative effect of these changes is, as Brady observes, "to rob the *View* of much of its polemical and rebarbative character" ("Crisis" 1986, 25).

For Ware, Spenser's *View* had become an anachronous text because, we might say, Anglo-Irish history was thought to have conformed, in the first three decades of the seventeenth century, to the trajectory plotted for it by Sir John Davies in 1612.[4] The country had been reduced to a peaceful state, Irish difference had been eliminated, and the various inhabitants of the island had become a single, united entity. As Ware himself observes (in what we might almost take to be an echo of James VI and I's union rhetoric): "Now we may truly say, *jam cuncti gens una sumus*" (now we are one whole people) (1633, 2). We find the same tropes of union and conjunction deployed thirteen years later in another text about Ireland, this one written by Sir John Temple, who, again looking back on the opening decades of the seventeenth century, notes that "the ancient animosities and hatred which the Irish had been ever observed to bear unto the English Nation . . . seemed now to be quite deposited and buried in a firm conglutination of their affections and Nationall obligations passed between them. The two Nations had now lived together 40 years in peace, with great security and comfort, which had in a manner consolidated them into one body, knit and compacted together with all those bonds and ligatures of friendship, alliance and consanguinity as might make up a constant and perpetuall union betwixt them" (B3v). Again, the echoes of Davies's Irish vision are striking here. But where Davies projects his image of unity into an imagined future, Temple, like Ware, reflects on an accomplished fact. Where Davies looks forward to the dawning of a harmonious age in which there would "bee no difference or distinction, but the Irish Sea betwixt" (Mm2v) the English and the Irish, Temple, by contrast, looks back to the first four decades of the Stuart reign as a period of peace and integration, in which there has been a "constant and perpetuall union betwixt them."

II.

Ware's moderated text of the *View* became the standard version for all subsequent editions until the Globe *Complete Works* of 1869, in which it was re-edited from a manuscript copy held at the British Museum.[5] But at least one seventeenth-century reader of the text found Ware's optimistic vision to be fatally misguided. This anonymous reader added marginal annotations to the *Historie,* offering a particularly telling comment opposite Ware's observation that "the troubles and miseries of the time when he wrote . . . doe partly excuse" Spenser's harshness: "for the rebellion of Oct. 23. 1641," the reader observes, "justified Spencers wisedom and deep insight into that barbarous nation" (quoted in Patterson, "Egalitarian Giant" 1992, 114).[6] For this reader, if, as Davies predicted and Ware had affirmed, the Irish game had turned and had delivered peace and uniformity of identity in the earliest decades of the seventeenth century, that vision had been shattered by a resurgence of violent Irish difference in the uprising of 1641.[7]

Turning back to Sir John Temple, we see that, by contrast with Ware, who celebrates union and concordance as the characteristics of his own time, Temple's vision is in fact nostalgic—a rueful remembrance of a lost era. For Temple—writing in 1646, in the wake of the uprising registered by Ware's anonymous annotator—the first four Stuart decades in Ireland constitute something of a golden age. And, in common with all other such visions, the image of this great era of Anglo-Irish harmony and integration is produced in retrospect, evoked from a darker time, in which the world, as Spenser himself writes in the opening to book 5 of *The Faerie Queene,*

> . . . from the golden age, that first was named,
> [Is] now at earst become a stonie one;
> And men themselves, the which at first were framed
> Of earthly mould, and form'd of flesh and bone,
> Are now transformed into hardest stone.
>
> (V Proem 2 1-5)

Temple's tract was one of a very large number of texts produced in response to the events of 1641. Temple himself served as Master of the Rolls in Ireland

and as an Irish privy councillor, and, as T.C. Barnard has noted, in his official capacity he "assisted in collecting and processing the details of Protestant sufferings and Catholic depradations" (1990, 51-52) in the wake of the uprising.[8] His text is thus very largely a catalog of horror, because he registers the outrages perpetrated against the English settler community in Ireland. For Temple, the rising was

so execrable in it self, so odious to God and the whole world, as no age, no kingdome, no people can parallel the horrid cruelties, the abominable murders, that have been without number, as well as without mercy committed upon the British inhabitants throughout the land, of what sexe or age, of what quality or condition soever they were. (B4v)

The following passage is indicative of the kind of horrors graphically documented by Temple in the work as a whole:

Some had their . . . Bellies ript up, and so left with their guts running about their heels. But this horrid kinde of cruelty was principally reserved by this inhumane Monsters for . . . Women, whose sexe they neither pitied nor spared, hanging up severall Women, many of them great with childe, whose . . . bellies they ripped up as they hung, and so let the little Infants fall out; a course they ordinarily tooke with such as they found in that sad condition . . . And sometimes they gave their Children to Swine, . . . Some the Dogges eat; and some . . . taken alive out of their Mothers bellies, they cast into the ditches. (M4v-N1r)

The great proliferation of tracts and pamphlets prompted by the uprising signaled what we might characterize as a kind of "return of the repressed," as the Irish difference that writers such as Jonson, Davies, and Ware conceived as being wholly erasable reerupted to shatter any imagined sense of quiescent unity.[9] This return of Irish difference is often figured in decidedly apocalyptic terms. The anonymous *Irelands Amazement,* for instance, offers us an account of an ominous vision witnessed in the skies over Dublin during the period of evolving crisis:

There did appear in the sight of the Jnhabitants of the City of *Dublin* a prodigious Apparition in the Firmament, the similitude whereof I shall truely demonstrate in this present Declaration; There appeared a great host of Armed men in the likenesse of horse and Foot, and according to humane supposition they seemed innumerable, when especially were notified to the eye of the aforesaid beholders of the City of *Dublin,* a traine of Artillery with great Ordnance and Field peeces, as necessary for Battell, where also was presented to the amazement of the beholders, Gunners giving fire in direfull and hideous manner, that the very likenesse of the flames thereof, strooke the beholders with great astonishment and admiration. (A2v)[10]

This celestial manifestation may well bring to mind Gerald's rather similar portentous dream vision, in which he sees "a great crowd of men all looking towards the sky as if in amazement at some strange new spectacle." Following their gaze, he sees a host of armed men wounding Christ and banishing him from his throne.[11] In each case, an eruption of suppressed difference threatens to invert and consume identity.

Similar images of voracious, consuming difference also occur throughout Temple's tract. The rebels, he tells us, had been heard to declare of Dublin "that they would burn and ruine it, destroy all Records, and Monuments of the English government; Make lawes against speaking English, and that all names given by English to places, should be abolished, and the ancient names restored" (B1r). Once Dublin had been dealt with, the rebels intended "to make a generall extirpation of all the English, root and branch; not to leave them name or posterity throughout the whole Kingdome" (H4r). Not even English farm animals were safe: "*The* Irish *in many places killed* English *Cowes and Sheep meerly because they were* English; *in some places they cut off their legges, or tooke a peece out of their buttocks, and so let them remain still alive*" (L2v; [original emphases]). The resurgence of Irish difference thus threatens the possibility of any last vestige of English identity persisting in Ireland.

But in Temple's account, the ambitions of the Irish extend even beyond this scheme utterly to eradicate any trace of Englishness from the island. Having once banished the English, Temple informs us, it was the intention of the rebels that "they would goe over into ENGLAND, and not leave the Memoriall of the ENGLISH Name under Heaven" (L3r). Thus, where Michael Neill perceptively speaks of Ireland as being "the indispensible anvil upon which the notion of Englishness was violently hammered out" in the Renaissance, here Temple imagines the re-eruption of Irish difference as potentially serving to hammer that sense of English identity utterly out of existence. If, as Neill rightly notes, "nationality can only be imagined as a dimension of difference" ("Broken English 1994, 3), then, ironically, the reemergence of an Irish difference that was considered to have been successfully suppressed threatens to destroy that newly established sense of self.

III.

There are, however, deeper historical issues at play here — issues that serve to return us from Temple's manichean world of binary differences to the more entangled realm of proximate connections. The fear that Temple registers of an Irish invasion of England was by no means an extravagant idle fantasy. Ireland, as we will recall from chapter 4, was always seen as offering a potential point of entry for hostile forces into England itself—a fear registered in Fynes Moryson's invocation of the "old prophesie": "He that will England winne, must with Ireland first beginne" (1617, 2:3)—a fear reinforced in 1601, when Spanish forces finally succeeded in landing at Kinsale.[12] The same anxiety resurfaced in the 1640s, with G. S. (a "Minister of Gods word in Ireland") warning the English: "for this your owne Backdoore of *Ireland;* for your owne sakes, have a care now in most needfull time" (B4r), and another, anonymous, writer elaborating on the same theme: "Ireland is not unfitly termed, a back doore into England: and of what dismall portendance it must needs be to you and your nation, to have the pope keeper of the keyes of your back dore, I shall not need to represent unto you. . . . If you let Ireland goe, the peace and safety of your own land and nation (it is much to be feared) will soone follow after it."[13]

These fears of a popish penetration of England, routed through Ireland, serve, of course, to emphasize once again Ireland's connection with continental Catholic Europe. This connection is explicitly noted by the author of a pamphlet entitled *More newes from Ireland: or, the bloody practices and proceedings of the papists in that kingdom at this present,* who feared that, "vnlesse some helpe and ayd be sent to relieve and rescue us, we shall vtterly be destroyed and rooted out of the Kingdome, for they surpasse us in strength and number, being ten to one, besides many supplyes from divers Papists in *England, Spaine* and *France,* to the vtter subversion and overthrow of the Protestants here, their estates, wives, and Children" (A2v).[14] The continental Catholic connection is also confirmed, we might say, by the fact that Hugh O'Neill's nephew, Owen Roe O'Neill, returned to Ireland in 1642 to take charge of the uprising, having spent the previous thirty years in Spanish military service. O'Neill was quickly followed by Thomas Preston, another Irish veteran of the Spanish forces. Patrick J. Corish has observed of O'Neill and Preston that "both of them, O'Neill especially, had over the years assimilated Spanish views on the religious nature of the European conflict as well as learning the art of war." "The same," he observes, "may be presumed to have been true of many of the other officers who returned with them" (1976, 296). Likewise, R.F. Foster notes that O'Neill's arrival on the scene serves as a reminder of the fact that events in Ireland must be perceived in a wider, continental context, being "part of the history of the later Counter-Reformation and the Thirty Years War" (1989, 90)—a fact confirmed by the arrival of the papal nuncio, Giovanni Rinuccini, in Ireland in 1645. Rinuccini would play a central role in Irish affairs over the course of the next four years.

The developing situation in Ireland was complicated, however, not just by the island's continuing continental connections. One of the tracts published in the period complained that the Irish rebels claimed "that they were for the King, and by the Kings Authority they did all that they did in *Ireland,* and so consequently all the Kings good Subjects that either resisted them in their cursed rebellion; or defended themselves in their owne Right . . . take up Armes against the King and fight against him" (T.B., W.B., O.B., and J.H., *Marleborowes Miseries* 1643, A2v). The Irish claim to monarchial fidelity registered here was, in fact, backed up with a document supposedly provided by the king himself. As Patrick J. Corish notes, on November 4, 1641, Sir Phelim O'Neill and Rory Maguire (the early leaders of the uprising) "issued a proclamation, purporting to come from Charles I, and sealed with the great seal of Scotland, authorising them to take arms in his defence" (292-93). While historians for the most part agree that the document in question was a forgery, it could, as Corish observes, "at the time . . . certainly . . . have borne the appearance of truth" (293).[15] The very fact that the rebels thought to advance the document at all indicates the complexity of the situation in Ireland and the extent to which Irish affairs were interwoven with contemporary developments in Britain.

This interweaving of events in the two islands became more clearly marked when relations between crown and parliament in London irretrievably broke down—a breakdown that was, as Keith Lindley has shown, in no small measure connected with events in Ireland.[16] As Raymond Gillespie (among others) has argued, "after the outbreak of the English civil war in August 1642," the Irish uprising became "part of the war of the three kingdoms" ("End of an Era 1986, 192).[17] In these circumstances, though the Irish may not exactly have carried out their imagined threat of launching a concerted invasion of England, many English people did suspect the king of complicity with the rebels and believed that his army had been supplemented by elements of the Catholic Irish. Lindley thus notes that, "in December 1642, the parliamentarians claimed not only that the catholics had 'a great party' in the king's army, but that there were 'sundry of the cruell and bloud-thirsty Irish papists in actuall rebellion there, that are now with the king's army.' Repeated references were, in fact, made in these early months of the English civil war to 'Irish cavaliers about his majestie,' and to his receiving 'divers papists of Ireland, some of which are indicted of high treason for their rebellion there, notoriously known to have been in actual rebellion'" ("Impact of 1641 Rebellion" 1972, 167).[18]

Fear of a Catholic Irish presence within the king's faction resonated with a general fear of the Catholic communities within England itself, who were thought by many to be in league with their Irish coreligionists. As Lindley observes, "as soon as news of the Irish rebellion reached England, suspicious eyes were turned on the catholic population at home" (155). Likewise, Michael Perceval-Maxwell has noted that, in the early stages of the uprising, "hardly a week passed without a letter being read to the Commons from an Irish official describing the treatment of Protestants, the need for help, or the links between the Irish and Catholics in England" (1994, 275). We can see anxieties of this nature registered in a text such as John Crag's verse pamphlet entitled *A prophecy concerning the Earle of Essex that now is,* in which Crag expresses his fears about those "seeming faithfull friends / Here plac'd amongst us" (A3v) and proclaims:

> packe hence those Lidgers proud papisticall,
> They still proiect, they seeke to worke our fall:
> They blaze such rumours, and su[c]h miste they cast,
> To hinder us to circumvent our haste:
> That so they may obtaine a longer time
> To bri[n]g in forces to subvert our climbe.
> Now haste with speed, now let it acted bee,
> presse souldiers now with courage bold and free. (A4r)

One way of viewing this intensification of the fear and suspicion of the native Catholic community would be to see it as indicative of a fracturing of any tentative sense of coherent unitary identity within England itself. Tom Healy offers a very fruitful reframing of the Helgersonian model of English national self-imagining when he observes that, in early modern England, "the idea of the national community may be replaced with that of the sectarian community: what predominantly fashions the imagined organisations of integrated self or state . . . is a sectarian identity founded on religious difference."[19] In the 1640s, we might say, the fissures of an English national community constructed along sectarian lines begin to show through, with the result that the differences that identity fails to incorporate become more visible and are perceived as multiplying, with the result that the imagined national community fragments and contracts.

In the tract literature of the period, this process of fracturing is associated with the Anglo-Irish connection, with a text such as *Marleborowes Miseries,* for instance, offering the subtitle *"or England turned Ireland."* Likewise, we find another tract from the period bearing the title *Englands division, and Irelands distraction. The feares and disasters of the one, The teares and distresses of the other; Being the just cause and sad occasion of both kingdomes deploration.* The author of this tract regrets the plight of "bleeding Ireland" and observes that "lamenting England is now somewhat near the like wofull condition. Difference in opinion hath bred difference in affection, and both these have wrought civill contention" (A4r). The linkage of the two territories in this way suggests that the reeruption of difference in Ireland is perceived as serving directly to contribute to the proliferation of difference within England itself.

IV.

Some of the complexities we have been tracking here are neatly registered in John Milton's tract on Ireland, generally referred to by critics as the *Observations on the Articles of Peace.* The unifying thrust of this critically convenient title serves to mask the complexity of the document itself and of its political and historical narrative. The full title of the publication reads as follows:

Articles of Peace, Made and Concluded with the Irish Rebels, and Papists, by James Earle of Ormond, for and in behalfe of the late King, and by vertue of his Autoritie. Also a Letter sent by Ormond to Col. Jones, Governour of Dublin, with his Answer thereunto. And A Representation of the Scotch Presbytery at Belfast in Ireland. Upon all which are added Observations.

As the full title indicates, the pamphlet offers a curious amalgam of documents: the text of the peace treaty concluded between the Protestant, royalist, Anglo-Irish James Butler, Earl of Ormond, and the Catholic-dominated Irish Confederacy, which had gradually emerged in the wake of the 1641 uprising; a letter sent by Ormond to the Governor of Dublin, soliciting his support for the heterogenous alliance thus effected; a policy document issued by a group of Belfast Presbyterians objecting to various actions of the parliamentarians in London, notably the trial of Charles I; and Milton's response to all three of these texts.[20]

The simple description of the constituent components of the pamphlet set out here should serve to indicate the entangled complexity of the situation Milton sought to address. Milton does, indeed, give some attention to the native Irish and attempts to characterize them as straightforwardly barbarous. Thus, he uses, for instance, the twenty-second article of the treaty as an index of an Irish lack of civility. This article, he notes, "obtains that those Acts prohibiting to plow with horses by the Tayle, and burne oates in the Straw, be repeald; anough if nothing else, to declare in them a disposition not onely sottish but indocible and averse from all Civility and amendment, and what hopes they give for the future, who rejecting the ingenuity of all other Nations to improve and waxe more civill by a civilizing Conquest, though all these many yeares better shown and taught, preferre their own absurd and savage customes before the most convincing evidence of reason and demonstration: a testimony of their true Barbarisme and obdurate wilfulnesse to be expected no lesse in other matters of greatest moment" (47). As Thomas Corns has suggested, Milton's presentation of Irish farming procedures here is meant to play on an English sense of civilizational superiority—Irish practices "could be perceived as evidence of primitivism: who but a savage couldn't manufacture a functional collar, especially after he'd seen one being used? [It offers] proof, too, of idiocy: who but a fool would ruin a good horse by mistreating it in this way?" (1990, 125-26).

We can see, then, that Milton's text clearly finds a place within the general tradition of writing on Ireland initiated by Gerald of Wales, and his sense of the savagery of the Irish is confirmed in his extraordinary estimate of the number of settlers killed during the 1641 uprising, when he speaks of "the blood of more then 200,000 . . . assassinated and cut in pieces by those *Irish Barbarians*" (49). As in the case of Spenser's *View,* however, Milton's *Observations* are less concerned with the native Irish than with those other elements within the Irish populace whose positioning serves to disrupt any possibility of viewing Ireland within clearly colonialist terms. A large proportion of his text is dedicated to an attack on Ormond, whose own location—as indicated by my characterization of him above as "Protestant, royalist, Anglo-Irish"—was peculiarly convoluted. Ormond does not easily fit with any of the standard categories that might have been employed to anatomize the Irish populace. He was of member of Spenser's hated Old English stock, but, unlike many of his Old English fellows, he was a confirmed Protestant. Apart from a brief engagement with the parliamentarians, he was loyal to the crown, and, on leaving Ireland in 1650, he entered into the personal service of Charles II. After the Restoration, he served Charles as Lord Lieutenant in Ireland. Ormond's own personal history is thus woven across the complex set of interrelations and fracturings between the islands of Britain and Ireland that prevailed at mid-century.

Equally symptomatic of the complexities of identity and fragmentation of the period is the fact that by far the longest section of Milton's *Observations* concerns itself not with the native Irish nor with Ormond but rather takes up the issue of a group of Scots Presbyterian settlers in Ulster who had objected to some of the policies of the English parliamentarians. Milton attempts to discredit the Scots by collapsing them into a kind of savage Celtic constituency, treacherous to their English sponsors: "By thir actions we might rather judge them to be a generation of High-land theevs and Redshanks, who beeing neighbourly admitted, not as the *Saxons* by merit of thir warfare against our enemies, but by the courtesie of *England* to hold possessions in our Province, a Countrey better then thir own, have, with worse faith then those Heathen, prov'd ingratefull and treacherous guests to thir best friends and entertainers" (64-65). Milton's Presbyterians are thus not unlike Spenser's Hugh O'Neill—that "frozen snake" who, "releived by the husbandman sone after he was warme, begane to hisse and threaten daunger even to him and his" (*View* 1949, 168). Much as Milton tries in this passage to stress the civilizationally inferior Celtic heritage of the Belfast Presbyterians, it is, however, important to recognize that there were also very strong connections between the Ulster group and their religious counterparts in England. Thus, as Merritt Hughes has noted, the majority of the members who had been purged from the English Parliament were also Presbyterians, and members of the Ulster community saw themselves as being clearly aligned with this group.[21] Milton's attack on the Presbyterians thus locates itself as much within contemporary English politics and the fragmenting of consensus within the English political community as it does within an Irish colonial narrative and again serves to indicate the close intertwining of the politics of both realms.

In this context, then, what Anglo-Irish proximity signals in the middle decades of the seventeenth century is less the unexpected emergence of sameness within desired difference than it is a general fragmentation of identity. What the 1640s offer us is another turn of Davies's Irish game. If Davies and Ware imagined that the mechanism of proximity could be used to collapse difference into an imposed identity, then 1641 and its aftermath clearly indicated not only that within proximity difference persists, but, indeed, that such difference had the potential to unravel identity itself.

Certainly, there were those in the 1640s who continued to hanker after a clearly marked and wholly stable binary distinction between the Irish and the English. Thomas Emitie, author of a tract entitled *New Remonstrance from Ireland* (1642), was just such a person. Emitie worried about the presence in England of what he called "Irish Renegadoes" and was deeply troubled by the fact that it might be difficult for the average English person to detect them. Helpfully, he provides "infallible Notes whereby they may be knowne and distinguished, together with the places they usually frequent, and many other things remarkable" (title page). In essence, he offers a four-part strategy, exhorting his readers to "observe these directions following":

1. Cause them to pronounce any word which hath the letter H in it, as Smith, Faith, &c which they cannot do, not one among an hundred, but pronounce Smith, Smit; and Faith, Fait.

2. To know their Religion, cause them to say their prayers, as the Pater Noster and the Creed, in English, which they cannot well do.

3. Vncover their bosomes, most of them weare Crucifixes, especially the women.

4. Concerning their false passes, separate them asunder, and so examine them. (B4r-B4v)

What Emitie seeks to establish here is a world in which, in the absence of immediately obvious markers of distinction, difference can none the less still be established. Covert signs of otherness can be brought to the surface (crucifixes uncovered, linguistic variances registered), and these signifiers can be seen as combining to provide a coherent and stable taxonomy of ethnic identity. But the very fact that Emitie feels these rituals of interrogation and exposure to be necessary in itself affirms the difficulty of fixing identity in an Anglo-Irish context. If our examination of Renaissance writing about Ireland indicates anything, it is surely that such distinctions simply cannot so easily be established; Irish difference cannot be mapped so clearly as to disjoin the Irish wholly from the English, nor can Irish difference be wholly mastered through the process of being mapped. For the English, we might say, Irish difference is finally at one and the same time both insufficient and excessive. Emitie's confidence is misplaced: the Irish can neither so easily be fully recognized, nor, being recognized, can they be so easily mastered.

V.

It is at this point in the Anglo-Irish historical narrative that I draw my study to a close. The remainder of the seventeenth century presents its own particular challenges and complexities, but I would hope that, by extending my analysis as far as this point, I have fulfilled my objective of tracking the trope of proximity across the course of the English Renaissance. My own feeling is that this textual and cultural history could well be extended, to register the relevance of the notion of proximity to later periods of Irish history. In the 1680s, for example, Anglo-Irish connections became, if anything, even more entangled than they had been forty years earlier, as the decisive battle between James II and William of Orange was fought on Irish soil, between two international armies—"Irish, French, Germans and Walloons" on one side, "versus Irish, English, Dutch, Germans, and Danes" on the other, as R.F. Foster puts it (148). And, as Charles Kingsley makes clear to us, as late as the middle decades of the nineteenth century, the proximate positioning of the Irish continued to intrude itself problematically into the English mind.[22] The consolidation of a native sense of Irish nationalism in the closing decades of that century served to complicate matters still further—especially, I would argue, since much of the cultural apparatus of that ideology of nationalism was constructed by a group of intellectuals whose own positioning as Anglo-Irish Protestant nationalists was itself profoundly liminal. There is much work to be done in all of these areas and, again, I look forward to the possibility that the present series might serve as a forum for such analysis.

Henry Louis Gates notes in his 1991 essay "Critical Fanonism" that "one of the signal developments in contemporary criticism over the past several years has been the ascendancy of the colonial paradigm" (457). Reacting in part against such a proliferation of analyses grounded in the colonialist model, Gayatri Spivak has argued against the extension of such analysis to situations that are not, historically, colonialist in nature. Spivak has thus observed that "the critique of imperialism is not identitical, and cannot be identical, with the critique of racism. Nor is our own effort to see the identification of the constitution of race within first world countries, identical with the problem of capitalist territorial imperialism in the context of the eighteenth-and nineteenth-centuries" (McRobbie 1985, 7). The question of the appropriateness of extending a colonialist analysis to the Irish situation is rather more complex, in that Ireland's experience has indeed been colonial in certain crucial senses, and, to a significant extent, it even continues to be colonial. For all that, as I have endeavored to demonstrate here, Ireland's experience has never been exactly consonant with that of other colonized territories. The Norman-English were involved in Ireland for centuries before the European colonization of the New World even got underway. Likewise, at the other end of the historical scale, the British government has remained in control of part of the island of Ireland long after Macmillan's "wind of change" has swept almost all of Britain's other colonies to independence.[23] These realities alone should serve to alert us to the fact that Ireland's situation has never been quite the same as that of other colonized territories elsewhere.[24] Therefore, to insist that the relationship between the Irish and their neighbors is *no more* than colonial — as David Cairns and Shaun Richards have done in declaring that "the reality of the historical relationship of Ireland with England [is of] a relation of the colonized and the colonizer" (1988, 1) — is to fail to appreciate the fundamental complexity of the Anglo-Irish situation.

I chose John Davies's phrase "but the Irish sea betwixt us" as my title for this study in order to try to indicate the essential structure of that complexity. There is a kind of fruitful (if unwitting) duality in the phrase: Davies himself clearly wishes to suggest that *only* the Irish sea lies between the two territories and their people, so that they are separated by a barrier that is readily permeable and that, in Davies's view, is finally wholly transcendable.[25] We could, however, also take that "but" in Davies's phrase as indicating not the inconsequential nature of the divide but rather as affirming its ineluctable existence, stressing that the two territories are indeed separated from each other, inhabited by populations who are possessed of different languages, legal traditions, patterns of living, and cultures. In this sense, Davies's Irish sea takes on the importance which Spenser's Eudoxus affords it when, in resisting Irenius's conflation of the Irish and the Scots, he observes, "We all knowe righte well that they are distinguished with a great sea rvnninge betwene them" (83). It is important, I feel, to hold both views in sight: to recognize the presence of both identity and difference; of continuity and separation. This has been my point in laying stress on the proximate, in emphasizing that these cultures are both like and unlike — simultaneously both familiar and alien to each other.

It seems to me that this complex dialectic of identity and difference has never fully been appreciated by any of the communities living in the islands of Britain and Ireland. All of these communities have, for the most part, pledged their allegiance to identities that are perceived as being distinctive and mutually exclusive and that, again as Michael Neill has noted, "can only be imagined as a dimension[s] of difference" (1994, 3). As a closing thought for this study of the Anglo-Irish past, I would suggest that perhaps an engagement with the complex dual mapping of difference and identity among these groups might well be a necessary part of the extremely difficult task of effecting a lasting agreement among these islands' divided peoples on what the future of their communities' communal lives should be.[26] Only in these circumstances might we anticipate a fruitful British, Irish, and Anglo-Irish future — a future different from the tragic shared history of our deeply troubled past.

Notes

Introduction

1. Alan Armstrong notes, in a special issue of *Literature & History* dedicated to "Historicizing Shakespeare," that "since 1980, a rising historicism has swept the field, to the extent that, as the editor of a prominent Shakespeare journal recently noted, nearly four-fifths of the essays now submitted for publication there are historically-based studies" (1996, v).

2. The great volume of this work would seem to negate Edward Said's observation (in *Culture and Imperialism*) that "it is generally true that literary historians who study the great sixteenth-century poet Edmund Spenser . . . do not connect his bloodthirsty plans for Ireland, where he imagined a British army virtually exterminating the native inhabitants, with his poetic achievement or with the history of British rule over Ireland, which continues today" (1993, 5). For extremely useful bibliographies of materials relating to Spenser and Ireland, see Willy Maley, "Spenser and Ireland: A Select Bibliography" (1991) and "Spenser and Ireland: An Annotated Bibliography, 1986-1996" (1996).

3. I am very grateful to Anne Fogarty for providing me with a copy of this issue of *IUR.*

4. A second volume of essays on the same topic, edited by Nicholas Grene and Dennis Kennedy, is anticipated to emerge from the 1997 "Shakespeare and Ireland" conference, held at Trinity College Dublin.

5. These interests are, of course, also registered in Greenblatt's seminal early article: "Invisible Bullets."

6. The significance of the particular chronological markers will be set out in chapter 1.

7. Two new books by Willy Maley, as well as books by Chris Highley and David Baker, were just on the point of being published as this book was being prepared for the press. I very much regret that it was not possible for me to include consideration of these works here.

8. I acknowledge, of course, that "share" may be a rather anodyne term, especially when one is talking about a "political heritage" that very often includes a history of oppression, dispossession, and displacement. The broader point I am making, however, is that the populations of the two islands have, by the Renaissance era, already established a longstanding set of relationships, not all of which are oppositional or antagonistic.

9. See "Of Mimicry and Man: The Ambivalence of Colonial Discourse" in *The Location of Culture* (1994), especially pp. 86, 89.

10. My particular critical location here may be indicative of a fault line that has run through the historicist project of the last decade or so. Whereas New Historicism has tended to see power as totalizing and as always serving ultimately to contain subversion and disjunction, Cultural Materialism, by contrast, has focused on the productive possibilities of irreconcilable contradictions and aporias that can be locatable within discourses of power. Thus, Alan Sinfield has observed that "cultural materialists read for *incoherence*" (*Cultural Politics* 1994, 38 [emphasis added]). It is precisely the incoherencies of English colonialist discourse on Ireland that interest me—by contrast with the clear binary coherence that some other critics find in such discourse. In this sense, I would entirely agree with Willy Maley's assertion (in "Shakespeare, Holinshed" [1997]) that, "while it is important to record and tabulate instances of discrimination against the so-called margins, it is equally valuable to look for fissures within the putative metropolis" (29).

11. See Hadfield and Maley's introduction to *Representing Ireland* (1993) and Neill's "Broken English and Broken Irish" (1994).

12. Maley has noted, in "Shakespeare, Holinshed," that "too often, criticism of English views of Ireland confines itself to the early modern period, overlooking the first phase of English colonialism that preceded the arrival of Spenser and others" (29).

13. For an assessment of this volume, see my review in *Irish Studies Review* (1995).

14. Neill himself actually writes "in the drama of the period," but I think his observation is more broadly applicable.

15. One text that has not found a place in my account is John Ford's *Perkin Warbeck*. For a masterful analysis of the location of this text in the broad British history of the time, see Willy Maley's "Fording the Nation" (1997).

16. See Ranajit Guha and Gayatri Chakravorty Spivak, eds., *Selected Subaltern Studies* (1988)—especially Spivak's "Subaltern Studies: Deconstructing Historiography" and Guha's essays on methodology. See also Spivak's "Can the Subaltern Speak?" (1988).

17. See Peter Lombard, *De Regno Hiberniae* (1857); Geoffrey Keating, *Foras Feasa ar Éireann* (1902-13); Philip O'Sullivan Beare, *Historiae Catholicae Iberniae Compendium* (1903); and David Rothe, *Analecta Sacra Nova et Mira de Rebus Catholicorum in Hibernia* (1884).

18. See O Riordan's *The Gaelic Mind and the Collapse of the Gaelic World* (1990) and Caball's comprehensive review of this text in *Cambridge Medieval Celtic Studies* (1993). See also Dympna Callaghan's chapter on Ireland in *Shakespeare Without Women* (forthcoming; my thanks to Prof. Callaghan for providing a copy of this material).

19. Steven Ellis has mapped out some of the problematics of using the terms "British" and "British Isles" to include Ireland in his introduction to *Conquest and Union*. He usefully notes that "the very fact that no single word, analogous to Japan or Indonesia, exists to describe the group of islands dominated by Britain and Ireland is itself significant: the very phrase 'the British Isles' also draws attention to an arrested process of state formation" (1995, 3).

20. To cite just four major collections: R.G. Asch, ed., *Three Nations: A Common History? England, Scotland, Ireland and British History c. 1600-1920* (1993); Brendan Bradshaw and John Morrill, eds., *The British Problem, c. 1534-1707: State Formation in the Atlantic Archipelago* (1996); Steven G. Ellis and Sarah Barber, eds., *Conquest and Union:*

Fashioning a British State, 1485-1725 (1995); and Alexander Grant and Keith J. Stringer, eds., *Uniting the Kingdom? The Making of British History* (1995). Willy Maley has reviewed the first two of these volumes in *History Ireland.* For two early articles which served to map out some of this territory, see J.G.A. Pocock, "British History: A Plea for a New Subject" (1975) and "The Limits and Divisions of British History: In Search of the Unknown Subject" (1982). Willy Maley and David Baker are currently planning what will undoubtedly by a very valuable collection of new essays on the topic of Renaissance literature and the British Problem.

1. "White chimpanzees"

1. In fact, there *is* a very small, but significant, black community native to Ireland. The question of how this community is represented is itself interesting. The complexities of that representation can be caught in the nickname of the Dublin-born soccer player, Paul McGrath, popularly known as the "black pearl." A similar set of incongruities can be traced through the career of Phil Lynott, a black rock musician from Ireland. See Shay Healy, dir., *The Rocker: A Portrait of Phil Lynott* (1996).

2. Some of the ambiguities inherent in Ireland's position are aptly caught by Clair Wills in "Language Politics, Narrative, Political Violence," when she observes that the history of colonialism in Ireland throws up contradictions which "stem primarily from the fact that Ireland is not one of Europe's 'others.' Is the Irish nationalist movement, the Easter Rising and its aftermath to be classed among the varieties of nineteenth-century Western nationalisms, or as a non-Western postcolonial movement for liberation, like the one it influenced in India?" (1991, 21). Wills goes on to note, as I have here, the difficulties presented by "the absence of the visual marker of skin colour difference" as a sign of colonial distinctions. See also Conor Gearty's perceptive comment: "Irish nationalism poses [to Britain] a threat not of liberation, but of dismemberment" (1996, 28).

3. See Alan Sinfield, *Faultlines: Cultural Materialism and the Politics of Dissident Reading* (1992).

4. Reviewing *Writing Ireland* in *Textual Practice*, Willy Maley has complained of "the stultifying dualism, the stupefying metaphysics, of certain forms of literary theory" (1989, 293). Likewise, Andrew Hadfield notes (in *Spenser's Irish Experience*) that "the very easy polarity of 'native' and 'colonizer' betrays the existence of a more complex history" (1997, 4).

5. The play in which Caliban appears—Shakespeare's *Tempest*—has often been seen as a text in which we find simultaneously inscribed a narrative of English colonial ventures in the New World and in Ireland. See, for example, Paul Brown, "'This Thing of Darkness I Acknowledge Mine'" (1985). See also Dympna Callaghan's forthcoming work on the play.

6. Eagleton does qualify his observation by noting that "however fundamentally indifferent colonialism may be to the nature of the peoples it does down, the fact remains that a particular people is in effect done down *as such*" (1990, 30). But, again, he sees this as a *universal* quality of colonialism, not as something that is specific to the Irish situation. His position does appear to have shifted somewhat in recent times, as he writes in *Heathcliff*

and the Great Hunger that "if the Irish had been black, unintelligible and ensconced in another hemisphere, their presence might have proved rather less unnerving" to the British (1995, 128).

7. For a very useful anthology of essays on revisionism and Irish historiography, see Ciarán Brady, *Interpreting Irish History* (1994); for important individual contributions to the debate, see Brendan Bradshaw "Nationalism and Historical Scholarship in Modern Ireland" (1989); Terry Eagleton "A Postmodern Punch" (1994); Seamus Deane "Muffling the Cry for a Hungry Past" (1995); Willy Maley "Varieties of Nationalism" (1996); and Steven G. Ellis, "Writing Irish History" (1996). Bradshaw's article is reprinted in Brady's collection.

8. I should make clear that it is specifically what I take to be Said's skewed interpretation of the *Irish* colonial situation that I am taking issue with here, not his analysis of colonial relations in general. Said's paradigm of "contrapuntal analysis" has very usefully been applied to early modern English texts about Ireland by Michael Neill, in "Broken English" (1994). For an assessment of Said's work within the broad theoretical framework of studies in colonialism, see Robert Young, *White Mythologies,* chapter 7.

9. On "hybridity," see Homi Bhabha, "Signs Taken for Wonders" in *The Location of Culture* (1994). See also Andrew Hadfield, "Translating the Reformation: John Bale's Irish *Vocacyon,*" in Bradshaw, Hadfield, and Maley, eds., *Representing Ireland* (1993), p. 52. I discuss the relevance of Bhabha's theories of colonialism to the Irish situation at section III below.

10. As will become apparent, my deployment of the term "proximity" here has much in common with Jonathan Dollimore's use of the term in *Sexual Dissidence* (1991).

11. Thus, for example, John Morrill notes of the middle decades of the seventeenth century that "more than a third of the land surface of Ireland moved from Irish Catholic to English Protestant ownership, and as a result the proportion of land held by those of recent English origin and who were effectively monoglot, anglophone and Protestant rose to almost 80 per cent" ("British Problem" 1996, 34). On the tendency of a certain strand of revisionist historiography to suppress or ignore "the catastrophic dimensions of the Irish past" and thereby "to marginalise a central dimension of the Irish historical experience and, indeed, in some cases virtually to write it out of the record," see Brendan Bradshaw, "Nationalism" (1989) pp. 338-41 (quotations here taken from pp. 340, 341).

12. On the appropriation of black history as a metaphor for oppression within the white community, see bell hooks's critique of the white suffragist movement in the United States in chapter 4 of *Ain't I a Woman: Black Women and Feminism* (1982). I wish to thank Charonne Ruth for drawing this material to my attention.

13. In terms of a broader critical project, I would agree with Eve Kosofsky Sedgwick's assertion that "a tiny number of inconceivably coarse axes of categorization have been painstakingly inscribed in current critical and political thought: gender, race, class, nationality, sexual orientation are pretty much the available distinctions" and that "every single theoretically or politically interesting project of postwar thought has finally had the effect of delegitimating our space for asking or thinking in detail about the multiple, unstable ways in which people may be like or different from each other" (1994, 22, 23).

14. The question of nomenclature is always fraught when one is writing about Ireland. As Hadfield and Maley have observed, "every neutral expression or anodyne appellation conceals a complex cultural reality" (1993, 2). I will take up this issue at greater length in chapters 2 and 3.

15. For an anthology of early modern prose texts about Ireland, see James P. Myers, ed., *Elizabethan Ireland: A Selection of Writings by Elizabethan Writers on Ireland* (1983). For an extremely useful more general annotated anthology of English texts about Ireland, see A.D. Hadfield and J. McVeagh, eds., *"Strangers to that Land": British Perceptions of Ireland from the Reformation to the Famine* (1994).

16. The particular significance of the years 1541 and 1641 will be registered in the analysis that follows.

17. Quinn's publications for the years 1932 to 1976 have been cataloged by Alison M. Quinn and P.E. Hair at pp. 303-309 of K.R. Andrews, N.P. Canny, and P.E. Hair, *The Westward Enterprise* (1978).

18. Hiram Morgan does, however, seem to be willing to go further than this. In "Mid-Atlantic Blues," he observes, "my first publication about the plantation attempt of Sir Thomas Smith in Ulster . . . followed the perspective developed by Quinn and Canny. However, having since researched the origins of the Nine Years' War which saw the completion of the Elizabethan conquest, I am convinced the colonialist approach is no longer tenable" (1991-92, 54).

19. Steven Ellis also makes the following point, in contrasting Ireland with Africa: "Ireland is only a few miles distant from Britain, whereas the nearest British colonies were a few thousand miles away. Thus the colonists arrived in much larger numbers in Ireland, over a far longer period, and their impact has been much more profound, lasting over eight centuries. This is a far longer time span than even the oldest European settlement in Africa, the Cape colony established in 1652" ("Writing Irish History" 1996, 10).

20. Barnard notes that "a passage on the long route between Cork and Pembroke could be had for 3s., rising with the quality of accommodation to 7s. 6d. or 16s." (1990, 43). On the significance of the transatlantic sea journey, see also Anthony Pagden's comment in his introduction to the Penguin edition of Bartolomé de Las Casas's *Short Account of the Destruction of the Indies* that "for Las Casas, as for so many other Europeans, the crossing to America came to seem something of a rebirth" (1992, xviii). On the perils of the crossing, see the extracts from the letters of Eugenio de Salazar included in J.H. Parry, ed., *The European Reconnaissance: Selected Documents* (1968), pp. 348-64.

21. See also Las Casas's own comment in the opening "Synopsis" of his book that the New World experience "seems . . . to overshadow all the deeds of famous men of the past, no matter how heroic, and to silence all talk of other wonders of the world" (*Short Account* 1992, 3).

22. For an analysis of this text, see Willy Maley, "'Another Britain'" (1995).

23. See, for example, the following passage from Columbus: "During that time I walked among the trees, which were the loveliest sight I had yet seen. They were green as those of Andalusia in the month of May. But all these trees are as different from ours as day from night and so are the fruit and plants and stones, and everything else. It is true that some

trees were of a species that can be found in Castile or could compare with them" (66). On this aspect of Columbus's writing, see Mary Campbell, *Witness* (1988), chapter 5.

24. See also Brady's "Court, Castle and Country" in Brady and Gillespie, eds., *Natives and Newcomers* (1988), p. 28.

25. Neill offers the interesting suggestion that, even when the colonialist paradigm appears to be in the ascendant, the harshest measures advocated may in fact, paradoxically, be driven by an assimilationist goal: "For these propagandists Irish difference was something that simply *ought not to exist;* it was an unnatural aberration that the English were morally bound to extirpate" ("Broken English" 1994, 5).

26. The Kildare Rebellion took place in 1534. In *The Chief Governors,* Brady observes that this year "deserves its place as a date of crucial importance in the Irish historical canon, but not as tradition would have it, as the starting point of an ever more triumphant Tudor conquest; it marked rather the beginning of a long series of misunderstandings, miscalculations and failures which were to constitute Ireland's political tragedy in the sixteenth-century" (1994, 1).

27. For further comments on the complexities of the deployment of the term "colony" in an Irish context, see Andrew Hadfield, "The Spectre of Positivism?" (1988), p. 10.

28. A more complex argument about the European context of the Anglo-Irish relationship than the one I set out in these pages could also be made and Brendan Bradshaw has gone some distance toward suggesting some of the outlines of this argument in "The Tudor Reformation." Bradshaw points out that "the major dynamic of early modern European state formation" was "the assimilation of peripheral territories by their cores under the impulse provided by Europe's consolidating Renaissance monarchs striving to transmute their disparate feudal patrimonies into centralised unitary realms by arrogating to themselves the absolute sovereignty vested in the Roman Emperor in the Civil Code of Justinian in accordance with the maxim of humanist jurisprudence, *rex est imperator in regno suo*" (1996, 42). Bradshaw sees Wales as conforming to this model, while Ireland resists. Thus, in a sense, Ireland offers a convoluted anomalous instance: conforming neither to the colonial type nor the European centralizing expansionist paradigm.

29. The source of the quotation Morgan reproduces is the *Calendar of the Carew Manuscripts Preserved in the Archiepiscopal Library at Lambeth, 1515-1624,* i, 308.

30. J.G.A. Pocock notes, in "The Atlantic Archipelago," that "non-Roman Ireland became Christian just as soon as did the ex-Roman provinces which were its neighbors, and can be said to have shared their Christian or European history" (1996, 187).

31. For a comprehensive account of Ireland and the Reformation, see Alan Ford, *The Protestant Reformation in Ireland, 1590-1641* (1987). For an interesting firsthand account of the attempt to introduce the reformed faith, see Johan Bale, *The Vocacyon of Joha[n] Bale to the bishoprick of Ossorie in Irelande* (1533; 1990).

32. For a useful comparison between the course of the Reformation in Wales and in Ireland, see Bradshaw, "Tudor Reformation" (1996).

33. My reference here is to an important series of articles on Ireland and the Reformation published in the *Journal of Ecclesiastical History:* Nicholas Canny, "Why the Reformation Failed in Ireland: *Une Question Mal Posée*" (1979); Karl Bottigheimer, "The Failure of

the Reformation in Ireland: *Une Question Bien Posée*" (1985); and Steven Ellis, "Economic Problems of the Church: Why the Reformation Failed in Ireland" (1990). Canny's article is in part a response to Brendan Bradshaw's "Sword, Word and Strategy in the Reformation in Ireland" (1978).

34. Bottigheimer has likewise observed that "the Reformation need not and might not have failed, and to assume otherwise is to attribute to Ireland a pervasive 'character' which it may, indeed, have acquired, but which was itself a changeable and changing product of other circumstances" ("Failure," 207).

35. Some of these ideas are set out by Thomas Healy in "Selves, States, and Sectarianism in Early Modern England" (1995). For the most part here, however, I am drawing on unpublished work that will eventually form part of a book on sectarian identity. I am extremely grateful to Professor Healy for making this material available to me.

36. Ireland's connectedness to a greater continental Catholic world can also be seen in the establishment in this period of various Irish colleges throughout Europe. Such institutions were established at, for example, Salamanca, Douai, Paris, Louvain, and Rome. See Helga Hammerstein "Aspects of the Continental Education of Irish Students in the Reign of Queen Elizabeth I" (1969). Edmund Spenser protests in *A View of the Present State of Ireland* about the Irish "sendinge theire younge men abroade to . . . vniuersities beyond the sea as Reymes doway Lovaine and the like" (1949, 222).

37. Morgan also offers, at pp. 219-21 of *Tyrone's Rebellion*, a sustained comparison of the Irish war with other, contemporary, European conflicts. See also his "Hugh O'Neill and the Nine Years' War in Tudor Ireland" (1993).

38. When he died in Rome, in 1616, O'Neill was buried at San Pietro de Montorio, beside the graves of his allies Hugh and Rory O'Donnell.

39. In stressing the "manichean" aspect of Fanon's theory I am, I realize, providing a rather reductive account of his conception of colonialism. Far from viewing the colonial situation purely in such strictly binary terms, Fanon clearly recognized the relentless reciprocity binding the colonizer and the colonized. As I will emphasize below, what Homi Bhabha's work serves to do is to bring out this aspect of Fanon's theorizing. As Bhabha himself has observed in the foreword to his Pluto Press edition of *Black Skin White Masks*, Fanon's sense of "the jagged testimony of colonial dislocation, its displacement of time and person, its defilement of culture and territory, refuses the ambition of any 'total' theory of colonial op[p]ression" (1986, x).

40. For an interesting and extremely suggestive account of the history of the Manichean paradigm of civility and barbarism within Anglo-Irish discourse, see Seamus Deane's "Civilians and Barbarians" in *Ireland's Field Day* (1986).

41. Henry Louis Gates has thus observed, in "Critical Fanonism" that, "if JanMohamed made of Fanon a Manichean theorist of colonization as absolute negation . . . Bhabha cloned, from Fanon's *theoria*, another Third World poststructuralist" (1991, 465). Gates's article provides a very useful introduction to the theoretical debate generally, as does Benita Parry's "Problems in Current Theories of Colonial Discourse" (1987).

42. Drawing on Bhabha's theories, David J. Baker has provided one of the clearest articulations of this position: "Colonial authority imposes a schema of essentialist categories

on an apparently undifferentiated populace, and insists that the difference thus created in-here in the natives themselves. . . . Colonialist discourse would thus seem to be as fully hegemonic as any instrument of power can be. And yet . . . as total as this colonial power is, it is not capable of insuring the stability of its own discourse. It is not capable of main-taining the distinctions it imposes" ("'Wildehirissheman'" 1992, 39).

43. For an extremely interesting deployment of Dollimore's theoretical frame in an analysis of the connections between homo/sexuality and colonialism in an Irish context, see Eibhear Walshe, "Sexing the Shamrock" (1996).

44. On Wilde's transgressive cultural positioning, see also Alan Sinfield, *The Wilde Century* (1994), and, more generally, Neil Bartlett, *Who Was That Man?* (1988).

45. For a further interesting analogous instance, see Robert Young's comment on the anomalous positioning of the European Jewish community within the framework of anti-Islamic and anti-Arab feeling: "In this context, the Jews come to represent the Orient within, uncannily appearing inside when they should have remained hidden, outside Eu-rope" (1990, 139).

2. "Ad Remotissimas Occidentis Insulas"

1. See also Kiberd's more recent volume, *Inventing Ireland* (1995).

2. The issue of naming is always a difficult one in an Irish context. Traditionally, the twelfth-century incursion into Ireland from the island of Britain has been known as the "Norman Invasion." However, recently, a number of historians have sought to provide a greater clarification of the make-up of the forces which came to Ireland in this period. As R.R. Davies has noted, "many of the leaders of the invasion might be classified as 'Nor-man,' 'Anglo-Norman,' 'Anglo-French' or 'Cambro-Norman' (all of them terms employed by historians); but the ordinary troops and above all the settlers were overwhelmingly English, with a good sprinkling of Welsh and Flemings" (1990, 13). While some histori-ans have moved in the direction of "hyphenated" identifying labels, such as Cambro-Nor-man, others (especially John Gillingham and Michael Richter) have argued for seeing the newcomers to the island simply as English—see, for instance, the uncompromising title of Gillingham's contribution to Bradshaw, et al.'s *Representing Ireland* (1993): "The Eng-lish Invasion of Ireland." In that article, Gillingham argues that "the best reason for saying that the invaders were English is that this is what contemporary narrative sources say they were" (30). Part of the problem here stems from the grounds on which identity is to be predicated. In an era predating the rise of what we typically regard as national entities and identities (Benedict Anderson's "imagined communities"), it is difficult to say how such identities can easily be assigned within a rapidly changing political and social situation. I have opted here to refer to the newcomers as "Norman-English" because, although I feel that Gillingham's and Richter's arguments are persuasive, it nevertheless seems to me that simply to use the term "English" masks the instability of identity and allegiance that pre-vails in this period. As Gillingham himself, for instance, observes regarding Gerald, he "began as pro-English, went first pro-Welsh, then pro-French" ("Invasion" 1993, 33). By retaining "Norman" in labeling the newcomers, I hope to maintain a sense of the mixed

history of this group and the general significance of indeterminate "hypenated identity" in the period.

3. Once again, the question of naming is an issue here. Traditionally, Gerald has been known by the Latin name "Giraldus Cambrensis"—Gerald of Wales—and Gerald's family did have strong Welsh connections. However, as John Gillingham notes, "Gerald never called himself Cambrensis" ("Invasion," 33), and his transitory allegiance to Wales indicates only one phase of Gerald's career as an ambitious churchman. Gillingham thus advocates the use of Gerald's family name "de Barri" (or, in Latin, "Barrensis"), which "is how he referred to his own brother and . . . is a form which does not, as it were, identify the whole man with just one stage of his career" (33). What is interesting here again is not so much the specific question of what Gerald should, or should not, be called but the fact that, as at a group level, so also at an individual level, the issue of identity and allegiance is problematic and uncertain.

4. For a "family tree" that outlines the relationship between Gerald and those who ventured to Ireland in the 1160s and 1170s, see Robin Frame *Colonial Ireland, 1169-1369* (1981), p. 5.

5. Likewise, R.R. Davies notes that "when Diarmait mac Maél na mBó, king of Leinster 1047-72, gave asylum to the sons of Harold Godwinson after 1066 and, quite possibly, employed Norman mercenaries in his service, such acts could well have initiated a relationship of dependence between Leinster and England a century before the 'conquest' of 1169" (1990, 5).

6. See also Elizabeth Rambo's observation, in *Colonial Ireland in Medieval English Literature,* that "before the devastating Viking raids of the ninth and tenth centuries, Irish monks had gained a far-reaching reputation for erudition and sanctity in England and on the Continent; even after the Vikings had disrupted the system in Ireland, exiled Irish monks in Europe were known for their high standard of learning" (1994, 73-74).

7. See also Said's comment in *Orientalism* that, from the seventh century onward, "Europe was shut in on itself: the Orient . . . was culturally, intellectually, spiritually *outside* Europe and European civilization, which, in Pirenne's words, became 'one great Christian community, coterminous with the *ecclesia. . . .* The Occident was now living its own life'" (1979, 71; Said's quotation is from Henri Pirenne *Mohammed and Charlemagne,* trans. Bernard Miall [New York: Norton, 1939], p. 283).

8. Lewis Thorpe, in his introduction to the Penguin edition of Geoffrey of Monmouth's *History,* notes strong similarities in the scope and content of the opening chapters of Geoffrey, Bede, Nennius, and Gildas (53).

9. The quotations throughout this chapter will be taken from John O'Meara's (1982) translation of the *Topographia Hibernica: The History and Topography of Ireland* and from A.B. Scott and F.X. Martin's translation of the *Expugnatio,* included in their annotated parallel text *Expugnatio Hibernica: The Conquest of Ireland.* Where a particular point of analysis requires reference to the Latin original I will, in the case of the *Topographia,* quote from J.F. Dimock's edition in volume 5 of the *Giraldi Cambrensis Opera.* In the case of the *Expugnatio,* such quotations will be taken from Scott and Martin's own Latin text.

10. Text in italics indicates chapter headings.

11. According to Bede, "there are no reptiles [in Ireland], and no snake can exist there; for although often brought over from Britain, as soon as the ship nears land, they breathe the scent of its air, and die. In fact, almost everything in this isle confers immunity to poison" (46). Gerald makes explicit reference to Bede's comments on Ireland at chapter 2 of section 1 of the *Topographia*.

12. In the original (emphasis added throughout): "Secure sub divo, securi nudo in marmore *dormimus*. Non auram vel algore penetrabilem, vel æstu periculosam, vel corruptione pestiferam *formidamus*. Et quod spirando *includimus*, et quo continenter *includimur*, benigna salubritate fœderatur" (70) and "De laudabilibus *hic* quarundam rerum defectibus. Sunt et aliarum quarundam rerum, sicut et vermium, defectus *hic* laudabiles. Terræmotus *hic* nunquam: vix semel in anno tonitruum audies. Non *hic* tonitrua terrent, non fulmina feriunt" (72).

13. Edward Said notes that the Orient is "one of [Europe's] deepest and most recurring images of the Other. In addition, the Orient has helped to define Europe (or the West) as its contrasting image, idea, personality, experience" (*Orientalism* 1979, 1-2).

14. See below, chapter 3, p. 68.

15. "Gens igitur hæc gens barbara, et vere barbara" (152) is the Latin original for "this people is . . . a barbarous people, literally barbarous."

16. For a comprehensive survey of the history of the concept of the "barbarian" from the classical period through the Middle Ages, see W. R. Jones "The Image of the Barbarian in Medieval Europe" (1971).

17. William of Malmsbury makes the same argument about the Irish: "The soil of Ireland produces nothing good, because of the poverty or, rather, the ignorance of the cultivators, but engenders a rural, dirty crowd of Irishmen outside the cities; the English and French, on the other hand, inhabit commercial cities and have a more civilized way of life" (quoted in Bartlett [1982], 159). William's views were not confined to the Irish but extended to the Celtic peoples generally. See John Gillingham, "The Beginnings of English Imperialism" (1992), p. 396 ff.

18. Gerald actually describes the Irish as "gens silvestris" (*Topographia*, 151).

19. On the wild man, see also Hayden White, "The Forms of Wildness: Archaeology of an Idea" in *Tropics of Discourse* (1978), and Richard Bernheimer, *Wild Men in the Middle Ages* (1952).

20. Spenser, in *A View of the Present State of Ireland*, makes a similar cultural concession, writing of the poems of the Irish bards: "I haue Cawsed diuerse of them to be translated vnto me that I mighte understande them and surelye they savored of swete witt and good invencion but skilled not of the goodlie ornamentes of Poetrye yet weare they sprinkled with some prettie flowers of theire owne naturall devise" (1949, 127).

21. See W.R. Jones "The Image of the Barbarian" (1971), pp. 390-92.

22. Note, however, that Gillingham argues that William of Malmsbury effects in this period the breaking of the link between Christianity and civility. Gillingham notes that William discards "the familiar concept of barbarian as equivalent to pagan and formulat[es] a new one — one which allowed for the possibility of Christian barbarians" ("Beginnings" 1992, 398); see also Gillingham's "Foundations of a Disunited Kingdom" (1995), pp. 59-60.

23. For a brief account of some of Gerald's reforming activities, see Lewis Thorpe's introduction to his translation of Gerald's Welsh texts, pp. 12-15.

24. In 1155, the Norman-English faction at Rome succeeded in convincing the British-born Adrian IV (Nicholas Breakspear) that the situation in Ireland was such that Henry II should be authorized to enter the country on the Pope's behalf and initiate a program of reform. Nothing came of this at the time, but in 1172 Alexander III renewed the papal approval for the Norman-English incursion into Ireland. For an introduction to the background of these issues, see Martin "Diarmait" pp. 50-52 and Bethell "English Monks and Irish Reform." For a more extensive account of the religious issue in an Irish context in this period, see J.A. Watt *The Church and the Two Nations in Medieval Ireland.* We might note here a parallel between Gerald writing, in the twelfth century, in a period of significant reform within the Church, and his early modern successors writing in a period when that Church had split, leaving the Irish and English at opposite sides of a religious divide. The Reformation of the sixteenth century to some extent served the same ends for his successors as the twelfth-century reform movement served for Gerald himself.

25. John of Salisbury made the same argument about the Welsh, observing that they "are rude and untamed; they live like beasts and though they nominally profess Christ, they deny him in their life and ways" (quoted in Gillingham, "Beginnings," 397).

26. In the original: "O quoties eadem hora et incontinenti vel sequitur vel prævenit, vel etiam inaudito more sanguinolentum divortium ipsam interrumpit desponsationem!" (167).

27. Said makes a similar point with respect to orientalism: "Since Mohammed was viewed as the disseminator of a false Revelation, he became as well the epitome of lechery, debauchery, sodomy, and a whole battery of assorted treacheries, all of which derived 'logically' from his doctrinal impostures. . . . the Orient and the Oriental, Arab, Islamic, Indian, Chinese, or whatever, become repetitious pseudo-incarnations of some great original (Christ, Europe, the West) they were supposed to have been imitating" (*Orientalism* 1979, 62).

28. These chapters are based on a sermon that Gerald preached before a synod in Dublin during Lent in 1186 (see O'Meara's introduction to Gerald's *History & Topographia* [1982], p. 135 n. 68).

29. Gerald makes direct references to Solinus twice in the *Topographia*—at pp. 35 and 68.

30. In the original, "verba de Deo sana subjunxit" (101)—literally, "he added [to his original exhortation] some sound words concerning God."

31. W.L. Warren notes the importance of this extended shift of focus in the narrative, as he observes in an article on "John in Ireland" that "Gerald was prone to digressions, but it is clear that he sees this not as a lengthy excursus but as an integral part of his book" (1976, 19).

32. "Hunc filium suum non in orientem sed in occidentem, non in Saracenos sed in Christianos . . . transmisit" (236).

33. "Ut sicut Hibernicis Angli, sic et Anglis Hibernici simus" (80).

34. For an extremely interesting article on Céitinn's Irish history and his views of the Norman-English, see Brendan Bradshaw, "Geoffrey Keating: Apologist of Irish Ireland" (1993).

3. "They Are All Wandred Much: That Plaine Appeares"

The epigraph is quoted in Sir John Davies' *Discoverie of the Trve Cavses Why Ireland Was Neuer Entirely Subdued* (1612; 1969), Aa3v-Aa4r. Davies informs us that it is an "olde Verse made, which I finde Written in the White Booke of the Exchequer, in a hand as auncient as the time of King E*dward* the third" (Aa3v).

1. It should be noted that Gerald's views were kept in circulation in the preprint era also. As Elizabeth Rambo notes in *Colonial Ireland in Medieval English Literature,* "It was Ranulph Higden . . . who spread Giraldus's views most liberally . . . Higden's midfourteenth-century *Polychronicon,* one of the most widely circulated works of the time, was . . . translated twice into Middle English, by John Trevias (1385-87) and later by another, anonymous writer" (1994, 36).

2. In 1586, Camden was a cofounder of the Society of Antiquaries, which met regularly for the next fifteen years "as a private organization, independent of any official authority, to read papers on English institutions, customs, and topography" (Helgerson 1992, 127). On Ireland and early modern historiography, see Andrew Hadfield, "Briton and Scythian" (1993).

3. Hadfield notes (in *Spenser's Irish Experience*) that "Gerald provided a picture of the Irish which was echoed throughout sixteenth-century chronicles, accounts, political analyses, and government reports on the Irish" (1997, 26).

4. On the history and provenance of this phrase, see Art Cosgrove, "Hiberniores Ipsis Hibernis." Cosgrove provides a very interesting example of the nineteenth-century appropriation of the cliché for romantic, nationalist ends, in citing a poem from Thomas Davis (though, in truth, it reads more like the work of Jem Casey), which includes the lines:

These Geraldines! these Geraldines! not long our air they breathed,

Not long they fed on venison, in Irish water seethed;

Not often had their children been by Irish mothers nursed,

When from their full and genial hearts an Irish feeling burst!

The English monarchs strove in vain, by law, and force and bribe,

To win from Irish thoughts and ways this "more than Irish" tribe. (1979, 4)

5. Steven Ellis has indicated some of the problems with the "surrender and regrant" scheme by contrasting Ireland with Wales: "A promising start was made, reducing racial tensions . . . . Yet progress was slow. Ireland was four times the size of Wales, which had taken seven years to assimilate administratively to England; Gaelic Ireland had yet to accept Tudor sovereignty; its peoples had no natural ties with the king, unlike the Welsh; and the extension of royal government in Ireland was not accomplished, as in Wales, by a corresponding increase in the size of the bureaucracy there" ("Tudor State Formation" 1995, 56).

6. This view of colonialism is an enduring one. In his *Discourse on Colonialism,* Aimé Césaire quotes from Carl Siger's *Essai sur la Colonisation* (Paris, 1907): "The new countries offer a vast field for individual, violent activities which, in the metropolitan countries, would run up against certain prejudices, against a sober and orderly conception of life, and which, in the colonies, have greater freedom to develop and, consequently, to affirm their worth. Thus to a certain extent the colonies can serve as a safety valve for modern society. Even if this were their only value, it would be immense" (Césaire, *Discourse* 1972, 20).

7. The career of Richard Boyle, Earl of Cork, provides the most spectacular example of how an Englishman of modest means could make his fortune and secure accelerated advancement by settling in Ireland. As Nicholas Canny has observed in his study of Boyle, "his meteoric rise from Kentish obscurity to enormous wealth, an Irish peerage and membership of the English privy council was without parallel in his own generation." Canny notes that Boyle himself "acknowledged that by moving to Ireland he had sidestepped the barriers to social advancement which existed in England" (*Upstart Earl* 1982, 41, 65).

8. Hiram Morgan summarizes the brief life span of the colony as follows: "By the spring of 1572, Thomas Smith had collected up to eight hundred men at Liverpool. Due to delays, however, many drifted away. It was not until 31 August that he landed in the Ards with a force of just over one hundred men. . . . Smith made little headway against the Irish. After some temporary success, Smith's position slowly deteriorated until he was killed on 20 October 1573" ("Colonial" 1985, 264).

9. See Michael MacCarthy-Morrogh, *The Munster Plantation.*

10. The question of terminology here is, as ever, contentious (see chap. 2, n. 2). Indeed, the issue of what to call the descendants of the original settlers and their early modern successors has led to an acrimonious exchange of footnotes between Nicholas Canny and Ciarán Brady (over the course of a series of articles in *Past and Present*). Karl Bottigheimer appends a useful "Note on Nomenclature" to his "Kingdom and Colony" (see also Cosgrove, "Hiberniores" 1979, passim). I will follow Bottigheimer and Canny here in adopting the term "Old English" to refer to the descendants of the Norman-English. Canny traces the term to the Old English themselves, noting a 1568 letter to Cecil "referring to the loyal Palesmen as the Queen's 'old ancient faithfull English subjects who never revolted sens the conquest'" (*Formation* 1970, 31, citing an anonymous letter to Cecil, February 1, 1568, S.P. 63/23/29). Brendan Bradshaw, by contrast, sees the origins of the deriving from the Irish: "The categories of *Sean-Ghaill* (Old English) and *Nua-Ghaill* (New English) [were] devised to distinguish the medieval from the early modern colonial settlers" ("Geoffrey Keating" 1993, 182). Canny notes that the term "Old English" "became popular even among the Old English themselves in the seventeenth century" ("Reviewing *A View*" 1996, 258).

11. The persistence of a sense of the attractiveness of Irish systems and culture for the English is registered by Edmund Tremayne, an Englishman sent to Ireland in various capacities in 1569 and 1573. In one of a series of reports to the authorities in London written between 1571 and 1575, he observed that "the sweetness and gain of the Irish government hath been such that it hath rather drawn our own nation to become Irish than any way wrought the reformation of the Irish to reduce them to English law" (quoted in Brady, *Chief Governors* 1994, 140, from BL Add. MSS, 48015, fol. 274).

12. The Old English themselves also produced a great many treatises and other texts about Ireland—Andrew Hadfield notes (in *Spenser's Irish Experience*) that the Old English responded to the New English attack by producing "a series of submissions sent directly to the Privy Council, arguing that they were the best suited to govern Ireland and that the forms of government they had evolved, rather than the aggressive solutions often advocated by the New English would enable a peaceful transformation from a divided to a

united country" (1997, 23). Again, further work needs to be done on this area, which lies outside the scope of the present study. For an interesting account of one Old English writer, see Colm Lennon, *Richard Stanihurst: The Dubliner, 1547-1618* (1981). Lennon's biography includes a translation of Stanihurst's *De Rebus in Hibernia Gestis.*

13. Hadfield notes (in "English Colonialism") that "the emergence of a fragmented colonial milieu complicated the problem of stable identity for those who were to form the basis of an 'Anglo-Irish' tradition" (1993, 70).

14. Pauline Henley produced the first book-length study of Spenser and Ireland in her still-valuable *Spenser in Ireland* (1928). Henley was among the first to realise that "Spenser was not always the unpractical weaver of magic fancies, but could become on occasion the ruthless apostle of coercive government, the grimly precise exponent of the statecraft of Elizabethan England" (7). Willy Maley has noted the recent tendency whereby "Ireland is at once the source and the destination of so much Spenser criticism that it threatens to overrun Spenser studies" ("Spenser and Scotland" 1996, 2) and offers a very useful corrective, by attempting to locate Spenser more clearly in a broader, British and Anglo-Irish context.

15. A number of other New English texts exist that serve as useful companion pieces to Spenser's Irish work—most notably, Sir William Herbert's *Croftus: sive de Hibernia Liber* (1992) and Richard Beacon's *Solon His Follie* (1594; 1996). For a discussion of Herbert and Beacon (and some other New English writers) in the context of Spenser's writings, see Andrew Hadfield, *Spenser's Irish Experience,* pp. 33-50. Willy Maley sets out some useful parallels between Beacon and Spenser in his review of Clare Carroll and Vincent Carey's edition of *Solon* (1996/97), p. 44.

16. Jean Brink, in "Constructing the *View of the Present State of Ireland*" (1990), has questioned whether the *View* can, indeed, be securely attributed to Spenser. I follow Christopher Highley in believing that, despite "the paucity of 'bibliographical evidence' linking *A View* with Spenser," nevertheless, "persuasive internal evidence for Spenser's authorship" can be found in the tract (Highley, in press). For a useful discussion of the generic status of the *View* and the status of the voices it presents, see John M. Breen, "Imagining Voices" and Hadfield's Response to Breen in "Who Is Speaking" (1994/95).

17. See above, chapter 2, pp. 47-48.

18. All quotations from *A View of the Present State of Ireland* will be taken from Rudolf Gottfried's text included in the Johns Hopkins variorum edition of *The Works of Edmund Spenser.* Gottfried's text is derived from the Ellesmere 7041 manuscript, held at the Huntington Library, Santa Monica, California.

19. See also Hadfield, "Briton and Scythian," and Maley, "Spenser and Scotland," pp. 8-11.

20. Jones and Stallybrass have observed that "one of the main aims of the English in the late sixteenth century was to disarticulate the Irish from the Spanish" (159)—a necessary denial, we might say, of Ireland's place within a greater European world and, from a more pragmatic point of view, an attempt to stop the Spanish from providing military assistance to the Irish.

21. "[The] two terms *change* and *degeneration* were not indicators of separate and distinct ideas. They were interchangeable. The mere passage of time, day to day, year to year, was enough to ensure the maintenance of the process" (Hodgen 1964, 265).

22. See *Topographia* pp. 101-102. See also above, chapter 2, pp. 46-47.

23. See Canny "Identity Formation" (1987), p. 169. Citing this passage he suggests that in Spenser's assessment "the Anglo-Norman invaders of Ireland . . . had been only half-civil and certainly had not been capable of promoting a civilizing mission."

24. Jones and Stallybrass note that the Old English are "here imagined as all male" (163).

25. Lane was a Northamtonshire soldier who fought in Ireland during the Nine Years' War, remaining on in Munster, where he served as master of horse to Sir Henry Brouncker, President of the province from 1604 to 1607. His unpublished poetic text on Ireland, *Newes from the holy ile,* was likely composed around 1619. I am very grateful to Alan Ford for providing me with a copy of his transcription of the text. Details of Lane's career are derived from Dr. Ford's "Reforming the Holy Isle: Parr Lane and the Conversion of the Irish" (in press).

26. The *OED* glosses the verb as "To render fierce, exasperate." For the related adjective "effere," the dictionary gives "excessively wild or fierce," significantly citing Hooker's translation of Gerald in Holinshed: "Let us returne to the historie of this effere . . . nation."

27. See Ford, "Reforming the Holy Isle."

28. On Spenser's more general relationship with Irish, see Clare Carroll, "Spenser and the Irish Language." Carroll registers Spenser's "ambivalent attitude to Irish language and literature—poised between its preservation and destruction" (1990, 290).

29. Martin Elsky notes the prevalence in the early modern period of theories which conceive of speech as an image of the mind, "the idea was popular enough to find its way into behaviour manuals such as Hoby's translations of *The Courtier,* Henry Peacham's *Compleat Gentleman,* where the idea is explicitly attributed to Cicero's *De oratore,* and Richard Brathwait's *English Gentleman.* Given the widespread currency of the idea, it is not surprising that it appears in a work that tries to square English with Lily's *Grammar,* John Hewes's *Perfect Survey of the English Tongue.* Grafting English *sermo* onto the conventionally established categories of the exterior Latin discourse, Hewes reminds his reader of the moral nature of inner discourse governing speech: '*Hominis character eius est oratio.* Speech (saith one) is the Character of a man, or the expresse image of his heart or minde'" (1989, 65).

30. See *OED* "affected" def. III.1. The *OED* quotes Donne's *Biathanatos*: "To confesse, that those times were affected with a disease of this naturall desire of such a death" (38).

31. Spenser's program is rather bizarrely described by Sheila T. Cavanagh as "a meticulously designed outline for peace" ("Such Was" 1986, 35), reflecting Spenser's "compassionate analysis of the situation" (29).

32. See Canny, "Debate" (1988). See also Brady's "Reply" in the same issue of *Past and Present.*

33. By contrast, Hadfield sees the *View* as "a fractured work which pulls the reader in multitudinous ways—something its author was probably all too painfully aware of"

(*Spenser's Irish Experience* 1997, 71). Likewise, Walter Lim writes of "the inability of the text to sustain its relentless imperial logic" (1995, 60).

34. Hadfield provides a subtly nuanced reading of the generic relationship between the two texts in *Spenser's Irish Experience*. He has also usefully observed (in "Political Discourse") that "the *View*, as a political tract designed to persuade powerful individuals to adopt a particular policy cannot admit the possibility that nothing will stop the inevitable onset of chaos. *The Faerie Queene*, as a literary work under no such propagandist obligation, tells another story" (1993, 194).

35. All quotations from the *Faerie Queene* will be taken from Thomas P. Roche and C. Patrick O'Donnell's Yale University Press edition of the text (1978).

36. See also *A View*, pp. 159-63. Spenser had come to Ireland in the first instance as Lord Grey's secretary. For a useful discussion of Spenser and Grey see Richard A. McCabe, "The Fate of Irena" (1978). See also Ciarán Brady's entry on "Arthur Grey de Wilton" in A.C. Hamilton, ed., *A Spenser Encyclopedia* (1990), pp. 341-42.

37. Shiela T. Cavanagh has very usefully argued that "the obstacles impeding the titular knights and other proponents of virtue in the epic are often located in sections of Faeryland which appear to form boundary zones correlating to Ireland, where civil and sexual temptations compete with 'the good' for the allegiance of both inhabitants and travellers" ("'Licentious Barbarism'" 1996, 268-69). For a study of the Irish colonial context of book 2 of the poem, see Stephen Greenblatt's seminal "To Fashion a Gentleman: Spenser and the Destruction of the Bower of Bliss," in *Renaissance Self-Fashioning* (1980).

38. Hadfield has also argued that the nature of Spenser's presentation of Ireland in book 5 necessitates a rereading of certain elements of the books that precede it. In particular, he notes that the characterization of Irena's realm as "'the salvage island,' forces the reader to re-read incidents in the narrative so that their significance in the light of later developments be considered; in other words, we are asked to go back, reconsider and qualify our earlier judgements. The reader is therefore invited to regard the representation of Ireland in terms of images of the savage and savagery which have preceded Book V (these include 'the wilde and salvage man' who tries to rape Amoret in IV, iv, Sir Satyrane and Artegall himself), as well as in terms of the images which make up a substantial part of Book VI (the salvage man, the salvage nation and the brigands who destroy the pastoral idyll)" ("Sacred Hunger" 1995, 31).

39. Gilbert ruled Munster by martial law from 1569 to 1571. His savage campaign was chronicled by Thomas Churchyard as part of his *Generall Rehearsall of Warres* (1579). In July 1575, Essex despatched a raiding party to Rathlin Island, which put to death the entire population. Grey likewise ordered the killing of the entire Irish and Spanish garrison at Smerwick in 1580 (see *A View*, pp. 159-63). Brendan Bradshaw notes that a "combination of atrocity *ad terrorem* and blatant disregard for the conventions of the code of honour was to recur with dismaying regularity down to the end of the sixteenth century" ("Nationalism" 1989, 338).

40. The glib was an Irish hairstyle in which the fringe was grown long and combed straight down, to cover the eyes. The mantle was a one-piece, loose-fitting cloak. Jones and Stallybrass note that "most colonizing tracts fixate on the Irish mantle as a garment

that masks and veils men and women alike" (165), and Hadfield notes that, in Spenser's view, "the mantle enables its wearer to oppose ordered society more effectively, whether as a common lawbreaker or as a dangerous rebel against Crown forces. Coupled with the 'glib,' both serve to disguise the wearer and avoid the adoption of a stable identity which can be recorded by the civil and military authorities who desire to impose a civilized order" (*Spenser's Irish Experience,* 104). On Malengin and the mantle, see Neill, "Broken English" (1994), p. 26. On the significance of the mantle as a traditional form of Irish dress, see also the discussion of Jonson's *Irish Masque at Court* in chapter 5. Also see *A View,* pp. 99-102. Irenius notes inter alia that when a thief "hathe rune himself in to that perill of lawe that he will not be knowen he either Cuttethe of his glibbe quite by which he becommethe nothinge like himselfe, or pulleth it so lowe downe over his eyes that it is verye harde to discerne his thevishe Countenaunce" (102). See also p. 151: "He is a flyinge enemye hidinge him self in woodes and bogges from whence he will not drawe forthe but into some streighte passage or perilous forde wheare he knowes the Armie muste nedes passe." We might note in passing that, like Gerald, Spenser here invokes the tradition of the *sylvestres homines* in describing the Irish (see chap. 2, pp. 46-47).

41. Hodgen notes that such ideas "could be found either in Genesis and the hexameral literature, or in the 'contemptus mundi' of the Hebrew prophets; in the verdict of some of the ancient Greeks that man was an altogether calamitous thing, or in the works of other pagan writers, who played with the notion that the world was old and tired, that its productivity in ideas and inventions was on the wane" (1964, 263).

42. It should in any case be noted that, in the closing decades of the sixteenth century, Spenser was writing at precisely the time when this trope of natural and ineluctable degeneracy was being vigorously challenged—particularly in the works of Louis Le Roy and Jean Bodin. Both these writers were very popular among English intellectuals and authors in the closing decades of the sixteenth century. Gabriel Harvey, for instance, noted that "you cannot stepp into a schollar's studye . . . but (ten to one) you shall litely finde open either Bodin's *de Republica* or Le Royes *Exposition*" (quoted in Hodgen 283).

43. For an alternative to the reading of the Radigund episode in relation to Ireland than that set out in the following pages see Brendan Bradshaw "Edmund Spenser on Justice and Mercy" (1987).

44. Jones and Stallybrass offer a fascinating reading of Spenser's suppression of the long-standing association of the Scythians with degenerative effeminacy in order to displace "the fantasy of a degenerate masculinity . . . from the barbarian [Irish] onto the . . . Old English" (163).

45. See also Shiela T. Cavanagh, "'Licentious Barbarism,'" pp. 278-79.

46. It may be worth noting in this regard that though Artegall's submission is presented in the text as a contractual obligation arising out of his having accepted Radigund's terms of combat, submission specifically to degendering is not the only option available to Artegall. Terpin has already made this clear to him:

But if through stout disdaine of manly mind,
Any her proud obseruance will withstand,

Vppon that gibbet, which is there behind,
She causeth them be hang'd vp out of hand;
In which condition I right now did stand.
For being ouercome by her in fight,
And put to that base seruice of her band,
I rather chose to die in liues despight,
Then lead that shamefull life, vnworthy of a Knight.

(V iv 32)

47. Clare Carroll suggests an "Irish etymology" for Radigund's name: "'rade' in Irish means to [']grant,' or 'bestow', while 'guna' means 'women's clothes'" (1990, 183).

48. The emergence of the Gaelic Irish into a *female* character in the narrative is none too surprising, given the already noted conflation of gender and degeneracy in Spenser and, more generally, the fact that, as William Palmer has observed, "during the sixteenth- and early seventeenth-centuries racial and gender prejudices intersected as English men fused their images of disorderly women and rebellious Irish men, and blamed Irish women in part for why Ireland was so difficult to govern" (1992, 699). Holinshed observed that Irish women were capable of "mak[ing] their husbands to become changlings as being turned from a sober mood to hornewood" (quoted in Palmer 1992, 701-702). It is also worth noting here Jonathan Dollimore's observation that "the woman was once (and may still be) feared in a way in which the homosexual now is—feared, that is, not so much, or only, because of radical otherness, as because of an inferior resemblance presupposing a certain proximity" (1991, 253).

49. See Hadfield, "Serena and Irena" (1996), especially p. 292.

50. In her article on representations of Elizabeth as an Amazon, Schleiner includes a map dated 1598, which figures Elizabeth as England, brandishing a sword against the armada. As Schleiner points out, the Amazonian connection is definitely established in the illustration by Elizabeth's "single, bare breast: Amazons supposedly removed one breast so as to handle a bow more conveniently" (1978, 167). On the deployment of Amazonian imagery with respect to Elizabeth, see also Louis Adrian Montrose, "Shaping Fantasies" (1983), especially pp. 75-78.

51. Andrew Hadfield provides an incisive extended analysis of the Irena episode in chapter 5 of *Spenser's Irish Experience.* Hadfield sees Irena as "an empty figure who stands for a blank Ireland" and observes that "Grantorto, the usurping Catholic tyrant, actually represents more of Ireland than Irena herself does" (156).

52. See, among others, Judson (1945), chapter 10.

53. Richard A. McCabe has usefully observed that Spenser, in his work, seeks to effect "the dissociation of Ireland from the Irish" (1989, 122).

54. I am much indebted to William Flesch for helping me to understand the complexities of Artegall's encounter with Grantorto.

55. There are also complex paradoxes inscribed within the relationship between Spenser's deployment of Chrysaor as a symbolic object and the mythological narrative of the sword's origins, as Andrew Hadfield notes, "Ironically, Astrea gives Artegall the sword of Jove . . . which he used to suppress the revolt of the Titans. She is seemingly unaware

that Jove overthrew his father in classical legend, thus marking one of the crucial stages which caused the degeneration of the world" ("Serena and Irena," 294).

56. See *A View,* pp. 147-58.

57. Harry Berger also registers the continuity between the two books, seeing them as, in some respects, a single unit: "Though strikingly different from each other, [they] are both unfolded within the ambience of the poet's contemporary world. They reflect not merely the process of imagination as such but the problems of the Renaissance poet trying to make sense of the world around him" (1988, 216).

58. See also Berger, *Revisionary Play,* pp. 217-18.

59. For instance, the hermit who attempts to cure Serena and Timias, who "The name of knighthood . . . did disauow, / And hanging vp his armes and warlike spoyle, / From all this worlds incombraunce did himslefe assoyle" (VI v 37 7-9), and Pastorella's father, who grows disillusioned with Court life and returns "to [his] sheepe againe" (VI ix 25 7). On the general trope of rejections of/by the court, see Martin Elsky, *Authorizing Words* (1989), pp. 188-90.

60. Hadfield has astutely noted that "*Colin Cloutes Come Home Againe* is a colonial poem of hybrid identity; Colin can preserve his English voice only at the cost of choosing exile and no longer being recognisably English, having to define himself against both hostile natives and the central culture of the court" (*Literature* 1994, 190). See also Hadfield's *Spenser's Irish Experience,* pp. 16-17. On the theme of Spenser and exile, see John Breen, "*The Faerie Queene,* Book I and the Theme of Protestant Exile" (1996) and, more generally, "Representing Exile" (1996).

61. "In pastoral," William Empson writes, "you take a limited life and pretend it is the full and normal one" (1968, 115). Likewise, Willy Maley observes that "colonial ventures can represent a retreat from the political, into pastoral, but as pastoral they constitute an exemplary site of political resistance" ("Spenser and Scotland" 1996, 2). See also Louis Montrose, "Of Gentlemen and Shepherds: The Politics of Elizabethan Pastoral Form."

62. Likewise, Judith Anderson argues that, in book 6, "the antique ideal becomes more simply a fiction, a poet's golden image detached from the realities of time and place to which it was moored in the Proem to Book II" (1987, 213).

63. Canny also interprets the incident as an explicit figuring of the failure of the poetic project, observing that Colin's breaking of his pipes symbolises Spenser's "decision to bring his epic to a precipitate conclusion, presumably because there was no longer any heroic accomplishment to be celebrated" ("Reviewing *A View*," 253-54).

64. See also Lupton (1990), pp. 134-35. Hadfield notes that the description of the Brigants' hidden retreat is reminiscent "of a crann[ó]g (a fortified lake dwelling) used successfully by Hugh O'Neill in the Nine Years War" (*Spenser's Irish Experience,* 184).

65. Hadfield notes in *Spenser's Irish Experience* that "the symbiotic relationship between grand metaphysical speculation and current political problems, so frequently established at crucial junctures throughout *The Faerie Queene,* dictates the ending of the poem as it brings the reader back into the sphere of contemporary political problems, factional disputes, and the search for patronage" (174).

66. On the political geography of Spenser's "Arlo Hill," see Patricia Coughlan, "Local Context" (1996), pp. 326-28.

67. See *Spenser's Secret Career,* p. 116. Also, see above, chapter 2, pp. 56-58.

4. "The Remarkablest Story of Ireland"

1. Elizabeth herself, in her correspondence with Lord Mountjoy, refers to O'Neill as the "Arch-Traitor"—see, for example, Moryson (2:201, 219).

2. As in the case of the *View,* there is some dispute as to whether the "Briefe Note of Ireland" is the work of Spenser. In his biography of the poet, Judson disputes Spenser's authorship and concludes that "perhaps this document—really three documents, different from each other in tone—is the joint work of several refugees, and its endorsement [by Spenser] the result of Spenser's having brought it to England along with Norris's dispatches" (1995, 200).

3. Quoted in Hiram Morgan, *Tyrone's Rebellion* (1993), p. 167, from PRO SP 63/174, 62 (1). A number of O'Neill's contemporaries also fall into this elusive, liminal category, including Thomas Butler, the Old English Earl of Ormond, who exercised palatinate jurisdiction in the period over the county of Tipperary. Chris Highley has noted of Ormond, in "Spenser and the Bards" (in press), that though he was "educated at the Protestant court of Edward VI, and a cousin and personal favorite of Elizabeth," he "negotiated a cultural position for himself at the intersection of English and Gaelic spheres," which made his true attachments often difficult to discern. Morgan notes that Butler "was as devious a customer as O'Neill and the question-marks over his conduct in the Nine Years' War are indelible. We need answers about his failures of generalship at certain crucial points . . . about his attitude to the New English settlers and about the peculiar escape of his estates from major damage" ("Tom Lee" 1993, 158). See also Baker, "Charting Uncertainty" (1996), pp. 88-90, and Ciarán Brady, "Thomas Butler, Earl of Ormond"(1989). Unlike O'Neill, Butler managed to survive intact both the Nine Years' War itself and the shifting politics of the English court, despite being accused of treason by the English "soldier, marauder, squatter, debtor, poseur, pamphleteer, mediator, conspirator and jailbird" Captain Thomas Lee (Morgan, "Tom Lee," 132). Lee himself, as Morgan's description of him indicates, is also an interesting figure. He presented himself as a go-between serving English interests in Ireland by maintaining a channel of communication with O'Neill and the rebel Irish. His ambiguous position is celebrated in Marcus Gheeraedts's 1594 portrait, in which he appears as an odd amalgam of English and Irish identities. As James P. Myers has noted, Lee's "pointed beard, his red military cape and white-and-delft-blue floral undergarment distinguish him readily as an Elizabethan; his high-peake morion, long spear, round shield strapped to his back, and his shoeless feet and hoseless legs mark him as an Irish chieftain" ("Early English" 1988, 11). For additional material on Lee's portrait, see Morgan, pp. 142-43, and Brian de Breffny, "An Elizabethan Political Painting" (1984). For other instances of Anglo-Irish liminal figures, see John Morrill, "The Fashioning of Britain" (1995), pp. 24-26, and the (unpublished) material by Vincent Carey, Tom Connors, and Jane Ohlmeyer to which Morrill draws attention.

4. No full-length scholarly biography of O'Neill has been published in recent times. By far the best study of O'Neill currently available is Morgan's *Tyrone's Rebellion: The Outbreak of the Nine Years' War in Tudor Ireland.* Morgan's study breaks new ground on O'Neill's early years and is very strong on the causes and early course of the war. His work does not extend, however, beyond 1596. For an interesting, but fanciful, account of O'Neill's life, see Seán Ó Faoláin's *The Great O'Neill* (1942). Ó Faoláin considered some historical materials in writing his account of O'Neill's life and his biography draws heavily on J.K. Graham's unpublished M.A. thesis "Hugh O'Neill, 2nd Earl of Tyrone," but his instinct is very much that of a novelist. Morgan has accused him, perhaps a touch harshly, of "wild inaccuracy, crass romanticism and faulty revisionism" (*Tyrone's Rebellion,* 12). Ó Faoláin's "novelization" of O'Neill's life has inspired another creative treatment of the subject—Brian Friel's play *Making History* (1988). Morgan has taken Friel to task for his Ó Faoláin-inspired inaccuracy and romanticism in "Making History: A Criticism and a Manifesto" (1990).

5. Fynes Moryson provides a genealogy of the O'Neills at book 2, pp. 5-7, of his *Itinerary.* Moryson was secretary to Lord Mountjoy, who was appointed Lord Deputy in Ireland in 1600. His *Itinerary,* published in 1617, includes a history of the Nine Years' War as part of his extensive memoir of his time in Ireland.

6. R.F. Foster has observed of Shane that he was "the antithesis of Hugh O'Neill, having no English qualities, not even the language" (1989, 30).

7. The Elizabethan section of William Camden's *Annales* was published in an English translation by R. Norton in 1630. All quotations from the work in this chapter are taken from this edition, entitled *The Historie of the Most Renowned and Victorious Princesse Elizabeth.* On Shane's visit to the English court, see James Hogan, "Shane O'Neill comes to the Court of Elizabeth" (1947).

8. Philip Sidney wrote a defense of his father's policies in Ireland, entitled *A Discourse on Irish Affairs.* Only a fragment of this text survives. See James P. Myers, ed., *Elizabethan Ireland: A Selection of Writings by Elizabethan Writers on Ireland* (1983), pp. 36-37. Friel, following Ó Faoláin, has O'Neill reflecting nostalgically on his days at Ludlow and Penshurst: "I'm remembering Sir Henry Sidney and Lady Mary, may they rest in peace. We spent the winters in the great castle at Ludlow in Shropshire. I've few memories of the winters. It's the summers I remember and the autumns, in Kent, in the family seat at Penshurst. And the orchards; and the deerpark; and those enormous fields of wheat and barley. A golden beneficent land. Days without blemish" (34).

9. See Morgan, *Tyrone's Rebellion,* pp. 12, 92-93, 214. Ciarán Brady has, however, in *The Chief Governors,* still been willing to assert that O'Neill was able to "win the confidence of a number of influential friends, notably Sir Henry Sidney, with whom it seems he spent some part of his early life" (1994, 289).

10. On the battle for the O'Neillship, see Nicholas Canny "Hugh O'Neill, Earl of Tyrone, and the Changing Face of Gaelic Ulster" (1970), especially pp. 20-23. Hugh's self-presentation as "The O'Neill" is, in itself, interestingly ambiguous in that he signed his letters in long hand, using the English form of his name. By contrast, his ally, Hugh O'Donnell, signed himself "Aodh O'Domhnaill," using Irish script—see Morgan, *Tyrone's Rebellion,* p. 188, and Cyril Falls *Elizabeth's Irish Wars* (1950), p. 195.

11. From the anonymous *Chronicle of Ireland 1584-1608,* first brought to publication by the Irish Manuscripts Commission in 1933 in an edition by Herbert Wood. Wood proposes that "it is quite evident" that the author was Sir James Perrot, the illegitimate son of Sir John Perrot who was Lord Deputy in Ireland from 1584 to 1588. On James Perrot's career, see Ciarán Brady, *The Chief Governors,* pp. 291-300.

12. Baker makes a similar point about Spenser's perceptions of Irish manipulations of the English legal system: "What especially bothers Irenius . . . is that the Irish can maneuver within the procedural boundaries of the common law and yet escape its jurisdiction," hence "common law in Ireland . . . degenerated into legal spectacle. Selves slipped in and out of categories which should fix them, and the declarations of these shifting [selves] took on different meanings within the conventions of different legal codes simultaneously" ("Some Quirk" 1986, 154, 155).

13. For a detailed history of military affairs in Ireland during the Elizabethan period, see (in addition to Morgan's history of the Nine Years' War) Cyril Falls, *Elizabeth's Irish Wars* (1950).

14. Perrot confirms the red coats in the *Chronicle of Ireland*: "The rebells beinge many more in number came on thicke, marching in redde coates (a manner not usually seene before that time emongst the meere Irishrie)" (94). Elsewhere Perrot notes that the "aleven hundred foote and above 400 horse" that O'Neill "had ordinarily about hym . . . were armed after the English maner" (89).

15. In *Poetry and Politics* (1984), Norbrook also suggests that "before he departed" for Ireland, Essex "arranged Spenser's funeral" (149). In "The Egalitarian Giant," Annabel Patterson has argued for seeing Essex as one of the figures indicated by the *Faerie Queene's* Artegall "in at least the early stages of his military career (the 1591 campaign in Normandy in support of Henry of Navarre)" (1992, 105). For an alternative account of the failure to license the *View,* see Baker, "Some Quirk," and Andrew Hadfield, "Was Spenser's *View of the Present State of Ireland* Censored?"

16. The extent of the levies imposed in support of the war is registered by Joel Altman: "An order went out for a fresh levy of 2,000 soldiers to be taken from Cornwall, Devon, Southampton, Oxfordshire, Somerset, and Wiltshire. At the end of November [1599], another 1,000 men were mustered for service from eight counties. In January 3,000 more and in mid-February another 2,000 were levied, in addition to the 2,000 taken from London and the southeastern counties in December, who were transported early in 1599 to the Low Countries as replacements for seasoned soldiers, who were shipped out to Ireland" (1991, 9).

17. This quotation is taken from a "Journall of the L. Lieutenants procedinges from the xxviijth Aug. tyll the viijth of Sept. 1599" included with John Harington's various writings in *Nugae Antiquae.*

18. John Dymmok's *Treatice of Ireland* was written *c.* 1600, but was not published for the first time until 1843. Richard Butler, the editor of the 1843 edition, noted that "of the author . . . nothing has been ascertained, but it is probable that he was an Englishman in attendance upon Essex, when he was Lord Lieutenant of Ireland" (1). Significant overlap exists between some of the material in Dymmok and the "Journall" included in Harington's *Nugae Antiquae.*

19. Gainsford, in his *History of the Earle of Tirone*, in a single paragraph-long sentence, details item by item Essex's progress from his "priuate parley with *Tyrone*" to "how his fortunes and Life ended" (1619, 24).

20. N.E. McClure includes a brief survey of Harington's career in his edition of *The Letters and Epigrams of Sir John Harington*. McClure also provides a summary of Harington's role in the Essex campaign at pp. 18-22. Harington wrote *A Short View of the State of Ireland* in 1605—essentially an extended letter jointly addressed to the Lords Devonshire (formerly Lord Deputy Mountjoy) and Cramborne, suing (unsuccessfully) for a joint appointment as Lord High Chancellor of Ireland and Archbishop of Dublin.

21. On the Irish as wolves, see above, chapter 2, pp. 50-53.

22. Andrew Hadfield observes of this encounter that "the exchange illustrates how close the two sides could appear at times, part of a shared culture rather than diametrically opposed polarities: the civilized and the barbarian" (*Spenser's Irish Experience* 1997, 47).

23. See above, chapter 3, p. 69.

24. Wotton was one Essex's personal secretaries. He was a member of the party of six English officials who negotiated the details of Essex's truce with O'Neill. Wotton was selected for this task because he was thought to be "the onely man in the armye fittest among the rest of the commissioners, that by the weight of his judgment, might be counterpoyzed the sharpnes of Hen. Ovengtons witt, Tyrones cheefest counseller" (Dymmok 1843, 50-51).

25. All quotations are from John T. Shawcross's edition of *The Complete Poetry of John Donne* (1967).

26. Likewise, in Spenser's *View*, Eudoxus asks, "is it possible that anye shoulde so far growe out of frame that they shoulde in so shorte space quite forgett theire Countrie and theire owne names," and notes "that is a moste daungerous *Lethargie*" (115 [original emphasis]). See above, chapter 3, p. 71.

27. For the dating of Shakespeare's plays, I rely on Stanley Wells and Gary Taylor, *Shakespeare: A Textual Companion* (1987). In his single volume Oxford edition of *Henry V*, Taylor notes that "the date of *Henry V* can . . . be established with—for Shakespeare—extraordinary precision" (1979, 7). Others have, however, been less convinced that the play can so readily be tied to the year 1599—see, for example, Warren D. Smith, "The *Henry V* Choruses in the First Folio" (1954), and Keith Brown, "Historical Context and *Henry V*" (1986).

28. Essex placed Southampton in charge of the cavalry, in contravention of Elizabeth's express wishes. One of the "fiue speciall crimes" Essex was accused of on his return was "his making the Earle of *Southampton* Generall of the Horse" (Moryson, II, 69). Shakespeare dedicated both *Venus and Adonis* (1593) and *The Rape of Lucrece* (1594) to Southampton. Taylor notes that "the allusion to the Irish expedition . . . is the only explicit, extra-dramatic, incontestable reference to a contemporary event anywhere in the [Shakespeare] canon" (*Henry V*, 7).

29. Throughout this chapter, all Shakespeare quotations will be taken from the first folio (F1) edition of the plays, using Charlton Hinman's facsimile edition. References are in the form of Hinman's through line numbers (TLNs). It should be noted, however, that

some of the plays discussed here were also published in this period in independent quarto editions, which differ significantly from the F1 text. See also n. 30, below.

30. It is worth noting that the 1623 F1 text of *The Life of Henry the Fift* is quite different in many respects from the 1600 quarto entitled *The Cronicle History of Henry the Fift* (Q1), and much of the play's Irish material is not present in the Q1 version (for a further analogous text, see the 1598 *Famous Victories of Henry the fifth*). The question of whether the Celtic material is a deletion from or addition to the play is taken up by, among others, Keith Brown, in "Historical Context and *Henry V*" (1986), and Thomas L. Berger, in "The Disappearance of Macmorris in Shakespeare's *Henry V*" (1985). See also Gary Taylor "'We Happy Few': The 1600 Abridgement," in Stanley Wells and Gary Taylor, *Modernising Shakespeare's Spelling, with Three Studies in the Text of Henry V* (1979). Annabel Patterson provides a very interesting historicist analysis of the differences between Q1 and F1 in *Shakespeare and the Popular Voice* (1989), pp. 71-92. A number of different facsimile editions of the Q1 text have been published, including one contained in Michael Allen and Kenneth Muir, eds., *Shakespeare's Plays in Quarto* (1981). T.W. Craik's Arden 3 edition of *King Henry V* (1995) includes, as an appendix, a reduced facsimile of the quarto text.

31. Spenser, in attempting to disjoin the contemporary English from their Anglo-Norman ancestors, writes, "the vse of all Englande was in the Raigne of Henrye the Seconde when Irelande was firste planted withe Englishe verye rude and barbarous . . . it is but even the other daye since Englande grewe Civill" (118). See above, chapter 3, p. 72.

32. It is symptomatic of this concern that the words "England" and "English" are used almost one hundred times during the course of the play. Philip Edwards is surely right when he refers to the play as "an English epic" (1979, 74).

33. Helgerson makes the suggestive argument that "For . . . Elizabethans, the way to an acceptable national self led through self-alienation. They had to know themselves as the barbarous or inferior other, know themselves from the viewpoint of the more refined or more successful cultures of Greece, Rome, and contemporary Europe, before they could undertake the project of national self-making. In this sense, to be English was to be other—both before their work began and after it had been accomplished. Before, it was the otherness of the barbarian, the inferior. After, it was the otherness of the model of civility into which they had projected themselves" (243). The implications for such a process of the ongoing contact between the English and their Irish neighbors, whose history of barbarity/civility was so intertwined with their own (that history being written—in the broadest sense—largely by the English themselves) seems profound. Yet Helgerson nowhere addresses the issue. It is noteworthy that the index to *Forms of Nationhood* contains no entry for "Ireland."

34. See Wells and Taylor, *William Shakespeare: Textual Companion,* pp. 117-8, where 1595 is suggested as the most likely date of the play. I offer a more extended reading of the trajectory of Shakespeare's history plays against the backdrop of the Nine Years' War in my "Shakespeare's Irish History" (1996).

35. On Gaunt's speech, see also Graham Holderness, "'What ish my nation?': Shakespeare and National Identities" (1991).

36. See *The First Part of King Henry the Fourth*, TLN 1726 fwd.

37. As Dollimore and Sinfield have pointed out, when the Chorus introduces the issue of treason it is not the traitors who next appear on the stage, but rather Nim, Bardolph, Pistol, the hostess, and the boy. Their appearance here raises the possibility of their being guilty of treason "by association," as it were. Helgerson sees this discrediting and purging of the Henriad's comic characters as symptomatic of a larger movement within Shakespeare's work generally. Commenting on *The First Part of King Henry the Fourth,* he notes: "By including Falstaff, the play maintained its stake in a popular theater that mingled kings and clowns, a theater that could imagine a political nation comprising both high and low. But in banishing him, it awoke and despised that dream" (227).

38. It is interesting that Q1's reading of these lines is "The Marches gracious soueraigne, shalbe sufficient / To guard your *England* from the pilfering borderers" (A3r). Q2 also gives "England" rather than "inland" here.

39. The issue is handled rather differently in the 1598 *Famous Victories of Henry the fifth,* in which the Archbishop warns

> it hath bene alwaies knowne,
> That Scotland hath bene in league with France,
> By a sort of pensions which yearly come from thence,
> I thinke it therefore best to conquere Scotland,
> And th[en] I think that you may go more easily into France

To which Oxford answers:

> He that wil Scotland win, must first with France begin:
> According to the old saying.
> Therefore my good Lord, I thinke it best first to inuade France,
> For in conquering Scotland, you conquer but one,
> And conquere France, and conquere both.

(D2r, D2v; Praetorius facsimile, pp. 27, 28; scene IX, lines 78-82; 88-92)

40. For a useful "historical study of the earliest Irish, Welsh and Scottish characters in English plays," see J.O. Bartley *Teague, Shenkin and Sawney* (1954). Bartley discusses "Shakespeare's Irish Soldier" at pp. 16-17.

41. It should be noted, however, that elsewhere in the play Welch is consistently referred to by his personal name, Fluellen (or by some variation on it, such as "Flu."). Fluellen's positioning in the play is peculiarly complex—even as, in common with Irish and Scot, he functions as an ethnic cipher (and is also the focus of much stage-Welsh comedy), he is also recruited to foreground a version of the Tudor myth of origins. Thus, he reminds Henry: "Your Maiesty takes no scorne to weare the Leeke vppon S. Tauies day," to which Henry replies, "I am Welch you know good Countriman" (TLN 2631-33; 2635). On the expedient limits of Henry's "Welshness," see Willy Maley, "Sceptred Isle" (1997), p. 103.

42. This insight serves to illustrate the importance of using contemporary texts rather than modernized editions. F1's ethnic headings were followed by Ff 2-4. Rowe's edition of 1709 replaced the ethnic tags with the Celtic characters' proper names. Every major edition since 1709 has followed Rowe's lead in this, thus obscuring the political weight that is carried by the prefixes in the 1623 folio text. For a more detailed exploration of this issue,

see my "Tish Ill Done': *Henry the Fift* and the Politics of Editing" (1997). Peter Stallybrass offers a rather different perspective on these matters, arguing that, in this period, the personal name indicates precisely a *lack* of politically effective identity. See forthcoming work of his on "naming, unnaming, and renaming" in Shakespeare.

43. For a differently inflected, fruitful, and persuasive reading of this passage, see Maley, "Shakespeare, Holinshed and Ireland" (1997).

44. Perhaps Edwards and those critics who follow him feel in some sense obliged to reject this reading on the grounds of context. If "what ish my nation?" is treated as a genuine question, the immediately following "Ish a villain and a bastard and a knave and a rascal" becomes a something of a non sequitur. The fact remains, however, that the potential reading of the question as a question is still present in the text. It is, in any case, precisely the ambiguity of the speech that I wish to stress—an ambiguity underlined by the fact that the subject of "ish a villain and a bastard . . . " is indeterminate. Seamus Heaney recognizes the force of Irish's phrase as a question in his poem "Traditions," when he writes:

> Morris, gallivanting
> round the Globe, whinged
> to courtier and groundling
> who had heard tell of us
> as going very bare
>
> of learning, as wild hares,
> as anatomies of death:
> "What ish my nation?"
>
> And sensibly, though so much
> later, the wandering Bloom
> replied, "Ireland," said Bloom,
> "I was born here. Ireland."
>   (*Wintering Out*, 22)

45. In contrast with the view which I set out here, Andrew Gurr, in "Why Captain Jamy in *Henry V*" (1989), sees the ambiguity over Irish's nationality as being related to his position specifically as a *mercenary* serving in the English army: "MacMorris's outburst in 3,3, might be said to fit his role in the English army as mercenary, just as well as it fits his Irishness. Mercenaries were thought to be rascals and knaves and villains, and had no nation, as the French Herald's segregation of them from the French dead affirms" (372).

46. Such a protonationalist interpretation of O'Neill's career must, of course, be tempered by awareness of the fact that this "nationalist" project was undertaken after O'Neill and his allies had solicited aid from Spain (offering sovereignty over Ireland in return) and that, in any case, throughout his life O'Neill continued to play all sides of the issue to his own personal advantage. Morgan sees both O'Neill and O'Donnell as fundamentally concerned with consolidating their *local* spheres of influence. In his view, it was the appeal to Spain itself which forced them "to couch their struggle in religious and national terms in order to broaden their support" (*Tyrone's Rebellion*, 213). For all that, the Nine Years' War

did represent a significant threat that the coalition of Irish leaders united under O'Neill would actually succeed in driving the English from Ireland, leading to the existence—for the very first time—of an independent entity of "Ireland" off England's shores.

47. For two differing accounts of the extent to which an Irish ideology of "nationalism" did (or could) exist in the early modern period, see Nicholas Canny, "The Formation of the Irish Mind: Religion, Politics and Gaelic Literature 1580-1750" (1982), and Brendan Bradshaw, "Native Reaction to the Westward Enterprise: A Case-Study in Gaelic Ideology," (1978). For an excellent survey of the materials relevant to a study of this issue, see Marc Caball, "*The Gaelic Mind and the Collapse of the Gaelic World*: An Appraisal" (1993).

48. It is interesting to note in this context Thomas Berger's suggestion that the actor who played Irish may have doubled the role with that of Exeter, Henry's English loyalist who "formally arrests Cambridge, Scroop, and Grey . . . [is sent] on embassy to the French court . . . [and] reads Henry's new titles to France in the final scene of the play" (1985, 20-21).

49. Hadfield's comment on Spenser's Irish project is also of relevance here. He observes that "Ireland is the place from where all chaos originates and which will suck in and consume all attempts to redeem it. It is the site where (the English) language turns against itself and ceases to be able to transform its 'other'" ("Political Theory" 1994, 18).

50. I am grateful to Gary Taylor for drawing my attention to this moment in the text. In his edition of the play, Prof. Taylor argues that the mistake "seems almost certain to be Shakespeare's own 'Freudian slip'" (1982, 18). The New Folger Library edition of the play (edited by Barbara A. Mowat and Paul Werstine [1995]) retains "Ireland" here.

51. Similarly, David Norbrook notes of *The Faerie Queene* that "the poem is full of prophecies of future ceremonies which will resolve all contradictions, most notably the marriage of Arthur and Gloriana. But these ceremonies are always deferred, and the emphasis is on the difficulty of completing the quests and the dangers of complacency" (1984, 110).

52. On Mountjoy, see F.M. Jones, *Mountjoy, 1563-1606: The Last Elizabethan Deputy* (1958).

53. On the siege and battle of Kinsale, see J.J. Silke, *Kinsale: The Spanish Intervention in Ireland at the End of the Elizabethan Wars* (1970). On O'Neill's Spanish connections generally, see Micheline Kerney Walsh, *Destruction by Peace* (1986) and *An Exile of Ireland* (1996).

54. On the Welsh leg of this journey, see Christopher Highley, "Wales, Ireland, and *1 Henry IV*" (199). O'Neill was attacked by local women as he and Mountjoy made their way through Wales. Highley offers a very interesting new interpretation of this incident, suggesting "that the women targeted Tyrone not because they were sharing in English hostility but because they looked upon him as the failed and discredited leader of a cause they had themselves supported" (91).

55. On O'Neill's career in Ireland after 1603, see Nicholas Canny, "The Treaty of Mellifont and the Re-Organisation of Ulster, 1603" (1970); "Hugh O'Neill, Earl of Tyrone, and the Changing Face of Gaelic Ulster" (1970); and John McCavitt, "The Flight of the Earls, 1607" (1994).

5. "The Irish Game Turned Again"

1. In "James VI, James I and the Identity of Britain" (1996), Jenny Wormald interrogates the traditional view that James was wholly commited to the project of complete union, interpreting James's stance as, instead, indicating both a strategic ploy to effect a general stregthening of the Scottish position and a bargaining tactic aimed at achieving as extensive a degree of union as would pragmatically be possible. For a thorough account of the union issue, covering the years between 1603 and 1707 (when the Act of Union was passed), see Brian P. Levack, *The Formation of the British State* (1987).

2. For these details, see Leah Marcus, *Puzzling Shakespeare: Local Reading and its Discontents* (1988), chapter 3, and D.J. Gordon, "*Hymenæi*: Ben Jonson's Masque of Union" (1975), pp. 168-74. The union project's troubled parliamentary history can be traced in Wallace Notestein, *The House of Commons 1604-1610* (1970).

3. We might recall here the string of first person plurals to be found at the end of the first section of Gerald's *Topographia*. See above, chap. 2, p. 38.

4. The position of Wales here is very interesting and, though it falls outside the remit of the present study, certainly warrants being investigated in its own right. England and Wales had been brought to complete union by acts of parliament in 1536 and 1543—as Conrad Russell notes, together they constituted "a unitary state, with one law, one Parliament, one church, one Privy Council, one judicial system" (*Causes* 1990, 40). The Welsh example was often invoked by supporters of the Anglo-Scottish union. John Thornborough (writing as John Bristol), for example, writes that Wales "never receaved any thing more beneficial for the people there, then vniting that Country to the crowne & kingdom of England. For whilest it was alone without his brother, it was subject to storme, ful of contentions, war & shedding of bloud b[eing comb]ined with his brother, it flourished with p[eace]; and at this day is blessed in the vniformity of government there established" (n.d., D3r; this page of the British Library copy has been torn and repaired, with the loss of some text—the bracketed text here is conjectural). Wales's subordinate status here is clear (it is the unilateral recipient of the benefits of union) and this status is reinforced by the fact that "Wales" and "Welsh" are constantly subsumed in the union debate under the terms "England" and "English." Thornborough's pamphlet is, for instance, entitled *The Ioiefvll and Blessed Revniting of Two Mighty & Famous Kingdomes, England & Scotland into their Ancient Name of Great Brittaine.*

5. For a useful collection of such tract literature, see Bruce R. Galloway and Brian P. Levack, eds., *The Jacobean Union* (1985). As an appendix to their volume, Galloway and Levack provide a brief summary of the tracts not included in the collection.

6. Gordon Donaldson, in "Foundations of Anglo-Scottish Union" traces the "many factors which contributed to the anglicization of Scotland," noting that "the beginnings of most of the developments which have brought the two nations together during their political partnership can be discerned in the period before the union of the crowns" (1961, 314).

7. There was much debate over the issue of what kind of union could and should be effected between England and Scotland. James initially argued for total union, calling, in one speech to parliament in 1607, for "a perfect Vnion of Lawes and persons, and such a Naturalizing as may make one body of both Kingdomes vnder mee your King, That I and

my posteritie (if it so please God) may rule ouer you to the worlds end" (292). On the various paradigms of unity, see Conrad Russell, *Causes* (1990), pp. 40-41.

8. See Marcus, *Puzzling Shakespeare* (1988), p. 122, and Gordon (1975), p. 171. Jonathan Goldberg includes a picture of this coin among the illustrations to *James I and the Politics of Literature* (1989).

9. Michael J. Enright places the marriage trope in its historical context of Celtic imagery in "King James and his Island." Enright interestingly notes that "James was not . . . the only British sovereign to use the metaphor, for Charles I insisted on wearing white at his coronation so that he might 'declare the Virgin Purity with which he came to be espoused to his Kingdom'" (1976, 29; quoting from Peter Heylyn, *Cyprianus Anglicus* [London, 1671], 138). For a reading of Elizabeth's "Rainbow Portrait" that explores its bridal imagery in an Irish context, see Michael Neill's "Broken English" (1994), pp. 29-31.

10. In a 1604 prounion pamphlet attributed to Jon Skynner and dedicated to "the Right Honorable and famous Cities London and Edenborough" (A3r), the marriage of the kingdoms promises also a fruitful union between the cities themselves: "at this marriage if you will daunce, you make the contract sure, and till death depart [sic]" (H2v-H3r). The tract ends with the tag "God *Hymen* long your coupled ioyes maintaine" (H3r).

11. With the exception noted at n. 14 below, all quotations from Jonson are taken from the first folio of 1616.

12. Other versions of the metaphor are, of course, assimilable to the Anglo-Irish situation. To take a contemporary instance, Seamus Heaney's poem "Act of Union" (in *North* [1975]) imagines a sexual relationship between Britain and Ireland, with Northern Ireland as the product of their union. On this poem, see Jonathan Allison, "Acts of Union: Seamus Heaney's Tropes of Sex and Marriage" (1992).

13. For a detailed account of the broad significance of cartography in the Renaissance see, in addition to Klein's excellent work, chapter 3 of Richard Helgerson's *Forms of Nationhood* (1992).

14. *Pancharis: The First Booke* "was entered on the Stationers' Register on 1 August 1603" (Herford and Simpson XI, 126-27). I have used Herford and Simpson's text of the poem, being unable to access a copy of the original.

15. The island is known as *Môn* in Welsh and was referred to as *Mona* by the Romans. (Milton refers to "the shaggy top of *Mona* high" in *Lycidas* [line 54].) Mona was the birthplace of Henry VII and so has a certain potency in the mythology of the Renaissance period as the geographic source of the Tudor dynasty. Spenser's Merlin prophesies that "a sparke of fire" will "Be freshly kindled in the fruitfull Ile / of *Mona*" (*FQ*, III.iii.48.2, 4-5). See Hadfield, *Literature, Politics and National Identity* (1994), p. 197. Leah Marcus notes that James VI and I's "descent from Henry gave him his right to the English throne; his identification with the first Tudor was so intense that when he died he was, at his own wish, buried in Henry VII's tomb" (1988, 131).

16. This island has also been invested with a medial significance by the twentieth-century Irish writer, Tom Murphy. Murphy's play *The Gigli Concert* includes a character called Mona who, in the political allegory of the play, is intended as an intermediate figure set between Britain and Ireland.

17. Certainly in a strictly legal sense, but in other ways also. See Bradshaw, "Tudor Reformation" (1996), and Levack, *Formation of the British State* (1987), pp. 17-22.

18. Willy Maley sees a similar narrative being played out in Jonson's "To the memory of my beloued, the Avthor . . .," included in the Shakespeare First Folio: "The Bard of Britain, in the wake of Anglo-Scottish Union and the subjection of Ireland, is set favourably against European literary figures both contemporary and classical. The subsequent reference to 'those flights upon the banks of Thames, That so did take Eliza and our James' reinforces the notion that Shakespeare is the poet of the British state, of two monarchs and four nations, whose power, artistic and administrative, centres on London" ("This Sceptred Isle" [1997], 87).

19. The Somerset marriage would prove, of course, to be even more scandalous still, as Howard and Carr would eventually be implicated in the murder of Carr's close friend Thomas Overbury, who had been opposed to the marriage. Lindley points out, however, that "there is no evidence that anyone entertained suspicions of murder at the time of the divorce and remarriage" (346). For the most recent account of the affair, see Lindley's *The Trials of Frances Howard* (1996).

20. This was not, of course, the only scandalous marriage with an Irish connection in this period. Mountjoy's career also ended in scandal, following divorce and remarriage.

21. Jonson thus sees Irish culture here as being complicit in its own destruction. In some respects, this is not quite as disingenuous as it might seem. Bernadette Cunningham has charted the breakdown of Irish bardic culture during this period and notes that several Irish poets sought patronage from precisely those people who were intent on destroying the very societal structures on which their culture had traditionally been dependant—see her "Native Culture and Political Change in Ireland, 1580-1640" (1986). See also Katherine Simms, "Bards and Barons: The Anglo-Irish Aristocracy and the Native Culture" (1989); Michelle O Riordan, *The Gaelic Mind and the Collapse of the Gaelic World* (1990); and Marc Caball, "*The Gaelic Mind and the Collapse of the Gaelic World*: An Appraisal" (1993). Interestingly, Hiram Morgan notes that "there is no evidence that O'Neill ever patronized the poets. Instead his preferred methods were proclamation and preaching" ("Hugh O'Neill" 1993, 27).

22. The mantle was a one piece heavy cloak which formed the traditional dress of men and women alike in Ireland. See above, chapter 3, p. 80.

23. The "u" in *garraue* here is likely a turned "n." Stephen Orgel, in his edition of *The Complete Masques,* gives the word as "garrans" (horses; from the Irish *gearrán*).

24. See above chapter 4, p. 107.

25. On this issue, see Nicholas Canny, "Identity Formation in Ireland."

26. PRO sp. 14, vol. 76.

27. See also Stephen Orgel's comment on Jonson's *Masque of Blackness* (1981). Noting Sir Dudley Carleton's criticism of the performance, Orgel writes: "Although . . . the masquers appeared in blackface by the queen's own command, Carelton cannot forget that however much they are the nymphs of the poet's fiction, they are also the queen and her ladies" (Jonson *Masques*, 5).

28. David Lindley suggests that Jonson may have derived the central transformative device of the *Irish Masque* from having read Davies's *Discoverie* ("Embarrassing Ben" 1986).

29. See Foucault's assertion in *Discipline and Punish* that discipline "imposes on those whom it subjects a principle of compulsory visibility" (1979, 187). "The perfect disciplinary apparatus," he suggests, "would make it possible for a single gaze to see everything constantly. A central point would be both the source of light illuminating everything, and a locus of convergence for everything that must be known: a perfect eye that nothing would escape and a center towards which all gazes would be turned" (173). An interesting anticipation of this trope of visibility occurs in John Derricke's *The Image of Ireland*, published in 1581, in which Derricke, in framing his task in the poem, imagines a pyramid being erected in Ireland, which gives him visual access to the entire island. "It was concluded on," he writes

> That of the famous Irishe soile,
> I should enlarge vpon.
> And least thereof in any parte,
> I might relate a misse:
> By reason of the longitude,
> or latitude, there is.
> A goodly braue Piramides,
> erected passyng high:
> from whence all corners of the lande,
> I might at large discrie.
>
> (26-27)

30. The reference to "Tirone" here is somewhat odd, in that O'Neill had, of course, left Ireland some five years before the publication of the *Discoverie*. The continued interest of the English authorities in his activities is registered by the number of references to him which persist in the state papers, right up to his death in 1616.

31. The novelty of Davies's position lies not in his espousal of the primacy of English law but in the manner in which he succeeded in extending the law throughout the island and in his forging of the law in service of his own ends. The prospect of extending English law throughout Ireland had been raised persistently throughout the previous century. To take just one example, Edmund Tremayne observed in one of his reports on Ireland written between 1571 and 1575 that "the Irish government is never to be reformed till the common law have its course" (Brady, *Chief Governers* 1994, 141, quoting PRO SP 63/32/66).

32. "[The Irish] scheme of succession, known to contemporary English observers as the custom of 'tanistry,' derived from the technical Gaelic term *tanaise rig*, meaning second or next to the king. The custom originally referred to the practice enshrined in eighth-century Irish law whereby the successor to a chief or king was nominated during the lifetime of such a leader" (Pawlisch 1985, 61). R.F. Foster has noted that "what struck English observers [of Irish society] was the fluidity of a structure where the social foundations of authority and even property were redefined in every generation; and they rationalized this as anarchy" (1989, 10).

33. A similar set of maneuvers was planned, but not executed, by William Fitzwilliam, during his second stint as Lord Deputy, in the early 1590s. See Morgan, *Tyrone's Rebellion* (1993), pp. 78-81.

34. On the Ulster plantation, see Philip S. Robinson, *The Plantation of Ulster* (1984), and Raymond Gillespie, *Colonial Ulster* (1985).

35. Joel Altman provides the following statistics: "Between 1593 and 1603 Elizabeth spent £1,924,000 on the war in Ireland, compared with £1,844,000 on the Low Countries and France combined in the period 1585-1603. Exchequer issues for Ireland in 1597-98 were £108,000 and in 1598-99, £336,000. This vast expenditure necessitated privy seal loans in 1597 and 1601, loans from the London Corporation in 1598-99 and from a London syndicate in 1601, and sales of Crown lands in 1599 and 1601 at below-market prices" (1991, 8).

36. Josias Bodley was the youngest brother of Sir Thomas Bodley, founder of the Bodleian Library. He served under Essex and Mountjoy in the Irish wars. His manuscript account of his journey into Ulster was written in Latin and entitled *Descriptio Itineris ad Lecaliam in Ultonia*. I quote here from the English translation of the work included in Richard Butler's 1843 volume of *Tracts Relating to Ireland*.

Conclusion

1. For the possible reasons for the long delay in publishing the tract (it had been entered into the Stationer's Register on April 14, 1598), see Andrew Hadfield's "Was Spenser's *View of the Present State of Ireland* Censored?" (1994); see also Jean Brink, "Constructing the *View*" (199). Patricia Coughlan notes that "Ware, a Protestant of English stock, embodied in his own repertoire of social roles the doubleness or multiplicity of perspectives often entailed upon those publicly active in colonial situations. He was, on the one hand, a trusted office-holder in Strafford's diverse and autocratic regime, and on the other an extremely important antiquarian, historian and collector of ancient Irish manuscripts, who maintained cordial communications with contemporary Gaelic poets and was responsible for the survival of precious early works" ("Cheap" 1990, 208).

2. On Hanmer and Campion, see Hadfield, "Briton and Scythian" (1993).

3. In "Was Spenser's *View of the Present State of Ireland* Censored?" Hadfield notes that Ware "obligingly cut out both references to major Anglo-Irish magnates and some of Spenser's harshest judgements on native Irish, old and new English inhabitants of Ireland in order to render the text less offensive and anachronistic" (460). Rudolph Gottfried provides a detailed list of the emendations at pp. 519-23 of his volume of Spenser's prose works.

4. Willy Maley notes, in "Another Britain" (1995), that "at the turn of the seventeenth century there was a genuine widespread belief that the Irish problems of England and Scotland were being solved. . . . The Flight of the Earls in 1607 left a political vacuum in Irish society. This vacuum was to be filled by an experimental British culture, planted in the wake of a union that was limited in scope, and largely unforeseen" (5).

5. Additional Manuscript 22022. *Globe* editor, Richard Morris, commented in his edition of *The Complete Works of Edmund Spenser* that "the prose Treatise on Ireland, as

printed by Sir James Ware, and followed by all recent editors, was found on examination to be very inaccurate and incomplete. It seemed scarcely fair to Spenser's memory to let this single piece of prose remain in so unsatisfactory a state" (1869, iii).

6. For an analysis of some other seventeenth-century reactions to the *View,* see Willy Maley, "How Milton and Some Contemporaries Read Spenser's *View*" (1996). For another politically minded annotator of Spenser, see Stephen Orgel's "Margins of Truth," forthcoming in my *Renaissance Text* collection.

7. For a comprehensive account of the uprising, see Michael Perceval-Maxwell, *The Outbreak of the Irish Rebellion of 1641* (1994).

8. Coughlan notes of this process that "the intention of the original Commissions of Enquiry was to record the quantity and value of money and property stolen from Protestants, but within a few weeks an equal or greater emphasis was being laid on the alleged atrocities committed" ("Cheap," 210).

9. For an indication of the extent to which English popular print was preoccupied with Ireland in the early 1640s, see Lindley's analysis of "the proportion of references to Ireland in Thomason's collection of tracts," at p. 144 of "The Impact of the 1641 Rebellion" (1972). On the provenance and politics of the tracts, see Perceval-Maxwell, *The Outbreak of the Irish Rebellion,* pp. 271-74.

10. Raymond Gillespie notes that an "indication of the tensions of the early weeks of the rebellion was the appearance of ghosts both to settlers and natives all over Ulster and the emergence of allegations of witchcraft . . . . Significantly, one deponent reported the story that a vision seen at Dungannon had also been seen before the rebellion of the earl of Tyrone in 1594. Such supernatural phenomena are not recorded in Ulster before 1641, and their appearance at this juncture is an indication of the fears and tensions experienced by both sides" ("End" 1986, 210). For an example of a further unnatural phenomenon in Dublin (a mass gathering of birds on Christmas Eve, 1641), see *Irelands Amazement* (1642), A3v-A4r.

11. See above, chapter 2, pp. 56-58.

12. John Morrill has said of the early modern period generally that "the increasingly obsessive concern of the English with Ireland can be seen as a growing fear that Catholic Ireland would be a staging post for their superpower Catholic enemies intent on undermining Protestant monarchy in England" ("British Problem" 1996, 15).

13. Quoted in Lindley, "Impact," p. 153, from *Irelands advocate: or, a sermon preached upon Novem. 14, 1641 to promote the contributions by way of lending, for the present reliefe of the protestants party in Ireland* (London, 1641), pp. 32-43.

14. The inclusion of *English* papists here is striking. On perceptions of the position of the Catholic community within England itself, see below.

15. For details of the historical arguments regarding the document, see Aidan Clarke, *The Old English in Ireland, 1625-1642* (1966), pp. 165-68. Perceval-Maxwell notes that "[n]o historian today accepts the validity of the commission" (218).

16. Lindley has argued that "any understanding of the events of 1641 to 1645 in England and Wales is seriously incomplete without a knowledge of the way in which those events were influenced by the Irish rebellion" (176). See also his Ph.D. thesis "The Part

Played by the Catholics in the English Civil War" (1968). Christopher Hill has characterized the 1641 uprising as "the catalyst which forced civil war in England because neither king nor parliament would trust the other with command of the army which all agreed must be sent to restore English power in Ireland" (1985, 36-37).

17. Likewise, Willy Maley has noted that "the much-vaunted 'English Revolution' was always 'Cogadh na d'Trí Ríocht' for Gaelic annalists, and 'The War of the Three Kingdoms' for earlier English commentators" ("This Sceptred Isle" 1997, 89). On this topic, see J.G.A. Pocock, "The Atlantic Archipelago and the War of the Three Kingdoms" (1996), and Conrad Russell, "The British Background to the Irish Rebellion of 1641" (1988) and "The British Problem and the English Civil War" (1987).

18. The sources of Lindley's quotations are given as follows: *A perfect diurnall of the passages in parliament, 13-20 September 1642* (London, 1642); *Speciall passages and certain informations from severall places . . . , 13-20 September 1642*, p. 47; *Lords' Journal*, v, 418. Joyce Lee Malcolm confirms the negative impact that Irish recruitment had on Charles's standing, even among royalists: "At Mostyn in Flint residents were terrified at the arrival of convoys that seemed to herald the long-dreaded catholic invasion. Royalist soldiers mutinied at Bridgwater when they learned Irish troops had landed nearby, while serious disturbances were reported among both gentry and commoners in Shrewsbury, Worcester, and in Cheshire. . . . commissioners for Cumberland and Westmorland ignored orders to recruit residents and prepare to join with the incoming Irish" (1979, 248).

19. Unpublished material. See chapter 1, n. 35.

20. Milton was instructed to report on the affairs in Ireland by the Council of State— see the Order Book of the Council of State in the Public Record Office, London, MS SP Dom 25/62, p. 125, under the date of March 28, 1649. My thanks to Prof. John T. Shawcross for providing this reference and for his very helpful comments on Milton and Spenser.

21. See Merritt Hughes, "The Historical Setting of Milton's *Observations*" (1949), pp. 1069-70. For further discussion of the politics of Milton's tract, see Maley's "Rebels and Redshanks" (1994).

22. On Kingsley, see chapter 1, pp. 11-13.

23. There is a certain interesting irony in the fact that, while the penultimate round of revisions was being carried out on this book, British rule in Hong Kong was coming to an end. In much of the British media coverage of the event, Hong Kong was being described as "Britain's last colony." Meanwhile, the then newly appointed Secretary of State for Northern Ireland (Marjorie Mowlam) was making efforts to revive the troubled "peace process" in Ulster.

24. The position of citizens of the Republic of Ireland within the British state is a further indication of Ireland's odd, anomalous status. Even before the evolution of the European Community extended a broad range of reciprocal rights and benefits across the EC territory, citizens of the Republic of Ireland enjoyed full settlement, employment, social security and voting rights in the United Kingdom—rights which were much more closely controlled for citizens of the Commonwealth, a body from which the Irish state had, in fact, excluded itself. As Robin Frame has observed: "whether through arrogance, absence of mind, muddle or guilt, [the United Kingdom] state, so strict in its treatment

of Commonwealth citizens, has never brought itself to regard the inhabitants of the bit [of the greater British state] that has seceded—the citizens of the Irish Republic—as aliens" ("Overlordship and Reaction" 1995, 65).

25. For Davies, of course, the barrier is permeable in one direction only: from Britain to Ireland; likewise, transcendance means (the legal fiction of) rendering the Irish English.

26. Hiram Morgan has usefully observed that "the Northern Ireland problem can no longer be declared unique. The revolutions of 1989 have revealed a dozen other 'Ulsters' in Eastern Europe in the wake of the communist regimes which were mere successor-states to the multiple-kingdoms in that region. Clearly, only a balanced assessment of Ireland's status as a kingdom and a colony on the western periphery of Europe can provide an adequate explanation of the country's persisting problems" ("Mid-Atlantic" 1991-92, 55).

Bibliography

Allen, Michael, and Kenneth Muir, eds. *Shakespeare's Plays in Quarto*. Berkeley: University of California Press, 1981.

Allison, Jonathan. "Acts of Union: Seamus Heaney's Tropes of Sex and Marriage." *Éire-Ireland* 27, no. 4 (1992): 106-21.

Altman, Joel B. "'Vile Participation': The Amplification of Violence in the Theater of *Henry V*." *Shakespeare Quarterly* 42, no. 1 (Spring 1991): 1-32.

Anderson, Benedict. *Imagined Communities: Reflections on the Origins and Spread of Nationalism,* rev. ed. London: Verso, 1991.

Anderson, Judith. "The Antiquities of Fairyland and Ireland." *Journal of English and Germanic Philology* 86, no. 2 (April 1987): 199-214.

Anderson, Perry. *Lineages of the Absolutist State*. London: Verso, 1979.

Andrews, K.R., N.P. Canny, and P.E. Hair, eds. *The Westward Enterprise*. Liverpool: Liverpool University Press, 1978.

Armstrong, Alan. "Editor's Preface." *Literature & History* 5, no. 1 (Spring 1996): v-viii.

Asch, R.G., ed. *Three Nations: A Common History? England, Scotland, Ireland and British History, c. 1600-1920*. Bochum: Universitätsverlag Dr. N. Brockmeyer, 1993.

Avery, Bruce. "Mapping the Irish Other: Spenser's *A View of the Present State of Ireland.*" *English Literary History* 1990 (Spring-Summer): 263-79.

Bacon, Francis. "Certain Considerations Touching the Plantation in Ireland." In *Resuscitatio, or bringing into publick light several pieces of the works, civil, historical, philosophical & theological, hitherto sleeping; of the right honourable Francis Bacon,* edited by William Rawley. London: 1657.

———. *A Briefe Discovrse, Tovching the Happie Vnion of the Kingdomes of England, and Scotland. Dedicated in Private to His Maiestie*. London: 1603.

Baker, David J. "Off the Map: Charting Uncertainty in Renaissance Ireland." In *Representing Ireland: Literature and the Origin of Conflicts, 1534-1660,* edited by Brendan Bradshaw, Andrew Hadfield, and Willy Maley, 76-92. Cambridge: Cambridge University Press, 1993.

———. "'Some Quirk, Some Subtle Evasion': Legal Subversion in Spenser's *A View of the Present State of Ireland.*" *Spenser Studies* 6 (1986): 147-63.

{ 201 }

————. "'Wildehirissheman': Colonialist Representation in Shakespeare's *Henry V.*" *English Literary Renaissance* 22 (1992): 37-61.

Bale, Johan. *The Vocacyon of Joha[n] Bale to the bishoprick of Ossorie in Irelande. . . .* (Rome [Fictitious colophon. Printed perhaps in Dublin]: 1553); reprinted by Peter Happé and John N. King, eds, as *The Vocacyon of Johan Bale.* Binghamton, N.Y.: Renaissance English Text Society, 1990.

Barnard, T.C. "Crises of Identity among Irish Protestants, 1641-1685." *Past and Present* 127 (May 1990): 39-83.

Bartlett, Neil, *Who Was That Man? A Present for Mr. Oscar Wilde.* London: Serpent's Tail, 1988.

Bartlett, Robert. *Gerald of Wales, 1146-1223.* Oxford: Clarendon, 1982.

Bartley, J.O. *Teague, Shenkin and Sawney: An Historical Study of the Earliest Irish, Welsh and Scottish Characters in English Plays.* Cork: Cork University Press, 1954.

Beacon, Richard. *Solon His Follie, or A Politiqve Discovrse, Tovching the Reformation of Common-weales Conquered, Declined or Corrupted.* Oxford, 1594. Modern edition edited by Clare Carroll and Vincent Carey, issued by the Centre for Medieval and Early Renaissance Studies, Binghamton, N.Y., 1996.

Beare, Philip O'Sullivan. *Historiae Catholicae Iberniae Compendium* (1621). Translated by M.J. Byrne as *Ireland under Elizabeth.* Sealy, Bryers & Co.: Dublin, 1903; reissued, Port Washington, N.Y., London: Kennikat Press, 1970.

Bede. *The Ecclesiastical History of the English People,* translated by Leo Sherley-Price. London: Penguin, 1990.

Berger, Harry. *Revisionary Play: Studies in Spenserian Dynamics.* Berkeley: University of California Press, 1988.

Berger, Thomas L. "The Disappearance of Macmorris in Shakespeare's *Henry V.*" *Renaissance Papers* (1985): 13-26.

Bernheimer, Richard. *Wild Men in the Middle Ages.* Cambridge, Mass.: Harvard University Press, 1952.

Bethell, Denis. "English Monks and Irish Reform in the Eleventh and Twelfth Centuries." In *Historical Studies VIII,* edited by T.D. Williams, 111-35. Dublin: Gill & Macmillan, 1971.

Bhabha, Homi. "Foreword" to Frantz Fanon, *Black Skin White Masks.* London: Pluto Press, 1986.

————. *The Location of Culture.* London: Routledge, 1994.

Bodley, Josias. "A Visit to Lecale, in the County of Down, in the Year 1602-03." In *Tracts Relating to Ireland,* edited by Richard Butler, 326-61. Dublin: Irish Archaeological Society, 1843.

Bottigheimer, Karl. "The Failure of the Reformation in Ireland: *Une Question Bien Posée.*" *Journal of Ecclesiastical History* 36, no. 2 (April 1985): 196-207.

————. "Kingdom and Colony: Ireland in the Westward Enterprise 1536-1660." In *The Westward Enterprise,* edited by K.R. Andrews, N.P. Canny, and P.E. Hair, 45-63. Liverpool: Liverpool University Press, 1978.

Bradshaw, Brendan. "The Beginnings of Modern Ireland." In *The Irish Parliamentary Tradition,* edited by Brian Farrell, 68-87. Dublin: Gill and Macmillan, 1973.

———. "Edmund Spenser on Justice and Mercy." In *The Writer as Witness: Historical Studies XVI*, edited by Tom Dunne, 76-89. Cork: Cork University Press, 1987.

———. "Geoffrey Keating: Apologist of Irish Ireland" In *Representing Ireland: Literature and the Origins of Conflict, 1534-1660*, edited by Brendan Bradshaw, Andrew Hadfield, and Willy Maley, 166-90. Cambridge: Cambridge University Press, 1993.

———. *The Irish Constitutional Revolution in the Sixteenth Century.* Cambridge: Cambridge University Press, 1979.

———. "Nationalism and Historical Scholarship in Modern Ireland." *Irish Historical Studies* 26, no. 104 (November 1989): 329-51.

———. "Native Reaction to the Westward Enterprise: A Case-Study in Gaelic Ideology." In *The Westward Enterprise*, edited by K.R. Andrews, N.P. Canny, and P.E. Hair, 65-80. Liverpool: Liverpool University Press, 1978.

———. "Sword, Word and Strategy in the Reformation in Ireland." *Historical Journal* 21, no. 3 (1978): 475-502.

———. "The Tudor Reformation and Revolution in Wales and Ireland: the Origins of the British Problem." In *The British Problem, c. 1534-1707: State Formation in the Atlantic Archipelago*, edited by Brendan Bradshaw and John Morrill, 39-65. Basingstoke: Macmillan, 1996.

Bradshaw, Brendan, and John Morrill, eds. *The British Problem, c. 1534-1707: State Formation in the Atlantic Archipelago.* Basingstoke: Macmillan, 1996.

Bradshaw, Brendan, Andrew Hadfield, and Willy Maley, eds. *Representing Ireland: Literature and the Origins of Conflict, 1534-1660.* Cambridge: Cambridge University Press, 1993.

Brady, Ciarán. *The Chief Governors: The Rise and Fall of Reform Government in Tudor Ireland, 1536-1588.* Cambridge: Cambridge University Press, 1994.

———. "Court, Castle and Country." In *Natives and Newcomers: Essays on the Making of Irish Colonial Society, 1534-1641*, edited by Ciarán Brady and Raymond Gillespie, 22-49. Dublin: Irish Academy Press, 1986.

———, ed. *Interpreting Irish History: the Debate on Historical Revisionism, 1938-1994.* Dublin: Irish Academic Press, 1994.

———. "Reply." *Past and Present* 120 (August 1988): 210-15.

———. "The Road to the *View*: On the Decline of Reform Thought in Tudor Ireland." In *Spenser and Ireland: An Interdisciplinary Perspective*, edited by Patricia Coughlan, 25-45. Cork: Cork University Press, 1989.

———. "Spenser's Irish Crisis: Humanism and Experience in the 1590s." *Past and Present* 111 (May 1986): 17-49.

———. "Thomas Butler, Earl of Ormond." In *Worsted in the Game: Losers in Irish History*, edited by Ciarán Brady, 48-70. Dublin: Lilliput, 1989.

Brady, Ciarán, and Raymond Gillespie, eds. *Natives and Newcomers: Essays on the Making of Irish Colonial Society 1534-1641.* Dublin: Irish Academic Press, 1986.

Breen, John. "*The Faerie Queene*, Book I and the Theme of Protestant Exile." *Irish University Review* 26, no. 2 (Autumn/Winter 1996): 226-36.

———. "Imagining Voices in *A View of the Present State of Ireland*: A Discussion of Recent Studies Concerning Edmund Spenser's Dialogue." *Connotations* 4, nos. 1-2 (1994/95): 119-32.

———. "Representing Exile: Ireland in the Formation of the English Nation, 1558-1603." Ph.D. thesis, Queen's University, Belfast, 1996.

Breffny, Brian de. "An Elizabethan Political Painting." *Irish Arts Review* 1, no. 1 (Spring 1984): 1-5.

Brink, Jean. "Constructing the *View of the Present State of Ireland*." *Spenser Studies* 11 (1990): 203-28.

Bristoll, John [John Thornborough, Bishop of Bristol]. *The Ioiefvll and Blessed Revniting of Two Mighty & Famous Kingdomes, England & Scotland into their Ancient Name of Great Brittaine*. Oxford: n.d.

Brown, Keith. "Historical Context and *Henry V*." *Cahiers Elisabethains* (1986): 77-81.

Brown, Paul. "'This Thing of Darkness I Acknowledge Mine: *The Tempest* and the Discourse of Colonialism." In *Political Shakespeare: Essays on Cultural Materialism*, edited by Jonathan Dollimore and Alan Sinfield, 48-71. Manchester University Press, 1985.

Burnett, Mark Thornton, and Ramona Wray, eds. *Shakespeare and Ireland: History, Politics, Culture*. Basingstoke: Macmillan, 1997.

Butler, Richard, ed. *Tracts Relating to Ireland*. Dublin: Irish Archaeological Society, 1843.

Caball, Marc. "*The Gaelic Mind and the Collapse of the Gaelic World*: An Appraisal." *Cambrian Medieval Celtic Studies* 25 (1993): 87-96.

Cairns, David, and Shaun Richards. *Writing Ireland: Colonialism, Nationalism and Culture*. Manchester: Manchester University Press, 1988.

Calendar of State Papers, Ireland, James I. 1603-1606, edited by C.W. Russell and John P. Prendergast. London: Longman, 1872.

Campbell, Mary. *The Witness and the Other World: Exotic European Travel Writing, 400-1600*. Ithaca, N.Y.: Cornell University Press, 1988.

Camden, William. *The Historie of the Most Renowned and Victorious Princesse Elizabeth*, translated by R. Norton. Vol. 4. London: 1630.

Canny, Nicholas. "Debate: Spenser's Irish Crisis: Humanism and Experience in the 1590s." *Past and Present* 120 (August 1988): 201-9.

———. "Edmund Spenser and the Development of an Anglo-Irish Identity." *Yearbook of English Studies* 12 (1983): 1-19.

———. *The Elizabethan Conquest of Ireland: A Pattern Established 1565-76*. New York: Barnes & Noble, 1976.

———. "The Formation of the Irish Mind: Religion, Politics and Gaelic Literature, 1580-1750." *Past and Present* 95 (1982): 91-116.

———. *The Formation of the Old English Elite in Ireland*. Dublin: National University, 1975.

———. "Hugh O'Neill, Earl of Tyrone, and the Changing Face of Gaelic Ulster." *Studia Hibernica* 10 (1970): 7-35.

———. "Identity Formation in Ireland: The Emergence of the Anglo-Irish." In *Colonial*

Identity in the Atlantic World, 1500-1800, edited by Nicholas Canny and Anthony Pagden, 159-212. Princeton, N.J.: Princeton University Press, 1987.

———. "The Ideology of English Colonization: From Ireland to America." *William and Mary Quarterly* XXX (1973): 575-598.

———. "Introduction: Spenser and the Reform of Ireland." In *Spenser and Ireland: An Interdisciplinary Perspective,* edited by Patricia Coughlan, 9-24. Cork: Cork University Press, 1979.

———. "Reviewing *A View of the Present State of Ireland.*" *Irish University Review* 26, no. 2 (Autumn/Winter 1996): 252-67.

———. "The Treaty of Mellifont and the Re-Organisation of Ulster, 1603." *Irish Sword* 9, no. 37 (Winter 1970): 249-62.

———. *The Upstart Earl: A Study of the Social and Mental World of Richard Boyle, First Earl of Cork, 1566-1643.* Cambridge: Cambridge University Press, 1982.

———. "Why the Reformation Failed in Ireland: *Une Question Mal Posée.*" *Journal of Ecclesiastical History* 30, no. 4 (October 1979): 423-50.

Canny, Nicholas, and Anthony Pagden, eds. *Colonial Identity in the Atlantic World, 1500-1800.* Princeton, N.J.: Princeton University Press, 1987.

Carroll, Clare. "The Construction of Gender and the Cultural and Political Other in *The Faerie Queene* 5 and *A View of the Present State of Ireland*: The Critics, the Context, and the Case of Radigund." *Criticism* 32, no. 2 (Spring 1990): 163-91.

Cavanagh, Shiela T. "'Licentious Barbarism': Spenser's View of the Irish and *The Faerie Queene.*" *Irish University Review* 26, no. 2 (Autumn/Winter 1996): 268-80.

———. "'Such Was Irena's Countenance': Ireland in Spenser's Prose and Poetry." *Texas Studies in Literature and Language* 28, no. 1 (Spring 1986): 24-50.

Certeau, Michel de. *Heterologies: Discourse of the Other,* translated by Brian Massumi. Manchester: Manchester University Press, 1986.

Césaire, Aimé. *A Tempest,* translated by Richard Miller. New York: UBU, 1985.

———. *Discourse on Colonialism,* translated by Joan Pinkham. New York: Monthly Review, 1972.

Churchyard, Thomas. *A Generall Rehearsall of Warres.* London: 1579.

Clarke, Aidan. *The Old English in Ireland, 1625-1642.* London: MacGibbon and Kee, 1966.

Clark, Aidan, and R. Dudley Edwards. "Pacification, Plantation, and the Catholic Question" in *A New History of Ireland.* Vol. 3: *Early Modern Ireland,* edited by F.X. Martin, W.E. Vaughan, A. Cosgrove, and J.R. Hill, 187-232. Oxford: Oxford University Press, 1976.

Columbus, Christopher. *The Four Voyages,* translated and edited by J. M. Cohen. Harmondsworth: Penguin, 1969.

Corish, Patrick J. "The Rising of 1641 and the Catholic Confederacy, 1641-45." In *A New History of Ireland.* Vol. 3: *Early Modern Ireland,* edited by F.X. Martin, F.J. Byrne, W.E. Vaughan, A. Cosgrove, and J.R. Hill, 269-316. Oxford: Oxford University Press, 1976-91.

Corns, Thomas N. "Milton's *Observations upon the Articles of Peace*: Ireland under English

Eyes." In *Politics, Poetics, and Hermeneutics in Milton's Prose,* edited by David Lowenstein and James Grantham Turner, 123-134. Cambridge: Cambridge University Press, 1990.

Cortés, Hernán. *Letters from Mexico,* translated and and edited by Anthony Pagden. New Haven, Conn.: Yale University Press, 1986.

Cosgrove, Art. "Hiberniores Ipsis Hibernis." In *Studies in Irish History Presented to R. Dudley Edwards,* edited by Art Cosgrove and Donal McCarthy, 1-14. Dublin: University College Dublin Press, 1979.

Coughlan, Patricia, ed. *Spenser and Ireland: An Interdisciplinary Perspective.* Cork: Cork University Press, 1989.

————. "The Local Context of Mutabilitie's Plea." *Irish University Review* 26, no. 2 (Autumn/Winter 1996): 320-41.

————. "'Cheap and Common Animals': The English Anatomy of Ireland in the Seventeenth Century." In *Literature and the English Civil War,* edited by Thomas Healy and Jonathan Sawday, 205-23. Cambridge: Cambridge University Press, 1990.

————. "'Some secret scourge which shall by her come unto England': Ireland and Incivility in Spenser." In *Spenser and Ireland: An Interdisciplinary Perspective,* edited by Patricia Coughlan, 46-74. Cork: Cork University Press, 1979.

Crag, John. *A Prophecy Concerning the Earle of Essex that now is.* London: 1641.

The Cronicle History of Henry the fift, With his Battell Fought at Agin Court in France. Togither with Auntient Pistoll. London: 1600.

Cunningham, Bernadette. "Native Culture and Political Change in Ireland, 1580-1640." In *Natives and Newcomers: Essays on the Making of Irish Colonial Society, 1534-1641,* edited by Ciarán Brady and Raymond Gillespie, 148-70. Dublin: Irish Academic Press, 1986.

Daniel, Samuel. *A Panegyrike Congratvlatorie to the Kings Maiestie. Also Certaine Epistles.* London: 1603.

Davies, John. *Discovery of the True Causes why Ireland was never Entirely Subdued.* London: 1612; facsimile reprint Shannon: Irish University Press, 1969.

Davies, R.R. *Domination and Conquest: The Experience of Ireland, Scotland and Wales, 1100-1300.* Cambridge: Cambridge University Press, 1990.

Dawson, Jane. "Two Kingdoms or Three?: Ireland in Anglo-Scottish Relations in the Middle of the Sixteenth Century." In *Scotland and England, 1286-1815,* edited by Roger A. Mason, 113-38. Edinburgh: John Donald, 1987.

Deane, Seamus, "Civilians and Barbarians." In *Ireland's Field Day,* 33-42. South Bend, Ind.: University of Notre Dame Press, 1986.

————. "Introduction." In *Nationalism, Colonialism, and Culture,* edited by Seamus Deane, 3-19. Minneapolis: University of Minnesota Press, 1990.

————. "Muffling the Cry for a Hungry Past." *Guardian,* June 17 1995, sec. 2, p. 1.

————, ed. *Nationalism, Colonialism, and Literature.* Minneapolis: University of Minnesota Press, 1990.

Derricke, John. *The Image of Ireland.* London: 1581; reprinted Edinburgh: Adam and Charles Black, 1883.

Dollimore, Jonathan. *Sexual Dissidence: Augustine to Wilde, Freud to Foucault.* Oxford: Clarendon, 1991.

Dollimore, Jonathan, and Alan Sinfield, "History and Ideology: The Instance of *Henry V.*" In *Alternative Shakespeares,* edited by John Drakakis, 206-27. London: Routledge, 1985.

————, eds. *Political Shakespeare: [New] Essays in Cultural Materialism.* Manchester: Manchester University Press, 1985; second edition: 1995.

Donaldson, Gordon. "Foundations of Anglo-Scottish Union." In *Elizabethan Government and Society: Essays Presented to Sir John Neale,* edited by S.T. Bindoff, J. Hurstfield, and C.H. Williams, 282-314. London: Athlone, 1961.

Donne, John. *The Complete Poetry of John Donne,* edited by John T. Shawcross. New York: Anchor, 1967.

Doyle, Roddy. *The Commitments.* New York: Vintage, 1989.

Dymmock, John. *A Treatice of Ireland.* In vol. 2 of *Tracts Relating to Ireland,* edited by Richard Butler, 5-51. Dublin: Irish Archaeological Society, 1843.

Eagleton, Terry. *Heathcliff and the Great Hunger: Studies in Irish Culture.* London: Verso, 1995.

————. "Nationalism: Irony and Commitment." In *Nationalism, Colonialism, and Literature,* edited by Seamus Deane, 23-42. Minneapolis: University of Minnesota Press, 1990.

————. "A Postmodern Punch." *Irish Studies Review* 6 (Spring 1994): 3-4.

Edwards, Philip. *Threshold of a Nation: A Study in English and Irish Drama.* Cambridge: Cambridge University Press, 1979.

Elliott, J.H. "Introduction." In *Colonial Identity in the Atlantic World, 1500-1800,* edited by Nicholas Canny and Anthony Pagden, 3-13. Princeton, N.J.: Princeton University Press, 1987.

Ellis, Steven G. "Economic Problems of the Church: Why the Reformation Failed in Ireland." *Journal of Ecclesiastical History* 41, no. 2 (April 1990): 239-65.

————. *Tudor Ireland: Crown, Community and the Conflict of Culture.* London: Longman, 1985.

————. "Tudor State Formation and the Shaping of the British Isles." In *Conquest & Union: Fashioning a British State, 1485-1725,* edited by Steven Ellis and Sarah Barber, 40-63. London: Longman, 1995.

————. "Writing Irish History: Revisionism, Colonialism, and the British Isles." *Irish Review* 19 (Spring/Summer 1996): 1-21.

Ellis, Steven G., and Sarah Barber, eds. *Conquest & Union: Fashioning a British State, 1485-1725.* London: Longman, 1995.

Elsky, Martin. *Authorizing Words: Speech, Writing, and Print in the Early Renaissance.* Ithaca, N.Y.: Cornell University Press, 1989.

Emitie, Thomas. *A New Remonstrance from Ireland. . . .* London: 1642.

Empson, William. *Some Versions of Pastoral.* London: Chatto and Windus, 1968.

Englands Division, and Irelands Distraction. . . . London: 1642.

Enright, Michael J. "King James and his Island: An Archaic Kingship Belief?" *Scottish Historical Review* 55 (1976): 28-40.

Falls, Cyril. *Elizabeth's Irish Wars.* London: Methuen, 1950.

The Famovs Victories of Henry the fifth: Containing the Honourable Battell of Agin-Court. London, 1598. Published in facsimile as *The Famous Victories of Henry the Fifth: The Earliest Known Quarto, 1598.* London: Praetorius, 1887.

Fanon, Frantz. *Black Skin White Masks.* London: Pluto, 1986.

———. *The Wretched of the Earth,* translated by Constance Farrington. New York: Grove Press, 1968.

Fogarty, Anne. "The Colonization of Language: Narrative Strategies in *A View of the Present State of Ireland* and *The Faerie Queene,* Book VI." In *Spenser and Ireland: An Interdisciplinary Perspective,* edited by Patricia Coughlan, 75-109. Cork: Cork University Press, 1989.

———, ed. Special issue of *Irish University Review* 26, no. 2 (Autumn/Winter 1996) on "Spenser in Ireland 1596-1996."

Ford, Alan. *The Protestant Reformation in Ireland, 1590-1641.* Frankfurt: Peter Lang, 1987.

———. "Reforming the Holy Isle: Parr Lane and the Conversion of the Irish." (in press).

Ford, John. *Fames Memoriall, or the Earle of Deuonshire Deceased.* London: 1606.

Foster, R.F. *Modern Ireland, 1600-1972.* London: Penguin, 1989.

Foucault, Michel. *Language, Counter-Memory, Practice: Selected Essays and Interviews,* edited by Donald F. Bouchard; translated by Donald F. Bouchard and Sherry Simon. Oxford: Blackwell, 1977.

———. *Discipline and Punish: The Birth of the Prison,* translated by Alan Sheridan. New York: Vintage, 1979.

Frame, Robin. *Colonial Ireland, 1169-1369.* Dublin: Helicon, 1981.

———. "Overlordship and Reaction, *c.* 1200-*c.* 1450." In *Uniting the Kingdom? The Making of British History,* edited by Alexander Grant and Keith Stringer. London: Routledge, 1995.

Friel, Brian. *Making History.* London: Faber & Faber, 1988.

Gainsford, Thomas. *The True and Exemplary and Remarkable History of the Earle of Tirone.* London: 1619.

Galloway, Bruce R., and Brian P. Levack, eds. *The Jacobean Union: Six Tracts.* Edinburgh: Clark Constable, 1985.

Gates, Henry Louis. "Critical Fanonism." *Critical Inquiry* 17, no. 3 (Spring 1991): 457-70.

Gearty, Conor. "Diary." *London Review of Books* 18, no. 23 (1996): 28-29.

Geoffrey of Monmouth. *The History of the Kings of Britain,* translated and with introduction by Lewis Thorpe. London: Penguin, 1966.

Gerald of Wales. *Expugnatio Hibernica/The Conquest of Ireland,* translated by A.B. Scott. Dublin: Royal Irish Academy, 1978.

———. *The History and Topographia of Ireland,* translated by John O'Meara. London: Penguin, 1982

———. *The Journey Through Wales/The Description of Wales,* translated and with introduction by Lewis Thorpe. London: Penguin, 1978.

———. *Topographia Hibernica.* Volume 5: *Geraldi Cambrensis Opera,* edited by James F. Dimock. London: Her Majesty's Stationery Office, 1867; reprint London: Kraus, 1964.

Gillespie, Raymond. *Colonial Ulster: The Settlement of East Ulster, 1600-1641.* Cork: Cork University Press, 1985.

———. "The End of an Era: Ulster and the Outbreak of the 1641 Rising." In *Natives and Newcomers: Essays on the Making of Irish Colonial Society, 1534-1641,* edited by Ciarán Brady and Raymond Gillespie, 191-237. Dublin: Irish Academic Press, 1986.

Gillingham, John. "The Beginnings of English Imperialism." *Journal of Historical Sociology* 5, no. 4 (December 1992): 392-409.

———. "The English Invasion of Ireland." In *Representing Ireland: Literature and the Origins of Conflict, 1534-1660,* edited by Brendan Bradshaw, Andrew Hadfield, and Willy Maley, 24-42. Cambridge: Cambridge University Press, 1993.

———. "Foundations of a Disunited Kingdom." In *Uniting the Kingdom? The Making of British History,* edited by Alexander Grant and Keith Stringer, 48-64. London, Routledge, 1995.

Goldberg, Jonathan. *James I and the Politics of Literature: Jonson, Shakespeare, Donne and their Contemporaries.* Stanford, Calif.: Stanford University Press, 1989.

Gordon, D.J. "*Hymenæi*: Ben Jonson's Masque of Union." In *The Renaissance Imagination: Essays and Lectures by D.J. Gordon,* edited by Stephen Orgel, 157-84. Berkeley: University of California Press, 1975.

Graham, J.K. "Hugh O'Neill, 2nd Earl of Tyrone." M.A. thesis, Queens University, Belfast, 1938.

Grant, Alexander, and Keith J. Stringer, eds. *Uniting the Kingdom? The Making of British History.* London: Routledge, 1995.

Greenblatt, Stephen. "Invisible Bullets: Renaissance Authority and its Subversion, *Henry IV* and *Henry V.*" In *Political Shakespeare: [New] Essays in Cultural Materialism,* edited by Jonathan Dollimore and Alan Sinfield, 18-47. Manchester: Manchester University Press, 1985; 2d ed., 1995.

———. *Renaissance Self-Fashioning: From More to Shakespeare.* Chicago: University of Chicago Press, 1980.

G.S. *A Briefe Declaration of the Barbarovs and Inhumane Dealings of the Northerne Irish Rebels. . . .* London: 1641.

Guha, Ranajit, and Gayatri Chakravorty Spivak, eds. *Selected Subaltern Studies.* Oxford: Oxford University Press, 1988.

Gurr, Andrew. "Why Captain Jamy in *Henry V?*" *Archiv fur das Studium der Neuren Sprachen uns Literaturen* 226, no. 2 (1989): 365-73.

Hadfield, Andrew. "Another Look at Serena and Irena." *Irish Studies Review* 26, no. 2 (Autumn/Winter 1996): 291-302.

———. "Briton and Scythian: Tudor Representations of Irish Origins." *Irish Historical Studies* 28, no. 112 (November 1993): 390-408.

———. "The Course of Justice: Spenser, Ireland and Political Discourse." *Studi Neophilologica* 65 (1993): 187-96.

———. "English Colonialism and National Identity in Early Modern Ireland." *Éire-Ireland* 28, no. 1 (Spring 1993): 69-86.

———. *Literature, Politics and National Identity: Reformation to Renaissance.* Cambridge: Cambridge University Press, 1994.

———. "The 'Sacred Hunger of Ambitious Minds': Spenser's Savage Religion." In *Religion, Literature, and Politics in Post-Reformation England, 1540-1688,* edited by Donna B. Hamilton and Richard Strier, 27-45. Cambridge: Cambridge University Press, 1995.

———. "The Spectre of Positivism? Sixteenth-Century Irish Historiography." *Text & Context* 3 (1988): 10-16.

———. "Spenser, Ireland, and Sixteenth-Century Political Theory." *Modern Language Review* 89, no. 1 (January 1994): 1-18.

———. *Spenser's Irish Experience: Wilde Fruit and Salvage Soyl.* Oxford: Clarendon, 1997.

———. "Spenser's *View of the Present State of Ireland*: Some Notes Toward a 'Materialist' Analysis of Discourse." In *Anglo-Irish and Irish Literature: Aspects of Language and Culture,* vol. 2, edited by Brigit Bramsbäck and Martin Croghan, 265-72. Uppsala: Uppsala University Press, 1988.

———. "Translating the Reformation: John Bale's Irish *Vocacyon.*" In *Representing Ireland: Literature and the Origins of Conflict, 1534-1660,* edited by Brendan Bradshaw, Andrew Hadfield, and Willy Maley, 43-59. Cambridge: Cambridge University Press, 1993.

———. "Was Spenser's *View of the Present State of Ireland* Censored? A Review of the Evidence." *Notes and Queries* 240, no. 4 (December 1994): 459-63.

———. "Who Is Speaking in Spenser's *A View of the Present State of Ireland?* A Response to John Breen." *Connotations* 4, no. 3 (1994/95): 233-41.

Hadfield, Andrew, and John McVeagh, eds. *"Strangers to That Land": British Perceptions of Ireland from the Reformation to the Famine.* Gerrard's Cross: Colin Smythe, 1994.

Hadfield, Andrew, and Willy Maley. "Introduction: Irish Representations and English Alternatives." In *Representing Ireland: Literature and the Origins of Conflict, 1534-1660,* edited by Brendan Bradshaw, Andrew Hadfield, and Willy Maley, 1-23. Cambridge: Cambridge University Press, 1993.

Hamilton, A.C., ed. *A Spenser Encyclopedia.* Toronto: University of Toronto Press, 1990.

Hammerstein, Helga. "Aspects of the Continental Education of Irish Students in the Reign of Queen Elizabeth I." *Historical Studies* 8 (1969): 137-53.

Harington, John. *The Letters and Epigrams of Sir John Harington,* edited by N.E. McClure. Philadelphia: University of Pennsylvania Press, 1930.

———. *Nugæ Antiquæ.* London: 1804.

———. *A Short View of the State of Ireland.* London: 1605.

Hayes-McCoy, G.A. "The Army of Ulster, 1593-1601." *The Irish Sword* 1 (1949-53): 105-17.

Healy, Shay, dir. *The Rocker: A Portrait of Phil Lynott.* Dublin: Safinia/RTE, 1996.

Healy, Thomas. *New Latitudes: Theory and English Renaissance Literature.* London: Edward Arnold, 1992.

————. "Selves, States, and Sectarianism in Early Modern England." *English* 44, no. 180 (Autumn 1995): 193-213.

Heaney, Seamus. *North.* London: Faber and Faber, 1975.

————. *Wintering Out.* London: Faber and Faber, 1972.

Helgerson, Richard. *Forms of Nationhood: The Elizabethan Writing of England.* Chicago: University of Chicago Press, 1992.

Henley, Pauline. *Spenser in Ireland.* Cork: Cork University Press, 1928.

Herbert, Sir William. *Croftus: sive de Hibernia Liber,* edited and translated by Arthur Keaveney and John A. Madden. Dublin: Irish Manuscripts Commission, 1992.

Highley, Christopher. "Wales, Ireland, and *1 Henry IV.*" *Renaissance Drama* n.s. 21 (1990): 91-114.

————. "Spenser and the Bards." *Spenser Studies* (in press).

Hill, Christopher. "Seventeenth-Century English Radicals and Ireland." In *Radicals, Rebels and Establishments,* edited by Patrick J. Corish, 33-49. Belfast: Appletree Press, 1985.

Hodgen, Margaret T. *Early Anthropology in the Sixteenth and Seventeenth Centuries.* Philadelphia: University of Pennsylvania Press, 1964.

Hogan, James. "Shane O'Neill Comes to the Court of Elizabeth." In *Féil Scríbhinn Tórna: Essays and Studies Presented to Professor Tadhg Ua Donnchadha,* edited by S. Pender, 154-70. Cork: Cork University Press, 1947.

Holderness, Graham. "'What ish my nation?': Shakespeare and National Identities." *Textual Practice* 5, no. 1 (1991): 80-99.

hooks, bell. *Ain't I a Woman: Black Women and Feminism.* London: Pluto, 1982.

I.H. [John Hayward]. *A Treatise of Vnion of the Two Realmes of England and Scotland.* London: 1604.

Hughes, Merritt Y. "The Historical Setting of Milton's *Observations on the Articles of Peace, 1649.*" *PMLA,* 65, no. 5 (1949): 1049-73.

Irelands Amazement, or the Heavens Armado. . . . London: 1642.

Ireland's Field Day. South Bend, Ind.: University of Notre Dame Press, 1986.

James I. *The Political Works of James I,* edited by Charles Howard McIlwain. Cambridge, Mass.: Harvard University Press, 1918.

JanMohamed, Abdul. "The Economy of Manichean Allegory: The Function of Racial Difference in Colonialist Literature." In *"Race," Writing, and Difference,* edited by Henry Louis Gates, 78-106. Chicago: Chicago University Press, 1986.

————. *Manichean Aesthetics: The Politics of Literature in Colonial Africa.* Amherst, Mass.: University of Massachusetts Press, 1983.

Jardine, Lisa. "Encountering Ireland: Gabriel Harvey, Edmund Spenser, and English Colonial Ventures." In *Representing Ireland: Literature and the Origins of Conflict, 1534-1660,* edited by Brendan Bradshaw, Andrew Hadfield, and Willy Maley, 60-75. Cambridge: Cambridge University Press, 1993.

————. "Mastering the Uncouth: Gabriel Harvey, Edmund Spenser and the English Experience in Ireland." In *New Perspectives on Renaissance Thought: Essays in the History of Science, Education and Philosophy in Memory of Charles B. Schmitt,* edited by John Henry and Sarah Hutton, 68-82. London: Duckworth, 1990.

Jones, Ann Rosalind, and Peter Stallybrass. "Dismantling Irena: The Sexualizing of Ireland in Early Modern England." In *Nationalisms and Sexualities,* edited by Andrew Parker, Mary Russo, Doris Sommer, and Patricia Yaeger, 157-71. London: Routledge, 1992.

Jones, F.M. *Mountjoy, 1563-1606: The Last Elizabethan Deputy.* London: Burns, Oates and Washbourne, 1958.

Jones, W.R. "The Image of the Barbarian in Medieval Europe." *Comparative Studies in Society and History* 8 (1971): 376-407.

Jonson, Ben. *The Complete Masques,* edited by Stephen Orgel. New Haven: Yale University Press, 1969.

———. *Complete Works.* London: 1616.

———. *The Complete Works,* edited by C.H. Herford and P. and E. Simpson. Oxford: Clarendon, 1947.

Judson, Alexander. *The Life of Edmund Spenser.* Baltimore: Johns Hopkins University Press, 1945.

Kearney, Richard. "Introduction." In *The Irish Mind: Exploring Intellectual Traditions,* edited by Richard Kearney, 7-14. Dublin: Wolfhound, 1985.

Keating, Geoffrey [Seatrún Céitinn]. *Foras Feasa ar Éireann,* edited and translated by D. Comyn and P.S. Dineen as *The History of Ireland.* London: Early Irish Text Society, 1902-1913.

Klein, Bernhard. "English Cartographers and the Mapping of Ireland in the Early Modern Period." *Journal for the Study of British Cultures* 2, no. 2 (1995): 115-39.

Kiberd, Declan. "Anglo-Irish Attitudes." In *Ireland's Field Day,* 83-105. South Bend, Ind.: University of Notre Dame Press, 1986.

———. *Inventing Ireland: The Literature of the Modern Nation.* London: Jonathan Cape, 1995.

Kupperman, Karen Ordahl. *Settling with the Indians: The Meeting of English and Indian Cultures in America, 1580-1640.* London: Dent, 1980.

Lane, Parr. *Newes from the Holy Ile.* Dublin: Trinity College Dublin Ms 786.

Las Casas, Bartolomé de. *A Short Account of the Destruction of the Indies,* translated by Nigel Griffin. London: Penguin, 1992.

Laurence, Anne. "The Cradle to the Grave: English Observations of Irish Social Customs in the Seventeenth Century." *Seventeenth Century* 3 (1988): 63-82.

Lennon, Colm. *Richard Stanihurst, The Dubliner, 1547-1618.* Dublin: Irish Academic Press, 1981.

Levack, Brian P. *The Formation of the British State: England, Scotland, and the Union, 1603-1707.* Oxford: Clarendon, 1987.

Lim, Walter. "Figuring Justice." *Renaissance and Reformation* 19, no. 1 (1995): 45-70.

Lindley, David. "Embarrassing Ben: The Masques for Frances Howard." *English Literary Renaissance* 16 (1986): 343-59.

———. *The Trials of Frances Howard: Fact and Fiction at the Court of King James.* London: Routledge, 1996.

Lindley, Keith J. "The Impact of the 1641 Rebellion upon England and Wales, 1641-5." *Irish Historical Studies* 18, no. 70 (September 1972): 143-76.

———. "The Part Played by the Catholics in the English Civil War." Ph.D. thesis, University of Manchester, 1968.

Lloyd, David. *Anomalous States: Irish Writing and the Post-Colonial Moment.* Dublin: Lilliput, 1993.

Lombard, Peter. *De Regno Hiberniae,* edited by John McClean. London, 1857.

Lupton, Julia Reinhard. "Home-Making in Ireland: Virgil's Eclogue I and Book VI of *The Faerie Queene.*" *Spenser Studies* 7 (1990): 713-35.

MacCarthy-Morrogh, Michael. *The Munster Plantation: English Migration to Southern Ireland, 1583-1641.* Oxford: Clarendon, 1986.

MacCurtain, Margaret. *Tudor and Stuart Ireland.* Dublin: Longmans, 1972.

Malcolm, Joyce Lee. "All the King's Men: The Impact of the Crown's Irish Soldiers on the English Civil War." *Irish Historical Studies* 22, no. 83 (1979): 239-64.

Maley, Willy. "'Another Britain'?: Bacon's *Certain Considerations Touching the Plantation in Ireland* (1609)." *Prose Studies* 18, no. 1 (April 1995): 1-18.

———. "Fording the Nation: The British Problem in *Perkin Warbeck* (1634)." *Critical Survey* 9, no. 3 (Autumn 1997): 11-31.

———. "How Milton and Some Contemporaries Read Spenser's *View.*" In *Representing Ireland: Literature and the Origins of Conflict, 1534-1660,* edited by Brendan Bradshaw, Andrew Hadfield, and Willy Maley, 191-207. Cambridge: Cambridge University Press, 1993.

———. "Rebels and Redshanks: Milton and the British Problem." *Irish Studies Review* 6 (Spring 1994): 7-11.

———. Review of Brendan Bradshaw and John Morrill, eds., *The British Problem. . . . History Ireland* (Winter 1996): 53-55.

———. Review of Clare Carroll and Vincent Carey, eds., *Solon his Follie. Irish Studies Review* 17 (Winter 1996/97): 44-45.

———. Review of David Cairns and Shaun Richards, *Writing Ireland: Colonialism, Nationalism and Culture. Textual Practice* 3, no. 2 (1989): 291-98.

———. "Shakespeare, Holinshed and Ireland: Resources and Con-Texts." In *Shakespeare and Ireland: History, Politics, Culture,* edited by Mark Thornton Burnett and Ramona Wray, 27-46. Basingstoke: Macmillan, 1997.

———. "Spenser and Ireland: A Select Bibliography." *Spenser Studies* 9 (1991): 227-42.

———. "Spenser and Ireland: An Annotated Bibliography, 1986-96." *Irish University Review* 26, no. 2 (Autumn/Winter 1996): 342-53.

———. "Spenser and Scotland: The *View* and the Limits of Anglo-Irish Identity." *Prose Studies* 19, no. 1 (April 1996): 1-18.

———. "'This Sceptred Isle': Shakespeare and the British Problem." In *Shakespeare and National Culture,* edited by John Joughin, 83-108. Manchester: Manchester University Press, 1997.

———. "Varieties of Nationalism: Post-Revisionist Irish Studies." *Irish Studies Review* 15 (Summer 1996): 34-37.

Marcus, Leah. *Puzzling Shakespeare: Local Reading and its Discontents.* Berkeley: University of California Press, 1988.

Martin, F.X. "Gerald of Wales, Norman Reporter on Ireland." *Studies* (Autumn 1969): 279-92.

————. "Diarmait MacMurchadha and the Coming of the Anglo-Normans." In *A New History of Ireland.*. Vol. 2: *Medieval Ireland, 1169-1534,* edited by F.X. Martin, F.J. Byrne, W.E. Vaughan, A. Cosgrove, and J.R. Hill, 43-66. Oxford: Oxford University Press, 1987.

Martin, F.X., F.J. Byrne, W.E. Vaughan, A. Cosgrove, and J.R. Hill, eds. *A New History of Ireland.* 9 vols. Oxford: Oxford University Press, 1976-91.

McCabe, Richard A. "The Fate of Irena: Spenser and Political Violence." In *Spenser and Ireland: An Interdisciplinary Perspective,* edited by Patricia Coughlan, 109-25. Cork: Cork University Press, 1989.

McCavitt, John. "The Flight of the Earls, 1607." *Irish Historical Studies* 29, no. 114 (1994): 159-73.

McRobbie, Angela. "Strategies of Vigilence: An Interview with Gayatri Spivak." *Block* 10 (1985).

Milton, John. *Observations on the Articles of Peace.* London: 1649.

Mitchell, John. *The Life and Times of Aodh O'Neill.* Dublin: James Duffy, 1846.

Montrose, Louis Adrian. "Of Gentlemen and Shepherds: The Politics of Elizabethan Pastoral Form." *English Literary History* 50 (1983): 415-59.

————. "'Shaping Fantasies': Figurations of Gender and Power in Elizabethan Culture." *Representations* 12 (Spring 1983): 61-94.

More Newes from Ireland: Or, the Bloody Practices and Proceedings of the Papists in that Kingdome at this Present. London: 1641.

Morgan, Hiram. "The Colonial Venture of Sir Thomas Smith in Ulster, 1571-1575." *Historical Journal* 28, no. 2 (1985): 261-78.

————. "Hugh O'Neill and the Nine Years War in Tudor Ireland." *Historical Journal* 36, no. 1 (1993): 21-37.

————. "Mid-Atlantic Blues." *Irish Review* 11 (1991-92): 50-55.

————. "Making History: A Criticism and a Manifesto." *Text & Context* (Autumn 1990): 61-65.

————. "Tom Lee: The Posing Peacemaker." In *Representing Ireland: Literature and the Origins of Conflict, 1534-1660,* edited by Brendan Bradshaw, Andrew Hadfield, and Willy Maley, 132-65. Cambridge: Cambridge University Press, 1993.

————. *Tyrone's Rebellion: The Outbreak of the Nine Years' War in Tudor Ireland.* Woodbridge, England: Boydell, 1993.

Morrill, John. "The British Problem, c. 1534-1707." In *The British Problem, c. 1534-1707: State Formation in the Atlantic Archipelago,* edited by Brendan Bradshaw and John Morrill, 1-38. Basingstoke: Macmillan, 1996.

————. "The Fashioning of Britain." In *Conquest & Union: Fashioning a British State, 1485-1725,* edited by Steven G. Ellis and Sarah Barber, 8-39. London: Longman, 1995.

Moryson, Fynes. *An Itinerary.* Vol. 2. London: 1617.

Murphy, Andrew. Review of Elizabeth L. Rambo, *Colonial Ireland in Medieval Literature. Irish Studies Review* 11 (Autumn 1995): 32.

———. "Shakespeare's Irish History." *Literature & History* 5, no. 1 (Spring 1996): 38-59.

———. "'Tish Ill Done': *Henry the Fift* and the Politics of Editing." In *Shakespeare and Ireland: History, Politics, Culture,* edited by Mark Thornton Burnett and Ramona Wray, 213-234. Basingstoke: Macmillan, 1997.

———, ed. *The Renaissance Text: Theory, Editing, Textuality.* Manchester: Manchester University Press, forthcoming 1999.

Murphy, Thomas. *The Gigli Concert.* Dublin: Gallery, 1984.

Meyers, James P. "Early English Colonial Experiences in Ireland: Captain Thomas Lee and Sir John Davies." *Éire-Ireland* 23 (Spring 1988): 8-21.

———, ed. *Elizabethan Ireland: A Selection of Writings by Elizabethan Writers on Ireland.* Hamden, Conn.: Archon, 1983.

Neill, Michael. "Broken English and Broken Irish: Nation, Language, and the Optic of Power in Shakespeare's Histories." *Shakespeare Quarterly* 45, no. 1 (Spring 1994): 1-32.

———. "*Henry V*: A Modern Perspective." In William Shakespeare, *Henry V,* edited by Barbara Mowat and Paul Werstine, 253-78. New York: Washington Square Press, 1995.

Norbrook, David. *Poetry and Politics in the English Renaissance.* London: Routledge and Keegan Paul, 1984.

Notestein, Wallace. *The House of Commons, 1604-1610.* New Haven, Conn.: Yale University Press, 1971.

Ó Faoláin, Seán. *The Great O'Neill.* London: Longmans, 1942.

Orgel, Stephen. *The Illusion of Power: Political Theatre in the English Renaissance.* Berkeley: University of California Press, 1975.

———. *The Jonsonian Masque.* New York: Columbia, 1981.

———. "Margins of Truth." In *The Renaissance Text: Theory, Editing, Textuality,* edited by Andrew Murphy. Manchester: Manchester University Press, forthcoming 1999.

O Riordan, Michelle. *The Gaelic Mind and the Collapse of the Gaelic World.* Cork: Cork University Press, 1990.

Oxford English Dictionary: Compact Edition. Oxford: Oxford University Press, 1971.

Pagden, Anthony. "Introduction." In *A Short Account of the Destruction of the Indies,* Bartolomé de Las Casas, xiii-xli. Translated by Nigel Griffin. London: Penguin, 1992.

———. *The Fall of Natural Man: The American Indian and the Origins of Comparative Ethnology.* Cambridge: Cambridge University Press, 1982.

Palmer, William. "Gender, Violence, and Rebellion in Tudor and Early Stuart Ireland." *Sixteenth Century Journal* 23, no. 4 (1992): 699-712.

Parry, Benita. "Problems in Current Theories of Colonial Discourse." *Oxford Literary Review* 9, nos. 1-2 (1987): 27-58.

Parry, J.H., ed. *The European Reconnaissance: Selected Documents.* London: Macmillan, 1968.

Patterson, Annabel. "The Egalitarian Giant: Representations of Justice in History/Literature." *Journal of British Studies* 31 (April 1992): 97-132.

———. *Shakespeare and the Popular Voice.* Oxford: Blackwell, 1989.

Pawlisch, Hans. *Sir John Davies and the Conquest of Ireland: A Study in Legal Imperialism.* Cambridge: Cambridge University Press, 1985.

Percevall-Maxwell, Michael. *The Outbreak of the Irish Rebellion of 1641.* Montreal: McGill-Queen's University Press, 1994.

Perrot, James. *The Chronicle of Ireland, 1584-1608,* edited by H. Wood. Dublin: Irish Manuscripts Commission, 1933.

Pocock, J.G.A. "The Atlantic Archipelago." In *The British Problem, c. 1534-1707: State Formation in the Atlantic Archipelago,* edited by Brendan Bradshaw and John Morrill, 172-91. Basingstoke: Macmillan, 1996.

————. "British History: A Plea for a New Subject." *Journal of Modern History* 47 (1975): 601-628.

————. "The Limits and Divisions of British History: In Search of the Unknown Subject." *American Historical Review* 87, no. 2 (1982): 311-36.

Quinn, David Beers. *The Elizabethans and the Irish.* Ithaca, N.Y.: Cornell, 1966.

Rambo, Elizabeth L. *Colonial Ireland in Medieval English Literature.* London: Associated University Presses, 1994.

Rambuss, Richard. *Spenser's Secret Career.* Cambridge: Cambridge University Press, 1993.

Richter, Michael. "The Interpretation of Medieval Irish History." *Irish Historical Studies* 24, no. 5 (May 1985): 289-98.

Robinson, Philip S. *The Plantation of Ulster: British Settlement in an Irish Landscape, 1600-1670.* Dublin: Gill & MacMillan, 1984.

Rothe, David. *Analecta Sacra Nova et Mira de Rebus Catholicorum in Hibernia* (Cologne: 1616-17), edited and translated by P.F. Moran, as *The Analecta of David Rothe, Bishop of Ossory.* Dublin: M.H. Gill, 1884.

Russell, Conrad. "The British Background to the Irish Rebellion of 1641." *Historical Research* 61, no. 145 (1988): 166-82.

————. "The British Problem and the English Civil War." *History* 72, no. 236 (1987): 395-415.

————. *The Causes of the English Civil War: The Ford Lectures Delivered in the University of Oxford, 1987-1988.* Oxford: Clarendon, 1990.

Said, Edward. *Culture and Imperialism.* London: Chatto and Windus, 1993.

————. *Orientalism.* New York: Vintage, 1979.

————. "Yeats and Decolonization." In *Nationalism, Colonialism, and Culture,* edited by Seamus Deane, 69-95. Minneapolis: University of Minnesota Press, 1990.

Sartre, Jean-Paul. *Anti-Semite and Jew,* translated by George J. Becker. New York: Shocken, 1976.

Schleiner, Winifried. "*Divina Virago*: Queen Elizabeth as an Amazon." *Studies in Philology* 75, no. 1 (January 1978): 163-80.

Sedgwick, Eve Kosofsky. *The Epistemology of the Closet.* Harmondsworth: Penguin, 1994.

Shakespeare, William. *Henry V.* Folger Library Edition, edited by Barbara A. Mowat and Paul Werstine. New York: Washington Square Press, 1995.

————. *Henry V,* edited by Gary Taylor. Oxford: Oxford University Press, 1982.

————. *King Henry V,,* edited by T.W. Craik, ed.. London: Routledge/Nelson, 1995.

————. *Mr. William Shakespeares Comedies, Histories, & Tragedies,* facsimile ed. Charlton Hinman as *The First Folio of Shakespeare.* New York: Norton, 1968.

Sheehan, Anthony J. "The Overthrow of the Plantation of Munster in October 1598." *The Irish Sword* 15 (1982-83): 11-22.

Sidney, Henry. *Memoire.* London: 1583; reprinted London: 1855.

Silke, J.J. *Kinsale: The Spanish Intervention in Ireland at the End of the Elizabethan Wars.* Liverpool: Liverpool University Press, 1970.

Simms, Anngret. "Core and Periphery in Medieval Europe: The Irish Experience in a Wider Context." In *Common Ground: Essays on the Historical Geography of Ireland,* edited by William Smyth and Kevin Whelan, 22-40. Cork: Cork University Press, 1988.

Simms, Katherine. "Bards and Barons: The Anglo-Irish Aristocracy and the Native Culture." In *Medieval Frontier Societies,* edited by Robert Bartlett and Angus MacKay, 177-98. Oxford: Clarendon Press, 1989.

Sinfield, Alan. *Cultural Politics: Queer Reading.* London: Routledge, 1994.

———. *Faultlines: Cultural Materialism and the Politics of Dissident Reading.* Oxford: Clarendon, 1992.

———. *The Wilde Century: Effeminacy, Oscar Wilde and the Queer Moment.* London: Cassell, 1994.

[Skynner, Jon.] *Rapta Tatio: The Mirrour of his Maiesties Present Gouernment, Tending to the Vnion of his Whole Iland of Brittonie.* London: 1604.

[Smith, Thomas.] *A Letter Sent by T. B. Gentleman Unto His Very Frende Mayster R. C. Esquire. . . .* Reproduced as an appendix to G. Hill, *A Historical Account of the MacDonnells of Antrim.* Belfast: 1873.

Smith, Warren D. "The *Henry V* Choruses in the First Folio." *Journal of English and Germanic Philology* 53 (1954): 38-57.

Speed, John. *Theatre of the Empire of Great Britaine.* London: 1611.

Spenser, Edmund. *A Briefe Note of Ireland.* In *The Works of Edmund Spenser: A Variorum Edition,* vol. 10, edited by Rudolf Gottfried, 233-45. Baltimore: Johns Hopkins University Press, 1949.

———. *The Faerie Queene,* edited by Thomas P. Roche and C. Patrick O'Donnell. New Haven, Conn.: Yale University Press, 1978.

———. *A View of the Present State of Ireland.* In *The Works of Edmund Spenser: A Variorum Edition,* vol. 10, edited by Rudolf Gottfried, 39-232. Baltimore: Johns Hopkins University Press, 1949.

———. *The Complete Works of Edmund Spenser,* edited by R. Morris. London: Macmillan, 1869.

Spivak, Gayatri Chakravorty. "Can the Subaltern Speak?" In *Marxism and the Interpretation of Culture,* edited by Cary Nelson and Lawrence Grossberg, 271-313. Urbana: University of Illinois Press, 1988.

Steevens, Paul. "Spenser and Milton on Ireland: Civility, Exclusion, and the Politics of Wisdom." *ARIEL: A Review of International English Literature* 26, no. 4 (1995): 151-67.

Strong, Roy. *Art and Power: Renaissance Festivals, 1450-1650.* Woodbridge, England: Boydell, 1984.

T.B, W.B., O.B., J.H. *Marleborowes Miseries, or, England Turned Ireland.* London: 1643.

Temple, Sir John. *The Irish Rebellion. . . .* London: 1646.

Walsh, Micheline Kerney. *Destruction by Peace: Hugh O'Neill After Kinsale.* Armagh: Cumann Seanchais Árd Mhacha, 1986.

———. *An Exile of Ireland: Hugh O'Neill, Prince of Ulster.* Dublin: Four Courts, 1996.

Index